Eliana,

to her —

Indian — and t[...]
beautiful and special Ayesha —
you just have to know what

8 STEPS TO INNOVATION

"JUGAAD)" is all about —

— love.

Rajni Masi

28/3/2014.

ADVANCE PRAISE FOR *8 STEPS TO INNOVATION*

'An extraordinary guide to a speedy and successful journey from mind to marketplace, embellished with lucid arguments, brilliant logic and backed by the sprinkling of inspiring lessons from great innovators and innovations'

—R.A. Mashelkar, former Director General, Council of Scientific and Industrial Research; National Research Professor; Chancellor, Academy of Scientific and Innovative Research (AcSIR); and President, Global Research Alliance

'Given the ringside seats that Rishikesha Krishnan and Vinay Dabholkar have had in observing how innovation works in all kinds of enterprises, this guide would be of immense value for practitioners'

—Kris Gopalakrishnan, Executive Co-chairman, Infosys

'Rishi and Vinay have distilled almost all the major ideas in systematizing innovation—complemented with excellent case studies—into an easy-to-implement, eight-step process. This is a must-read book for all those in leadership positions or interested in becoming a leader'

—Sukumar Rajagopal, Senior Vice President, CIO & Head of Innovation, Cognizant Technology Solutions

'Kudos to Rishi and Vinay for having accomplished a fine balance between the theoretical and practical aspects of innovation through this book'

—L.R. Natarajan, Chief Executive (New Business), Titan Industries

'In a vast and often confusing literature devoted to innovation, this book stands out as a practical guide for implementing systematic innovation processes at enterprise level. It will be useful to individuals and corporates irrespective of where they stand today in their innovation journey'

—Dr Ardhendu G. Pathak, Vice President, Airbus Innovation Cell, India

8 STEPS TO INNOVATION

Going from Jugaad to Excellence

VINAY DABHOLKAR

RISHIKESHA T. KRISHNAN

COLLINS BUSINESS

An Imprint of HarperCollinsPublishers

First published in India in 2013 by Collins Business
An imprint of HarperCollins *Publishers* India

ISBN: 978-93-5029-358-4

4 6 8 10 9 7 5 3

HarperCollins *Publishers*
A-53, Sector 57, Noida, Uttar Pradesh 201301, India
77-85 Fulham Palace Road, London W6 8JB, United Kingdom
Hazelton Lanes, 55 Avenue Road, Suite 2900, Toronto, Ontario M5R 3L2
and 1995 Markham Road, Scarborough, Ontario M1B 5M8, Canada
25 Ryde Road, Pymble, Sydney, NSW 2073, Australia
31 View Road, Glenfield, Auckland 10, New Zealand
10 East 53rd Street, New York NY 10022, USA

Typeset in 12/16 Goudy Old Style at
SÜRYA

Printed and bound at
Thomson Press (India) Ltd.

For my parents
Padmakar and Usha

—Vinay

Contents

Introduction

'Once your mind stretches to a new level, it never goes back to its original dimension'[1]

—A.P.J. Abdul Kalam

ANYONE CAN INNOVATE

→ India's new symbol for the rupee was designed by D. Udaya Kumar, an architect-turned designer from Tamil Nadu. Kumar's main interest is in Tamil typography, but his moment of fame came in 2010 when the symbol he designed—integrating the best of international design creativity with a distinctive Indian flavour—was accepted by the Reserve Bank of India.[2]

→ Thiyagarajan Ramaswamy, an engineering student, and son of a Pondicherry-based weaver, reworked the design of commercially available wet-grinders (used to make batter for idlis, a south Indian rice cake) so that his mother could make idlis as soft as the ones made from a traditional hand-ground batter. His design won him several national awards and was finally adopted by a number of commercial manufacturers.[3]

→ Anandraj Sengupta became the first young Indian to be featured on the cover of the prominent international business magazine *Businessweek* in 2003, as an icon of India's emerging strength in technology and innovation. An employee of General Electric's John F. Welch Technology Centre, the largest multidisciplinary multinational research and development (R&D) centre in India, Anandraj was well known for his system-level innovations, including his contribution to a new method to enhance the effectiveness of rail track inspections using ultrasound transducers, which was awarded a US patent.[4]

→ Anand Kumar, then a mathematics student at Patna University, started the Ramanujam School of Mathematics in 1992 to further his love for mathematics. When Anand was unable to take up a scholarship to attend Cambridge University because of his poor financial condition, he used the Ramanujam School to train poor but talented students for competitive examinations. Since 2003, Anand has selected thirty poor and talented students every year and trained them for the joint entrance examination (JEE) to India's prestigious Indian Institutes of Technology (IITs). In the last eight years, 212 of the 240 'Super 30' students have qualified for admission to the IITs.[5]

→ Nagaraja, a diploma-holder working at Bharat Electronics Limited, came up with an idea to replace gold-headed transistors with nickel-headed ones, leading to savings of more than Rs 18 crore for his company. In recognition of his efforts, Nagaraja was given the Government of India's Shram Ratna Award for the Year 2008.[6]

→ An innovation by factory employees participating in various programmes in the Innovation School of Management at Titan Industries' jewellery manufacturing division has led to deskilling of the mould-setting process, a cumulative savings of Rs 43 crore and the Tata Group's award for the best innovation.[7]

'Everyone can fly,' promised low-cost aviation pioneer Captain Gopinath, and the examples given in the box suggest that there is much more that everyone can do—perhaps anyone can innovate. 'Maybe,' you might be thinking, 'as long as the conditions are right.' Can we create organizations that can provide support for innovation? Are there ways in which organizations can ensure a steady stream of innovations? Is it possible to promote 'systematic innovation'?

An emphatic 'yes' is the answer to all these questions. Read on, to find out how.

JUGAAD VS SYSTEMATIC INNOVATION

In 1959, the Hindustan Machine Tools (HMT) Factory in Bengaluru started the assembly of radial drilling machines mainly out of imported components from Kolb in Cologne, Germany.[8] Dr S.M. Patil, who would later go on to become the chief executive officer and managing director, was a general manager then. In 1960, when the manufacture of the machines was indigenized, the machines started making jerky noises while ascending and descending.

It was found that a worn-out screw was causing the malfunctioning. A workaround was devised and implemented, which only served to increase the customer complaints. The unit was assigned to expert assemblers yet the defect persisted. In fact, the rate of failure increased and one in five machines started getting stuck. Eventually, an assembly foreman of the same section was sent to Kolb to study the methods followed there. After three weeks the foreman returned, confident that he could fix the problem. The confidence didn't last long as he realized that the problem persisted even after close monitoring of the assembly process.

One day in 1961, Patil was taking a walk through the shop floor when the foreman of the heavy parts planning section—let's call him Rajappa—told him that he had a solution for the problem. Rajappa also requested Patil to allow him to demonstrate his idea through a few prototypes. Patil gave him a chance despite resistance from the section managers. Rajappa designed a simple solution. He made sure that the arm that was carried throughout the assembly was always placed vertically. The simple solution solved the problem permanently. Rajappa was promoted to a deputy manager's position.

A story of this kind usually doesn't make it to any report, let alone an autobiography. In fact, Dr S.M. Patil, who narrates it in his autobiographical account *25 Years with HMT*[9] writes the story more as a digression. After all, it is a story where nothing earth-shattering happened. No new product or service was created. It didn't reverse a trend of deserting customers. In the 1960s, it is quite likely that even if customers wanted to desert, they wouldn't have been able to since they didn't have too many options.

We consider this story an important early example of innovation because in this case we have an idea and its implementation that resulted in the improvement of an important parameter: product quality.

Let's compare this story with one that happened in a town called Jamshedpur, about a couple of thousand kilometres away from Bengaluru, around the same time as the Rajappa–Patil chance meeting.

P.K. Chakraborty, then charge-man in the Loco Shops at Tata Engines and Locomotives Company (Telco, now Tata Motors) gave a suggestion to the works manager.[10] On 31 May 1957, he suggested a simple milling fixture for milling bolt heads, nuts, pins etc. Until then the work was carried out on costly dividing heads imported from foreign countries. He also attached a sketch of the fixture. A prototype of the machine was made from scrap materials, and it ran satisfactorily, impressing everyone. Operators found it easier to handle because it was lightweight and the chance of any error in indexing was minimized. It saved 25 to 30 per cent time and required less maintenance. Chakraborty received a cash award of Rs 50 from the director-in-charge. He also received a letter from R.H. Broacha, then manager (Loco), which read: 'Your excellent effort in designing and constructing a milling fixture for the production of hexagonal heads has been greatly appreciated by the management.'[11]

Rajappa and Chakraborty's stories reinforce the idea that anyone can innovate. But they differ in an important way. Unlike HMT, Telco went ahead and turned the insight that ideas can come from anybody—even shop-floor workers—into a process called the suggestion box scheme that was rolled out in 1959. Tisco (now Tata Steel) started a suggestion scheme even earlier in 1932 though it was formalized as a suggestion box in 1945.[12]

Through a typical suggestion box scheme, the management invites ideas from employees on how to improve things in the workplace. On a regular basis, say once a month, ideas are evaluated by a committee and some ideas are implemented. A suggestion scheme has an associated incentive scheme where people who submit ideas and/or those whose ideas are implemented get rewarded.

When innovation happens in the organization only through ad hoc means and chance meetings like that between Rajappa and Patil, it seems more like jugaad. The word has its origin in north India where transportation vehicles are made by sourcing locally available parts, including the engine. We can call it 'ad hoc creative improvisation' as well. On the other hand, when an organization has a disciplined way of generating, selecting, nurturing and implementing ideas, like the suggestion scheme of Telco, we call it 'systematic innovation'.

This is a book to help managers steer their organization from jugaad to systematic innovation. Before we explore the other dimensions of systematic innovation, let's clarify what we mean by 'innovation' itself.

WHAT IS INNOVATION?

Innovation happens when an idea is implemented to create an impact. It has three elements: idea, implementation and impact. In a for-profit organization, the impact is typically measured as either cost saving or as an increase in revenues—both resulting in higher profits. We have already seen two examples of cost saving that originated as ideas from Rajappa and Chakraborty. An innovation also happens when a new phone model is launched by a Nokia or an Apple or a Micromax and results in profits.

In a not-for-profit organization where profits are not an important criterion, the impact of innovation could be measured on different parameters. For example, an engineering college pioneering an innovative curriculum may use the quantity and quality of student placements as one of the measures of the effectiveness of its innovation. For a hospital it could be the number of footfalls as compared to its competitor.

Innovation is classified into different types. One useful classification comes from the magazine *Businessweek*, which publishes a list of the most innovative companies every year.[13] The list also gives the type of innovation the company is known for. The four types of innovations *Businessweek* uses are: process, product, customer experience and business model. Let's look at each category:

Process: Rajappa's innovation belonged to this category because it improved the way the radial drilling machine was being manufactured. Chakraborty's innovation falls in the same category as he devised a new way of milling nuts and bolts. When internal procedures in a bank are automated, it is a process innovation too. Typically, a process innovation results in improvement of efficiency, thereby reducing the cost of production. Hence, sometimes people refer to it as 'efficiency improvement' and not 'innovation'. However, we look at it as another form of innovation because it also involves an idea, its implementation and an impact in the form of cost reduction.

Product: A new motorcycle like the gearless Jive or hybrid scooter Streak launched by TVS Motor or a prepaid gift card launched by the State Bank of India are classified as product innovations. For many people, innovation is synonymous with product innovations. That is also because products are more tangible and visible as compared to say, a process change inside an organization. Note that a product that is new to a company need not be new to the market. For example, the new autorickshaw launched by TVS called TVS King is a new product for TVS but not to the market. However, we consider it as a product innovation as far as TVS Motor is concerned. A new product often involves setting up new internal processes. Hence, a product innovation often involves process innovations as well.

Product and process innovation can be closely tied together in some industries. For example, the development of new semiconductors with thinner (and even thinner) wafers is limited more by manufacturing processes than by semiconductor design.

Customer experience: When a courier company such as DTDC or the Indian Post Office provides a facility to track your consignment on the internet, it is creating a new customer experience. The basic process of taking the packet from the customer to its destination doesn't change. However, the customer is happier because he can track its progress till it reaches the consignee; he knows that he can virtually control the packet's movement. Retail stores like Big Bazaar and Crossword keep changing their store layout periodically so that the customer gets a better experience. The product being sold, like vegetables or rice or books, doesn't change but the purchasing experience changes each time. We also put a brand campaign like the ZooZoos of Vodafone in this category.

Business model: The Indian Premier League (IPL) is about playing an old game of cricket in a totally new fashion and with high stakes. For example, in 2010, the IPL made Rs 1,200 crore from official broadcaster Set Max and sponsors and advertisers such as DLF, Pepsi, Hero Honda, Vodafone, Kingfisher Airlines, Citibank, MRF and others.[14] From the central pool of Rs 1,200 crore, 20 per cent (Rs 240 crore) was retained by the Board of Control for Cricket in India (BCCI). The balance of 80 per cent (Rs 960 crore) was earmarked for distribution among the franchisee teams. In short, each of the teams got a minimum of Rs 100 crore from the central pool without lifting a finger. Here, cricket lovers are getting a new value proposition packaged in a different form. When an innovation such as IPL redefines the way a game is played in terms of who the customer is or how to reach him or how to charge the customer, it is called a business model innovation. Note that the IPL business model existed in other parts of the world; for example, the English Premier League (soccer) and National Football League in the US (football). However, for the Indian market, the IPL would be considered a business model innovation.

Similarly, at Aravind Eye Hospital headquartered in Madurai, only 30 per cent of its patients pay; in fact, they pay less than what they would elsewhere.[15] The remaining 70 per cent are treated for free or they have to pay a nominal amount. Yet,

Aravind still has a 35 per cent operating profit—and this is a hospital that treats 2.4 million outpatients and conducts 286,000 cataract surgeries every year. Aravind Eye Hospital has pioneered a business model innovation (besides several process innovations as well!).

In today's hyper-competitive world, relying on just one dimension of innovation is often inadequate for commercial success. In fact, some of the most successful innovations—in market terms—incorporate multiple dimensions of innovation. Take Apple's iPod for instance. Though not the first MP3 player in the music market, it incorporated some new features like large storage space as well as easy search of and access to songs that allow us to qualify it as a product innovation. However, many believe that the iPod's success was more due to a business model innovation (the facility to download individual songs from the iTunes store) and the enhancement it provided to the overall customer hearing experience.

On the other hand, what is not an innovation? Let's look at Sheikh Jehangir's idea that reached the masses through a Hindi box-office hit, the Aamir Khan starrer *3 Idiots*. Jehangir is a fifty-year-old carpenter from the small town of Jalgaon, Maharashtra. He can't read or write and has not been trained in any vocational skill. However, Jehangir already has one patent to his name and he has applied for a second one. He has demonstrated that you can create a scooter-powered flourmill. This is the same scooter that is shown in the background when Rancho (Aamir Khan) reunites with his college buddies in *3 Idiots*. Jehangir's flourmill idea has a prototype implementation but it hasn't created an impact because it hasn't gone into production. Hence it is not an innovation yet. In fact, Jehangir has not been able to raise money to work on his idea. But, for all you know, by the time this book is out in the market, the scooter-powered flourmill may have crossed the barriers to commercialization and can, therefore, be called an innovation.

Jehangir's example highlights the difference between an invention and an innovation. Jehangir is certainly an inventor but he has some way to go before the invention becomes an innovation. Every invention does not result in innovation. Research in the US shows that only about 5 per cent of the inventions covered by patents get either produced or licensed for royalty.[16] Similarly, an inventor need not be the person who creates a product or service out of an invention. For example, Jehangir could very well sell the right to commercialize his invention to someone else. On the flip side, every innovation is not associated with an invention. Remember Rajappa, Chakraborty or even IPL. None of these innovations involved any invention. In this book, we are concerned with all types of innovations, some of which would be based on inventions.

Apart from the fact that each innovation involves an idea, implementation and impact, are there any characteristics common to all types of innovations? And, are there any common misconceptions as to what innovation is about? Let's look at the following story about Jamsetji Tata, one of the founders of Indian industry, to answer these questions.

THREE MYTHS OF INNOVATION

As R.M. Lala relates in the book *For the Love of India: The Life and Times of Jamsetji Tata*, Tata 'launched his real career as a textile magnate' at the age of thirty-five when he established Empress Mills in 1874.[17] James Brooksby was the chief engineer of Empress Mills.

While on leave in Lancashire in 1883, Brooksby came across

ring spindles invented in America. At the time Empress Mills, like all the other mills in India, was using the older technology of mule spinning. On a technical level, the two methods are fundamentally different.[18] The mule spins intermittently, that is to say, it spins approximately five feet of yarn, and then winds that section of yarn onto the spindle before spinning the next five feet. The ring, in contrast, spins and winds in one action, and is thus able to spin continuously. The ring spindle produced more yarn per hour than the mule, but at a cost of treating the raw cotton more harshly. This required the use of a better grade of raw material for any given type of yarn. Mule spindles were operated by relatively highly paid men, and ring spindles by relatively lowly paid women.

Jamsetji bought two ring spindle frames and asked Brooksby to try them out. The stated speed of 6,000 revolutions was soon exceeded and the ring frame produced 9,000 to 12,000 revolutions. Jamsetji requested his supplier, Platts Brothers and Co. Ltd (at that time the world's largest supplier of textile mill equipment), to supply ring spindles. But ring spinning was yet to catch on even in Lancashire, which is why Platts refused to supply ring spindles, preferring to stick to the older technology of mule spinning.

Consequently, Jamsetji changed his supplier to a rival manufacturer, Brooks and Doxey, who was willing to supply ring spindles. To bring about perfection in the technology, every defect was reported to the supplier. By the time Platts adopted the new technology, rivals like Brooks and Doxey had taken the lead.

Before we analyse the story further, let us make sure that it is indeed an innovation we are looking at here. Shifting from mule to ring spindles did involve an idea, its implementation and finally an impact in terms of improved business productivity. It is a 'process' type of innovation because it changed the way cloth was being made by making use of a newer and more efficient technology. This example highlights three myths associated with the process of innovation. Let's look at each one of them.

Where does innovation begin? When we think of innovation, the first thing that comes to mind is creativity. In fact, it is not uncommon for people to refer to these two terms interchangeably 'creativity and innovation'. It is as though they are inextricably linked since many innovation programmes begin and end with creativity exercises or idea brainstorms. Lots of ideas get generated and everyone goes home thinking, 'I did some innovation today.' We believe this is a very limited notion of what innovation is about.

Instead, let's ask where Brooksby got the idea of using ring spindles. He got it during his Lancashire visit by observing some of the earliest mills that had adopted ring spindles. He must have asked himself a question: 'Can this work in Empress Mills?' He must have become curious about the technology before he got thinking about how it could be useful in the Indian context. Innovation begins with curiosity and not creativity. This doesn't mean that creativity is not important, but the way you identify and define a challenge is perhaps even more important than how you address the problem it throws back and solve it.

This factor has significant implications for systematic innovation because as an organization we need to first check, 'What are we curious about?' It means identifying key areas that the customer is unhappy about. It also means being watchful and taking note of various emerging technologies like stem cell or cloud computing and asking whether any of them could be useful to our business. This is no different from Brooksby asking the ring spindle question. As we will see in this book, identifying challenges and building a 'challenge book' is one of the important first steps in systematic innovation.

The second myth revolves around the question: 'How does an idea move forward?' One of us was present at a client meeting where ideas were being assessed and selected for further development, out of which there was an idea that the innovation committee liked. The leader of the committee asked, 'When can we implement this?' This question gives an impression that an idea moves in a linear fashion from conception to implementation. We believe that this linear view is inappropriate.

We are certain that Jamsetji didn't say to Brooksby, 'Good idea! Let's implement it.' What Jamsetji is likely to have said instead is, 'Good idea! Let's first experiment with it.' That is how the idea of buying two ring spindle frames must have come about. The idea of adopting the ring spindle certainly held promise. But there were a number of uncertainties associated with it. To first validate the assumption that the ring spindles indeed improve productivity, his team would have had to set up a couple of frames and actually see how productively they could be operated. This process of validating assumptions associated with an idea is called experimentation. And the speed of experimentation is one of the important levers that determine how fast ideas can move forward.

The third myth about innovation is: 'Innovation is about risk-taking'. It is common to lament about the Indians' inability to take risks. After all, wasn't Jamsetji taking a risk by shifting the technology from mule to ring spindles? Well, perhaps he was, but only partly so. He was not only taking a risk but assessing and mitigating it as well.

A better way to put it would be to say that Jamsetji was managing the risk associated with the ring spindle opportunity. How did he assess the risk? We have already seen one element: experimentation. He would have also assessed the risk while negotiating with Platts, the original supplier. Perhaps he would have asked the prospective supplier other relevant questions, such as who else he supplied. Jamsetji mitigated the risk by making sure that the supplier would support him when defects were reported on the ring spindle. Thus innovation is about risk-taking, assessment and mitigation, three factors put together. People will take a risk if they learn to assess and mitigate it better.

TABLE 1.1: INNOVATION MYTHS VS REALITY

Myth	Reality
Innovation begins with creativity.	Innovation begins with curiosity.
Innovation is a smooth linear process.	Innovation is iterative and the outcome of a series of experiments.
Innovation is about risk-taking.	Effective innovation involves risk-taking, assessment and mitigation.

For every idea like Brooksby's ring spindle that goes from concept to cash, there are several ideas that go from concept to crash. Hence, organizations depict the idea pipeline in the form of a funnel. The objective is to show that many ideas enter the idea funnel but selectively fewer and fewer reach the next stage. And finally, only a few reach the market. Systematic innovation is basically about managing the idea funnel effectively. The question here is: 'What does it mean to manage an idea funnel?' Let's look at a brief history of systematic innovation next.

THREE GOALS OF IDEA MANAGEMENT SYSTEMS

William Denny's Shipyard

One of the earliest idea management systems was developed by William Denny at his shipyard in Dumbarton, Scotland.[19] This system, which Denny called 'Rules for the awards committee to guide them in rewarding the workmen for inventions and improvements', was started in 1880 and, eventually, was successfully adopted across England. Denny created a two-people committee to select good ideas and recognize innovators. In order to bring fairness to the system, one of the two members of the committee came from outside the company. Alan Robinson and Sam Stern present Denny's pioneering system in their book *Corporate Creativity: How Innovation and Improvement Actually Happens.*[20] The rules said that an employee could claim a reward for inventing or improving a machine or a hand tool. Ideas were also welcome for improving a process, reducing cost or improving quality.

Each accepted idea received a cash award from £2 to £15 according to its assessed value by the committee. For a patentable idea, the company not only gave an award of £15 but also paid the expense for patenting the idea in the inventor's name. The company didn't mind the inventor pursuing any other opportunity arising out of the patent so long as it retained the right to use the idea as well. In 1884, a further incentive was added: award money would be doubled for any employee submitting five or more ideas. By 1887, Denny's idea management system received more than 600 ideas, of which every third idea (196) got accepted and awards of £933 were paid out. The company also built the world's first commercial ship model experiment tank in 1882 known as The Denny Ship Model Experiment tank.

The first thing to notice about Denny's approach is that it created a continuous stream of ideas to be tested and selectively implemented. This stream of ideas is typically called an idea pipeline and building an idea pipeline is an important step common to all idea management systems. In the case of Denny, the scope of ideas was quite broad—it included both inventions and improvements. In all likelihood, Telco's suggestion scheme did not include inventions when it started. But perhaps the most remarkable aspect of Denny's scheme was a more basic assumption that its design had, which was quite radical for the time. It is that workers can actually identify and solve problems. To understand how bold this move was, we should contrast it with what a US Steel executive had famously said, 'I have always had one rule. When a workman sticks up his head, hit it.'[21]

Thomas Edison's Invention Factory

Around the same time Denny was designing his system, Thomas Alva Edison was creating his own unique version of an idea management system as described in the book *Edison on Innovation*. In 1876, Edison founded the first industrial research laboratory in the world called the 'Invention Factory' in Menlo Park, New Jersey.[22] This factory was designed to produce a stream of new products and bring about improvements in the existing products. It produced inventions such as the phonograph, the high-resistance incandescent lamp, the kinetographic camera, the electrical automobile and many improvements in telegraphy. Edison had set himself a goal of producing 'a minor invention every ten days and a big thing every six months or so'.[23] Edison ended up filing eighteen patents a year over a working lifetime of sixty-one years—not far from his original goal.

Edison made a systematic study of potential new markets, and kept track of products he could improve upon. A friend of Edison and a successful businessman, Henry Ford (founder of Ford Motor Co.), wrote about Edison:[24] 'First he determines the objective, that is exactly what he wants to accomplish. He may start to improve some crude device already in existence, as he did with the telephone, typewriter, dynamo and scores of other bits of apparatus. In any case he gets before him all that is known on the subject.' On the next step, Edison said, 'When I am after a result that I have in mind, I may make hundreds or thousands of experiments out of which there may be one that promises results in the right direction. This I follow to its legitimate conclusion, discarding the others, and usually get what I am after.'[25]

If building an idea pipeline is the first step in managing an idea funnel, then ensuring idea velocity is the second step.[26] Edison and his team performed rapid experiments to eliminate various possibilities and selected the most appropriate idea.

Edison's method can be summarized in three of his quotes:[27]

1. To have a great idea, have a lot of them. 2. I have not failed. I've just found 10,000 ways that won't work. 3. As soon as I find that something I am investigating does not lead to practical results, I drop it.

Edison systematically went about seeking opportunities,

generating ideas, performing experiments and finally, taking a few promising ideas to the market. The method of innovation Edison adopted had some similarities with Denny's method. Both involved a systematic management of an idea funnel; both involved workers contributing to the process; and both built a laboratory for experimentation. However, the methods differed in one important aspect. While Denny's method involved his team, Edison's method was autocratic in that he was the only one managing the idea funnel.

Let's fast forward to the twenty-first century and ask how systematic innovation is different today. The following story from Procter & Gamble (P&G) highlights the changes over time.[28] P&G was able to accelerate Pringles Prints, in which designs were imprinted on the Pringles snacks themselves, from its concept to its launch in less than a year, and at a fraction of what it would have otherwise cost. Here is how it happened.

Procter & Gamble's Connect and Develop

In his book *The Game-changer*, the then P&G chief executive officer (CEO), A.G. Lafley, relates how P&G changed the way it looked at innovation. Early on in the process, in 2002, they faced what seemed to be a simple challenge: how do you make snack foods more exciting?[29] One of the team members suggested that different images should be carried on Pringles chips. It was decided to try this idea out, but early experiments using the dough for chips and an ink-jet printer to create the images resulted only in rendering the printer unusable! It became clear that printing would have to take place after the potato chips were fried but were still hot, that every chip would have to be printed individually, that this would have to be done at high speed but without losing the quality of the image, and that new edible dyes would be required to make this happen. In P&G's traditional method of R&D-driven innovation, this looked like a long-drawn-out innovation process.

However, embracing the new open-innovation platform that Lafley was championing, P&G created a writeup on what problems they were trying to solve, and circulated it across the world to see if they could find someone who had a solution that could be quickly adapted as a solution to the problem at hand. And what did they find? A professor in Bologna in Italy ran a bakery where he printed images on cakes using custom-made equipment. Seizing the opportunity to adopt this method, P&G collaborated with him to modify the process for use with chips, and this innovation became a growth engine for the Pringles business.

When P&G opened the idea funnel for external partnerships right from the front-end, it increased the *capacity* of the innovation engine manifold. Suddenly, there were more people batting and creating partnerships, some hitting fours and sixes. In fact, A.G. Lafley established a simple goal in 2002: for every two ideas that hit the market, one should have a partner outside P&G.[30] The ratio achieved was at 15 per cent in 2000; it reached 35 per cent around 2005 and crossed 50 per cent in 2007. A global division called 'Connect and Develop' was created to facilitate the process. The outcome was that for every two products P&G launched in the market, one succeeded. This is the trickiest part of managing the idea funnel. If you decide to play safe and hit only singles then your score can never be high. On the other extreme, if you try to hit a sixer on every ball, again your score may be low. What matters is the batting average, how much impact innovations make on the company over a given period such as a financial year. We believe that after the idea pipeline and idea velocity, improving the batting average is the third most important goal for managing the idea funnel.

We have identified three goals in managing the idea funnel. One, building and sustaining an idea pipeline; two, improving idea velocity; and three, improving the batting average. How to do this systematically is what this book is about. But before we get to the 'how' part, let's understand some key hurdles.

TWO VILLAINS

We have seen examples of systematic innovation, for example, Denny's shipyard and Edison's invention factory, which are more than a hundred years old. If systematic innovation has been around for such a long time, and has evolved further, why isn't it practised everywhere? Why don't we have active idea management systems like Denny or P&G in many organizations?

There are definitely more P&Gs around. We have Indian companies like Marico, Tata Motors and Titan that have demonstrated a high level of innovation stamina over the last two decades. However, these are more of an exception than the rule. Systematic innovation is certainly not as ubiquitous as, say, quality management. The question is: Why?

Like any good story, our tale has two villains, both of whom have been around for a long time. To understand the first one, we will go back to the HMT story where Rajappa suggested an idea to fix a burning problem related to radial drilling.

The exact conversation between Patil and the manager of the radial drilling machine division is not known. However, we can imagine what might have happened. When Patil suggested to the manager that Rajappa's idea should be given a shot, the manager would have said, 'Why do we want to waste time? The problem has been tackled by the best engineers we have and we haven't found a solution. Do you think a matriculate can solve the problem?'

What we see in this kind of answer is a huge amount of resistance to the idea. There could be many reasons for this: one could be the deeply ingrained notion that an engineer is a better problem solver than a matriculate; another one could be that since the idea had originated outside the department, the resistance was a manifestation of the common 'not invented here' syndrome.

It is very easy for us to fall in the trap of making the manager the 'villain'. However, history shows otherwise. Practically every idea worth its salt has had to face resistance. And we believe that this 'resistance to change' is the chief villain of our story.

Retail wizard Kishore Biyani, chairman and MD of Future Group, experienced this mindset during his final year in college when he began to visit the office of Bansi Silk Mills in Kalbadevi in Mumbai.[31] It was a family business run by Kishore's father and his five brothers as well as two older cousins. The business was focused primarily on trading in various kinds of fabrics with the company acting as an intermediary between the textile mills in Mumbai and the garment manufacturers. Margins were low and there was hardly any growth. When Kishore questioned this way of conducting business, he was put in his place by being assigned the job of typing letters for official correspondence. As Kishore observed, 'preserving status quo' was the norm.[32] Anything that he tried to change was met with a 'no-no'.

Resistance to change goes beyond the company. When Ratan Tata proposed a partnership with an industry body to create an

Indian car in the 1990s, everybody scoffed at the concept. People said, 'Why doesn't Mr Tata produce a car that works before he talks about an Indian car?'[33] Eventually, Tata produced the Indica. Many times, however, the resistance to an idea may not be so visible. It is expressed by just ignoring ideas, let alone giving encouragement or inputs.

Implementing idea funnel management involves, at the very least, openness to ideas, some of which will challenge traditional beliefs. Many managers find this thought intimidating. After all, managers are supposed to be in control of the situation, and experimenting with new ideas would mean inviting uncertainty. What if the idea doesn't work?

The anxiety is natural and we will soon see how innovative companies overcome it. However, resistance to change isn't the only villain we need to worry about. There is a co-villain. To understand the second villain, we will go back to the Empress Mills story and put ourselves in the shoes of the manager of Platts, the manufacturer supplying mule spindles to Empress Mills.

When Jamsetji asked him to supply ring spindles, he had to decide whether to start a new product line with a new technology. Now, how would he have come to a decision? If he looked only in the rearview mirror, the answer would have seemed very clear: away with mule spindles. But let's say, he was a wise guy and he looked through the windshield. What did he see? A hazy picture, showing him that all his customers were still using mule spindles. The best he could have then done was to extrapolate the past into the future and make a prediction: mule or ring spindles? As Nassim Taleb brings out in *The Black Swan*, we can't predict a winning horse accurately,[34] a drawback we call the 'prediction disability'. But the most interesting part is that we forget that we have a disability.

The Rs 3,300-crore Arvind Mills features among the top three denim companies in the world, with an annual capacity of 110 million metres.[35] Sanjay Lalbhai, chairman and MD of the Arvind Group, introduced denim in India in 1988. Looking at the rising demand, Lalbhai went in for massive expansion of the mill's denim capacity, largely funded by loans. Later, when denim prices came crashing down due to excess capacity, it hit Arvind hard, heralding the bad phase that began in 1997 and ended more than half a decade later, when the group started seeing profits again.

When Sanjay was asked why he didn't see it coming, he said, 'If I had seen it coming, I wouldn't have done it. We did all the wrong things. We leveraged on the balance sheet and then everything went wrong.'[36] Sanjay admitted that he 'didn't see it coming'. Learning to manage this disability of 'not being able to see things coming', or in other words, prediction disability, is an important aspect of a systematic innovation process.

How deep-rooted are 'resistance to change' and 'prediction disability'? Why can't we find a magic pill that gets rid of these two? Well, it looks like these biases are indeed difficult to uproot. In the last few decades, psychologists have converged on a model of thinking that explains these biases. According to this model, human thinking can be seen as a combination of two distinct systems or processes of thinking at work all the time.[37] The first one is intuitive and emotional. It is the part that makes your right foot reach out for the brake when the vehicle in front slows down or makes you nervous when you enter into an annual appraisal meeting with your boss. The second part is the one that deliberates, analyses and looks into the future. It is the part that makes a New Year's resolution to go for a morning walk three times a week.

When you are talking to a friend while driving, both the systems are active at the same time. The automatic part is doing the driving while the conscious one is doing the talking. Sometimes the two systems fight. For example, the planning side sets an alarm for getting up early in order to go for a morning walk, but in reality, when the alarm actually rings it is the instinctive side that presses the snooze button.

Chip and Dan Heath use an analogy in their bestselling book *Switch*, which we find very useful.[38] In this analogy, the emotional side is like an elephant and the deliberating side is like a tiny human rider sitting on top of the elephant. The rider feels that he is the leader and things work fine as long as the elephant and the rider agree on where to go. However, anytime there is a conflict between the two, there is no surprise who will win. The elephant has a six-ton advantage and the tiny rider is rendered helpless by the mammoth beast.

'Resistance to change' is the case where the elephant sticks to his good old ways and overpowers the rider. On the other hand, 'prediction disability' shows where the rider fails to correct the incorrect instinctive verdict given by the elephant, perhaps under emotional euphoria or depression. How do we manage the elephant–rider conflict?

THE ELEPHANT AND RIDER CONFLICT

Idea management in India may be more than half a century old as we saw in the story about Telco's suggestion box. However, it gained momentum only in the late 1980s. There were two primary drivers: one was the arrival of the total quality management (TQM) movement in India from Japan and the second one was the opening up of the Indian economy, bringing in competition from foreign players. TQM was the bigger force of the two and hence led to idea management systems with the scope of ideas limited to 'continuous improvement'. Let's look at how this happened in the case of Maruti Suzuki India Ltd, a company that, unlike HMT, successfully transitioned from the licence-permit raj era.

Idea Management at Maruti

Chairman R.C. Bhargava narrates Maruti Udyog's experience in implementing an idea management system in his book *The Maruti Story*.[39] Maruti Udyog was set up in the early 1980s by the Government of India in collaboration with Japan's Suzuki Motor Company (SMC) to manufacture small cars. As a successful manufacturer of cars in Japan, SMC was keen to introduce its 'best practices' in Maruti Udyog. One such practice was the employee suggestion scheme, which unfortunately, the Indian managers did not respond to positively. They felt that it was more important to faithfully follow the manufacturing processes followed in Suzuki's Japanese plants. They doubted that Maruti's inexperienced workers would be able to make value-adding suggestions. But, on SMC's insistence, the company went ahead with the suggestion scheme. To attract ideas, initially a small amount was paid for every idea submitted irrespective of its quality or practicality. The result: generation of several useless ideas, in addition to some good ones. But, with time, the quality of the ideas improved, and the company shifted to paying incentives only for those ideas that were implemented.

The company found different ways of recognizing contributors to the suggestion scheme. These ranged from posting the names of employees giving suggestions on the notice board to giving the top annual idea generators the opportunity to have a meal, along with their family, with the top management of the company.

SMC introduced another 'best practice' in Maruti—the quality circle. A quality circle is a team of four to ten workers that understands the methodology of identifying and solving problems and applies this to issues that come up on the shop floor.[40] But transplanting this practice to Maruti was not easy either—in Japan, quality circles meet after the shift is over, but in India, where employees often live far away from the factory and depend on company transportation to reach home, staying late is difficult. So, this practice was adapted to Indian conditions and quality circle activity was allowed in company time. To encourage this further, a competition was held between quality circles, with the winners getting a trip to the SMC factory in Japan.

In this story, you would have noticed the elephant-rider fight when SMC recommended the suggestion scheme to Indian managers. The managers felt, 'What could the workers suggest about the process which Japanese engineers have put in place?' Research in psychology tells us that there is nothing unique about this reaction. It is the elephant side of thinking that is talking, based on past experience. However, the story also brings out various mechanisms that help the rider and the elephant move together in greater harmony.

The introduction of a suggestion scheme is typically associated with awareness and education sessions for the workers. During the training sessions, techniques for identifying and analysing problems are presented; this took place in Maruti Udyog too. Suzuki trainers would have shared examples of suggestions from the Japanese factories and explained the format for the suggestion form to be filled. Essentially, the rider gets a clear message as to what needs be done. The Heaths call this 'Directing the Rider'.

For a tiny rider, getting the direction is not sufficient. The elephant needs the motivation as well. That is where incentives in different forms help. The monetary rewards Maruti gave are just one part of the story. Perhaps what is a bigger motivation is to see your name on display on the notice board or an opportunity to have lunch with the managing director. Imagine the effect when a shop-floor worker tells stories of the lunch meeting with the MD to his friends during the lunch break. It is quite possible that there are more in the group who start wondering, 'If he can do it, why can't I?' The Heaths call this 'Motivating the Elephant'.

Imagine if Maruti had decided not to give the one-hour-a-month time for quality circle activity. Does it mean that the flow of ideas would have stopped? Perhaps not. But this practice makes it that much easier for workers to contribute. The Heaths call this 'Shaping the Path'. It is similar to your corner grocery shop offering home delivery. You may still shop at the shop even if he doesn't deliver things home but 'home delivery' makes grocery shopping easier. When your bank ATM ensures that you remove your card before it gives you the cash, it is also shaping the path,[41] because it is ensuring that you don't leave your card in the ATM even by mistake.

In this book we show how other companies in India and abroad are applying the techniques of directing the rider, motivating the elephant and shaping the path in order to overcome the elephant–rider conflict and manage the idea funnel.

The Further Evolution of Idea Management at Maruti

The Indian economy has undergone a sea change since the early days of Maruti. A company that took a decade to launch its second passenger car model Zen now launches many new models every year. Competition has brought its market share down from a near monopolistic 90 per cent to less than 50 per cent yet it is still the undisputed leader with the next car maker making less than half the cars that Maruti does. Maruti is selling at a run rate of 1 lakh cars per month and sold for the first time over a million cars in 2010.[42] How has all this impacted idea management at Maruti?

The continuous improvement activity has continued to evolve and Maruti consistently features in the benchmark figures published by the Indian National Suggestion Scheme Association (INSSAN).[43] The process was made more efficient by automating the logging of ideas. A fulltime programme manager was put in place to track the activity. As a result the savings resulting from employee ideas have gone up from Rs 2 crore in 1990 to Rs 479 crore in 2009. However, the most significant changes in innovation management at Maruti came not from the continuous improvement side but on the new product development side.

In December 2009, the managing director of Maruti Shinzo Nakanishi announced, 'Right now we have eight platforms and we would want to bring that down to three in the future with the Alto, WagonR and Estilo line continuing as our mainstay as it is now.'[44] A platform is a common architecture for multiple car models that covers design, engineering, production and major components. If we rip an Alto and a WagonR apart we will see the same bone structure underneath. What this means is that Maruti can develop new car models based on the existing platforms much faster and at a lower cost. Maruti is thinking not only in terms of new products but also in terms of platforms. This has meant building internal capabilities for R&D, market research, industrial design and laboratories for crash testing. It has also meant creating a career path for specialists who get the same benefits as managers.

Not all innovation programme stories are as positive as Maruti's. We got to hear about an innovation programme which started with all the fanfare like any other launch, when a web-based idea tool was put in place. A campaign with a logo was launched and a selection committee was formed to select and fund good ideas. The initial buzz created a flurry of activity on the innovation portal. And then gradually, the flow of ideas slowed down.

Among the few dozen ideas logged in the system in the first few months, only one was considered worthy of further evaluation. The author of this idea was given a business plan template and asked to prepare a business plan, but the poor fellow had no idea about preparing one. He never got back, and news went around that the idea system was 'not for them'. Soon the innovation committee lost interest too. The programme simply failed to motivate the elephant.

In this book, we show you how to run innovation programmes in a robust manner. We would like your innovation programme to progress more like Maruti's than the other one, which died a premature death.

We look at three steps in managing an idea funnel: Build and sustain the idea pipeline, improve the idea velocity and increase the batting average. In each step, we look at several ways in which we can help the rider and the elephant to move together in the right direction.

Key Takeaways

→ Innovation happens when an idea is implemented to create an impact.

→ Anyone can innovate provided the conditions are right.

→ An organization that practises systematic innovation has a disciplined way of generating, selecting, nurturing and implementing ideas.

→ There are four key types of innovation: process; product; customer experience; and business model. Some of the most successful innovations incorporate multiple dimensions of innovation.

→ Innovation begins with curiosity.

→ Innovation is an iterative process rather than a linear one, depending on a series of experiments. Innovation is not just about risk-taking, it's also about assessing and mitigating risks.

→ Managing the idea funnel involves pursuing three goals: One, building and sustaining the idea pipeline; two, improving idea velocity; and three, improving the batting average.

→ Successful idea management involves two major challenges: overcoming resistance to change and overcoming prediction disability.

→ Resistance to change can be easily understood in terms of the conflict between an elephant (tradition, emotions, inertia) and its rider (logic and rationality). Companies can use different methods to direct the rider, motivate the elephant and shape the path in order to overcome the elephant–rider conflict.

Things to do

→ Think of one change that you embraced in the last one year. Was there resistance to that change? What made you overcome it?

→ List some of your favourite innovations. Classify them into: product; process; customer experience; and business model.

→ Think of an innovation in which you played a role. What was the role? Now that you are familiar with the elephant–rider model, what could you have done differently to support the innovation process?

Part 1

BUILD AN IDEA PIPELINE

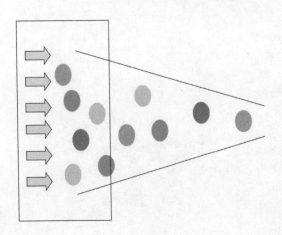

| Innovation programme | Challenge book | Build participation |

chapter one

STEP 1
Lay the Foundation

'We started from the premise that it is possible to run an innovation programme in much the same way we run a factory'[1]
—A.G. Lafley

WHY START AN INNOVATION PROGRAMME?

When Anand Mahindra became the head of R&D of the Mahindra & Mahindra Group of Companies in 1991, it was the company's most neglected department.[2] His first successful bet was a new chassis design idea from an engineer—Sandhesh Dahanukar, an M&M veteran. The M&M team had observed that the chassis design in use by M&M often broke down in the face of overloading. The existing design could be made more robust, but this would involve several crores of investment in new presses.

Instead, Dahanukar proposed the development of a new tubular design,[3] as noted in the book *Innovation at Mahindra and Mahindra*. He had developed his idea by observing what other automakers did. Anand Mahindra sanctioned Rs 6 lakh for developing a prototype and had Dahanukar report to him directly. In less than two years, Dahanukar not only came up with a working prototype, but also developed a corresponding manufacturing process. M&M benefited by creating more robust vehicles.

Anand Mahindra's tenure as the head of the R&D department was perhaps one of the turning points in M&M's innovation journey. Soon Mahindra realized that the R&D department carries significant creative potential and is under-leveraged. This is when the idea of setting up a system of new product development (NPD) came up. Mahindra set up a team to study NPD systems of companies such as Daimler-Benz, Samsung, Chrysler and John Deere. Subsequently, the team rolled out the Mahindra NPD system—a six-stage process involving multiple departments and several design review gates. In parallel, the automotive division of M&M created an integrated design and manufacturing (IDAM) system under the leadership of a former General Motors executive, Pawan Goenka. Some of the new products M&M launched, like the Scorpio, became a big hit in the market.

Why do organizations start innovation programmes or initiatives? The M&M example illustrates a typical scenario where a person in a leadership position is convinced that innovation can and should be managed in a more systematic way for the organization's well-being.

Why did a company like M&M, founded in the 1940s, wait for half a century to focus on innovation? Well, in the pre-1991 era, also known as the pre-liberalization era, the government made the role of an innovation manager irrelevant by deciding who will produce what, how much and where. And the government also provided protection to the goods produced in

India by limiting competition. In other words, there wasn't much of an incentive to innovate.[4] That situation changed when the economy opened up and global players stepped in. And, along with this change, came the innovation initiatives.

The trigger to systematize innovation was different at 3M, a company often considered to be one of the most consistently innovative companies in the world. When the then CEO of 3M, William McKnight, reviewed his product portfolio some time in 1940, he discovered that it had been almost six years since 3M had launched a profitable product.[5] In fact, the launch of some of their most successful products such as Wetordry waterproof sandpaper, Scotch masking tape and Scotch transparent tape dates back to 1921, 1925 and 1930 respectively. So, on 12 October 1940, McKnight wrote to 3M's head of research, '3M is spending a substantial and an increasing amount on research every year. It's time to create a department to cooperate with all interested parties in studying the commercial value of each research project upon which money is being spent.'[6] This memo led to the founding of 3M's New Products Department.

An important point to note is that organizations don't start innovation programmes to become innovative. All organizations are innovative—only the degree, scope and most importantly, the way the innovation is managed vary. Prior to launching the innovation programme, both M&M and 3M would have launched new products and services. However, there comes a time when innovation needs to be managed as a disciplined activity with cross-functional coordination. In some sense this is a step of going from jugaad to systematic innovation.

General Electric traces its origin to Edison General Electric, a company founded by Thomas Edison. And yet, when Jeffery

Immelt became the CEO in 2001, one of the initiatives he launched was called 'Imagination breakthroughs'.[7] It was a process of managing a pipeline of ideas, each of which had the potential of creating billion dollars of revenue. Why would GE have to launch a programme of this kind when it had a century-old history of managing innovation? As the organization grows, its research centres can become isolated islands. Immelt says, 'One of the big fears is that you develop this blue-sky place that's totally isolated from reality. I want a whole series of leaders to be able to come through there and share that reality, while at the same time they become better technology managers.'[8] Similar to the Crotonville Centre where GE runs management development programmes, Immelt has turned the global research centre near Schenectady, New York, into a place where scientists and business leaders share technology strategy and find its linkages with market trends.

Innovation programmes are launched to improve the effectiveness of how innovation is managed. Where does an innovation programme begin? What kinds of challenges does it face? And what are the indicators that it is moving in the right (or wrong) direction? Perhaps there is no better example to answer these questions than Toyota's idea management journey, which began in 1951.

TOYOTA'S FORTY YEARS, 20 MILLION IDEAS

Toyota rolled out two separate idea management systems—one for invention and the other for improvements—in 1949 and 1951 respectively. The former was called an invention and idea system and it awarded grants to technicians and engineers who produced inventions and ideas related to business. The latter, called the creative idea suggestion system, focused on continuous improvements.

Yuzo Yasuda's book *40 Years, 20 Million Ideas* in 1991[9] presented a detailed account of the management philosophy, idea management process, challenges in its rollout etc., which supported the creative idea suggestion system. As the title suggests, Toyota employees clocked 20 million ideas cumulatively in the first forty years after the system's inception. Toyota's suggestion system differed from its Western counterparts in one fundamental way. It emphasized participation and learning as much if not more than the business impact.

In its first year (1951) there were 789 suggestions and a participation rate of 8 per cent. But the quantity and quality of ideas were poor. Since the employees thought that 'ideas' meant great inventions, not many came forward. This led to the management clarifying that not everything had to be a great idea, that it was the quantity of ideas, not their quality, that mattered.

Several improvements were put in place in the next few years. A training programme was formulated that taught employees the tools and techniques to identify and solve problems in their workplaces. A field trip was organized for employees who made outstanding suggestions. A call for problem suggestions was announced—which meant that there would be more focus on the problems selected by the subcommittees. An individual annual award system was put in place by December 1952. The first call to all employees for a special company-wide topic was sent in 1955, and the topic was ashtrays!

What was the scope of these ideas? Who selected them? And how? The ideas involved improvement in quality, safety, hygiene or reduction in cost due to material, space or effort-saving.

Apart from its impact, each idea was evaluated for its adaptability and originality. A whole pyramid of committees was organized plant-wise to promote and select ideas. Rewards were given every month and included cash prizes starting from a few dollars to $300. The reward ceremony would be presided over by members of the top management.

Toyota realized that involving the workers was necessary but not sufficient to sustain the programme. The managers' engagement was important too and various mechanisms were put in place to involve them. During the screening of the 'superior' suggestion, it wasn't the idea author who made the presentation to the top management—it was the manager of that person's section. Why? The reason was that the manager was expected to understand the details of his workplace enough to explain the ideas to others.

The Toyota story illustrates the three building blocks of an innovation programme: the idea management process, the buzz creation process (prizes, exhibitions, campaigns) and the training and development process. To use the elephant–rider model, processes such as idea management shape the path for the elephant. They make it easier for the employees to participate in the innovation activity and tools and methodologies learned in the training programmes help direct the rider. Similarly, the buzz creation process both motivates the elephant through the rewards and directs the rider through a theme for the campaign. Let's look at each of these one by one.

FIGURE 2.1:
KEY PROCESSES IN AN INNOVATION PROGRAMME

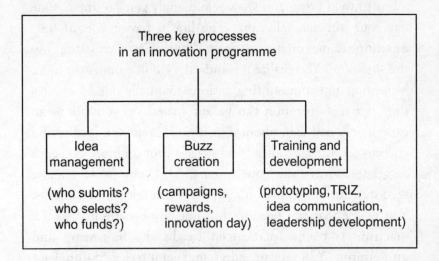

THE IDEA MANAGEMENT PROCESS

One of the key components of the innovation programme is the idea management process. What kinds of decisions are involved in designing the process? How does it differ in different contexts? What is common in the process creating the programme? In Toyota, it involved setting up a process for managing ideas. This meant creating forms for submitting an idea and setting up a hierarchical committee for selecting and implementing ideas. However, that is not the only way to implement an idea management system. There are several choices an organization can make in order to make the process relevant for the given context and culture. To understand what those key levers of the idea management process are, let's study a few variations in its implementation, starting with Toyota.

Suppose you are Akihiko Hasegawa working as a metal worker at the company headquarters' factory in 1980.[10] Every day your job is to weld boxes and shelves and apply paint to them. One day your foreman tells you, 'The line is having a hard time mounting frames on the conveyer. Why don't you try to improve the situation?' You realize it is indeed a troublesome operation. Mounting and unmounting is done manually one block at a time but this operation can be automated. So you talk to an experienced colleague about your idea. He refines it further and encourages you to go ahead and suggest your solution. You get a suggestion form from your foreman and start filling out the sections: current situation, improvement idea and benefits. You realize that you need to do some cost-benefit analysis if a machine is to be introduced to do the mounting and unmounting. You prepare a draft and get it reviewed from your colleague and eventually submit it to your foreman. Two months later, you hear your foreman shouting, 'Hey Hasegawa! You've done a good job. That was really an outstanding suggestion!' You know that your idea is selected for implementation and you have got an award for it.

Suppose you are a scientist working at Galaxy Surfactants headquartered in Navi Mumbai with annual revenue of Rs 900 crore.[11] Galaxy is a thirty-year-old organization and a leader in surfactant technology. Surfactants are used in personal care and home care products. Galaxy supplies sodium lauryl sulphate to all toothpaste manufacturers in India. If you have brushed your teeth using a toothpaste in India, then Galaxy products have touched your life (or at least your teeth!). Let's say you are working in the innovation department at Galaxy. One day, you get an idea about a new pathway that achieves an anti-aging effect. As a first step, you do a literature and patent search to figure out if someone else has got this idea before and how crowded this area is. You provide this information to the innovation committee, which clears the idea at the first gate. This idea gets checked for market attractiveness and whether it leverages Galaxy's existing capabilities and strengths. Once it passes this stage, it enters the feasibility study phase where a process is developed in the laboratory and checked for various parameters including eco-friendliness—a key component of Galaxy's core identity. At this stage there would be a decision about whether the idea is suitable for a connect-and-develop process with research partners such as the National Chemical Laboratory (NCL), Pune. Once it clears this stage, the idea moves to the capability development stage where cosmetic scientists are involved in preparing application formulation and field testing the product with end consumers. As of 2010, one in three ideas that entered the Galaxy funnel reached the market in this way.

Now suppose you are a software engineer working in Intuit's India development centre at the Eco-space campus on the Outer Ring Road in Bengaluru.[12] Intuit is a twenty-eight-year-old software products company helping 50 million customers in the US to file their taxes or do their finances. As an Intuit India engineer you may ask yourself questions like: 'How might we help poor farmers in rural India to manage their finances better?' You write the idea on a post-it note and paste it on the notice board. Within the next few days you hear from a mentor who calls for an informal session, called 'Speaker's corner', where interested people come to the innovation lab and you get an opportunity to explain your idea to them. Once your idea gets a favourable response, it moves to the next stage. In this stage, you may get help from a caricature expert to create a storyboard where the beneficiary and the benefit get highlighted. The storyboard is presented to a set of experts, and checked for further validity. Once it passes this stage, you join hands with another engineer or manager and make a field visit—at Intuit this is called 'Follow-me home'.[13] The idea is to actually visit a potential customer and observe him in action. With the insights from the field, you are expected to develop a quick prototype and show it to potential consumers for a feedback. In the next stage your idea is presented to relevant product managers for possible business sponsorships. Rapid iteration of ideas and experimentation is given a lot of importance at Intuit and your idea may reach the market within five to six months. As of mid-2012, Fasal—the most successful innovation coming out of Intuit India—is empowering close to a million farmers to find the best price for their produce through SMSes. Early results have shown that 90 per cent of the farmers benefit and 15–20 per cent have greater price realization as a result.[14]

The innovation processes at Toyota, Galaxy and Intuit may be different in some of their details. However, all idea management systems need to answer the following questions:

1. Source: Where will ideas come from? (Any employee, only certain employees—shop-floor workers, employees and customers, employees, customers and partners, anyone on the internet?).

2. Scope: What is the scope of ideas? (Process improvement, product improvement, new product, customer experience, business models, any of these).

3. Stages: How many stages will an idea go through before it is either implemented or parked? In M&M, a new product idea would have to go through six stages.

4. Technology: In what form will ideas be gathered, stored, searched and presented? Will it be a physical suggestion box, or a bulletin board where people write or an intranet website where people submit ideas? Or a combination of these?

5. Selection: How will ideas be selected for further development? Will it be through a committee or through open voting or through some other mechanism? What is the criterion for selection?

6. Sponsorship: How and what kind of resources will be allocated to the selected ideas? Will the sponsorship be in the form of time-off from the existing project ('Take two weeks off and create a prototype') or money ('Take this and show us the next level of prototype') or mentoring.

The six levers of the idea management systems are depicted in the figure below.

FIGURE 2.2: SIX LEVERS OF AN IDEA MANAGEMENT SYSTEM

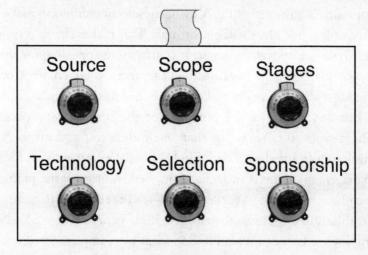

Idea Box

Among these, some key questions you need to answer are: Do we select only big-ticket ideas or even small ideas? Should the emphasis be on quantity or quality?

IDEA SELECTION: SMALL VS BIG IDEAS

Saito, the chairman of Toyota's idea management system[15], was worried about the participation in the first year. He realized that there was anxiety in the minds of employees who probably asked themselves: 'Will my idea be worthy of an innovation? What will others say if my idea is not selected? What will my manager say?' These are the thoughts that prevent employees from submitting their ideas. What did Saito do to tackle this mindset? He began emphasizing quantity over quality and changed the font in the programme logo to reflect the openness envisaged for the exchange of ideas.

'Should we focus only on the big ideas or emphasize small ideas as well?' This is the question that needs to be answered by every creator of an innovation programme. The big-idea-only approach is quite tempting. A stringent selection criterion makes sure only a few ideas will go through. This makes the selection and resource allocation easier. It is also more appealing for the senior management because they can focus their energies on the ideas that can really make a difference to the business.

But Toyota shows the potential of the opposite approach. The Toyota story shows us that small ideas can add up to 20 million over a period. The INSSAN publishes statistics on idea management systems in India, compiled from its participating members.[16] For the year 2009, in twenty-eight participating organizations, there were 640,258 ideas generated by 81,429 employees. Out of these, 440,838 ideas were implemented and resulted in a saving of Rs 1,649 crore. In the Bhilai plant of the

Steel Authority of India (SAIL), there were 5,970 ideas generated in 2008–09 and 18,729 employees participated. In TVS Motor, every employee generated, on an average, forty-one ideas per year. That is almost like every employee giving an idea a week.

Tata Motors generated twenty-five ideas per person during 2008–09.[17] In the same year the company also launched twenty-eight new models/variants, including low-floor buses (both CNG and diesel), Ace and Magic CNG versions, Winger, Xenon XT, trucks like the 2518 Turbo Gold, the Lift Axle Truck 3118 etc. During the same period, Tata Motors filed more than 305 applications for intellectual property rights (IPRs), and was granted more than forty-six patents.[18] The Tata Motors story illustrates that a company can emphasize both small and big ideas at the same time—one doesn't have to happen at the cost of the other.

As Toyota's former CEO, Katsuaki Watanabe, observed, 'When seventy years of very small improvements accumulate, they become a revolution.'[19] But that's not the only reason why small ideas are important. Alan Robinson and Dean Schroeder point out in their book *Ideas Are Free* that small ideas are the *best* sources of big ideas.[20] In fact, a big idea may begin by helping one individual in a small way.

That is how it began for Muhammad Yunus in 1976 in Chittagong, Bangladesh. Yunus was the head of the Economics Department at Chittagong University. The famine of 1974 had created a deep impact on Yunus and he had realized how far removed his elegant mathematical equations were from reality. That's when he decided to help poor people. His meeting with twenty-one-year-old Sufia Begum, a poor bamboo stool-maker, turned out to be the turning point. During the conversation with Sufia, Yunus realized that Sufia borrowed bamboo for five taka (equivalent to 22 cents). She sold the bamboo stools at the end of the day to repay her loan and make a 50 paisa profit (equivalent to 2 cents). At times, the moneylender charged an interest rate of 10 per cent per week. This shocked Yunus. He sent a student to the village to figure out how many Sufias existed and how much money they needed.

Within a week the list was ready. It had forty-two people who had borrowed 856 taka in all, a total less than $27. On the spur of the moment, Yunus decided to lend $27 to all the forty-two women, allowing them to repay the amount whenever they could afford it. Yunus had no idea that this act would eventually create a completely new market called micro-credit.[21]

Perhaps the biggest benefit of encouraging small ideas is in building a culture of innovation. When an organization says small ideas are welcome, and demonstrates that they matter, it helps reduce anxiety among employees. To use the elephant–rider model, small ideas make the change appear more easily doable to the elephant. It provides an opportunity to experience what it means to implement ideas that are less risky. This builds creative confidence and innovation muscle and prepares them for bigger ideas.

Openness to small ideas comes at a cost though. It increases the effort required to filter these ideas for further development. This may potentially slow down the selection process. As the Toyota example shows, the best way to handle this is to distribute the effort across the hierarchy. Most small ideas relate to the specific knowledge of local circumstances. This knowledge usually resides in the place where the idea originates. In fact, often idea selection is very effective as a part of regular team meetings because the members of the team are in a privileged position to review the ideas and choose those that are likely to work.[22]

Out of the three key processes of an innovation programme: 1. the idea management system; 2. buzz creation; and 3. training and development, we have so far looked at the first one. Now, let's see where the second one—buzz creation—begins.

DESIGNING A CAMPAIGN: POSITIVE VS NEGATIVE EMOTION

On 8 February 2011, the internet was abuzz with an internal memo sent by the CEO of one of the leading handset makers in the world to its employees.[23] The memo began by invoking a metaphor called 'burning platform'. It narrated a story about a man who was working on an oil platform in the North Sea. He woke up one night when he heard a loud explosion, following which the oil platform started burning as a fire engulfed it completely. He barely made it to the edge of the platform. However, he had to make a choice between jumping into the icy waters of the sea about a hundred feet below, or face death by burning on the disintegrating rig. The man was standing upon a 'burning platform' and he decided to jump. He eventually survived the ordeal. After he was rescued, he noted that the 'burning platform' caused a radical change in his behaviour.

Finally the memo said: *Folks, our platform is burning.*

The 1,200-word memo highlighted how competitors had changed the game with new products. It said that the company had some brilliant sources of innovation inside but that they weren't brought to market fast enough.

Is 'We have a burning platform, it's time to jump' a good campaign to transform the company into becoming more innovative?

It is quite clear that a 'burning platform' message creates an important ingredient known to bring about change—a sense of urgency.[24] You visualize yourself engulfed by the fire all around you and you naturally ask, 'What do I do now?' The emotion evoked is fear. The question is: does this prompt people to act in a desired direction? Well, studies have shown that it does indeed help in circumstances where the action is precisely defined.

Let's take the example of a successful HIV/AIDS prevention campaign launched by the India division of Population Services International (PSI) from January 2001 to December 2005.[25] The campaign began in Mumbai with a tagline 'Balbir Pasha ko AIDS hoga kya?' (Will Balbir Pasha get AIDS?) and then rolled it out to other port cities such as Vizag, Chennai and Kolkata.[26] One of the teasers said, 'Balbir Pasha goes only to Manjula . . . but others go to Manjula too . . . Will Balbir Pasha get AIDS?' The campaign brought the tabooed topic of HIV/AIDS out in the open and raised the awareness of high-risk sexual activity and the importance of using a condom. The campaign became so popular that Amul came out with a hoarding 'Amul butter, regular item'.

In the case of the Balbir Pasha campaign, negative emotion worked well because the behaviour it tries to induce is very specific: wear a condom during high-risk sexual activity. However, when you want your engineers to become more innovative, would evoking fear work?

Psychologists have concluded that the answer is 'no'. In fact, Barbara Fredrickson, a torch-bearer of the positive psychology movement, has found that if you want to broaden your search space, you should evoke positive emotions.[27] Innovation by its very nature is about uncertainty. It is about experimentation with multiple ideas and then selecting the best one. If I am an engineer in an organization that wants to be more innovative and my manager tells me to jump because the platform is burning, I wouldn't know what to do. The situation would perhaps be different if we want to foster a culture of safety. It would perhaps mean that I wear safety goggles and a helmet in case I am a civil engineer on a field visit.

Contrast this with the 'Power of Ideas' campaign launched by the *Economic Times* first in 2009.[28] One of the ads for the campaign said, 'Of all the things you can lose your heart to, an idea is the most obstinate. It will set your heart aflutter with whispers of success and riches. It will share your bed, your shower, your desk. It will sit next to you at dinner. Some learn to ignore it. Some learn to love it. People call them entrepreneurs.'[29] Finally the punch line says, 'Start up'. The campaign received 12,000 entries out of which 5,000 got a feedback on their ideas, 1,000 were mentored, 254 got individual mentoring and nine eventually got funding.

Clearly, an innovation campaign that evokes a positive emotion like the 'Power of Ideas' is better than one that evokes a negative emotion like 'Burning platform'. This does not mean that constraints imposed by adversity—a sudden downturn or a natural calamity like a tsunami—don't play a role in innovation. They do. In fact, we will see in chapter eight how constrained creativity forms an important part of systematic innovation.

Is every positive emotion campaign equally good?

HEAVIER, FASTER AND LONGER

Indians take pride in the railway network and its role in integrating India. However, over time, it no longer dominates the transportation sector in India as it did once. By 2004, its share of domestic freight had come down to 40 per cent and its share of domestic passenger traffic to 20 per cent from levels of nearly 90 and 70 per cent respectively soon after independence.[30] To make matters worse, government budgetary support for the railways had declined, and the railways' own ability to generate funds for investment was impaired by populist pricing policies. In 2004, the Indian Railways seemed to be heading for trouble.

In their book *Changing Tracks*, V. Nilakant and S. Ramnarayan present the initiatives undertaken by the Indian Railways to turn itself around in 2004 and 2008.[31] Under the leadership of Railway Minister Lalu Prasad Yadav, Sudhir Kumar, an officer on special duty in the railways, reviewed the report of a committee headed by economist Rakesh Mohan that had studied the financial health of the railways. This committee attributed the decline in the railways' market share of freight traffic to high freight rates, which were fixed in order to subsidize passenger fares. The response to high freight rates was not uniform across the board; in some commodities (steel, cement) the railways had lost market share, but in others (iron ore, coal) there was no major change. This made him wonder, 'What could be the explanation for this phenomenon?'

Sudhir Kumar discovered that for some commodities, the railways provided a door-to-door service, while for others the service was only from one station to another. Yet, the prices charged for both services were similar. It was no surprise that the railways had more loyal customers in the first case! Raising passenger fares would not be politically acceptable and raising freight rates further was not possible. Also, many of the costs incurred by the railways were outside their control. Sudhir Kumar soon realized that the best bet for the railways was to improve the volume of goods and passengers carried by the railway system. For freight trains, it was decided that the railways had to (1) Modify freight rates to target high-value commodities; (2) Carry more freight per train; and (3) Increase the number of trains by reducing their turnaround time.

The extension of this logic to passenger trains meant carrying more passengers per train.

'Heavier, faster and longer' was the slogan the railways adopted to popularize this campaign.[32] 'Heavier' meant more freight or more passengers per train, while 'faster' referred to the turnaround time for the trains. 'Longer' indicated the length of the train in terms of the number of wagons or coaches.

The different zones of the railways and its operational units worked on new ideas to put this philosophy into practice. One innovation that emerged was the Garib Rath—a low-cost, affordable, air-conditioned train service for the common man. Garib Rath was a twenty-four-coach train with each coach having the capacity of carrying 20 to 30 per cent more people. If Garib Rath meant making the train heavier and longer, another innovation involved improving the end-to-end examination practice, thus turning the trains around faster. To go back to the elephant–rider model, a good campaign not only motivates the elephant, it also directs the rider. 'Heavier, faster and longer' directed the rider of the railway employees and focused their energies in one direction.

Titan, the innovative company known for its watches and jewellery, has used campaigns effectively throughout its innovation journey. Since 2004, when the innovation programme began in Titan, it has launched a new campaign theme every year. For example, in 2007, the campaign theme was, 'Simplify and automate'.[33] This prompted the workers to look at the diamond bagging process. When a work order was received from the retail store, a team of twenty people picked the appropriate diamonds, put them in a bag and sent the bag to the production department. People realized that if the volume of production were to grow substantially as predicted, this process could become a bottleneck. That led to the automation of the process where a robot senses through a code which diamonds are ordered, picks them and packs them in a bag. L.R. Natarajan, chief manufacturing officer of Titan's jewellery division, said it was the first time this process got automated across the globe.[34] Note how 'Simplify and automate' gave a clear direction to the employees where to focus their energies and creativity.

The bigger the organization, the more critical is the campaign design. We have found that not every company is able to give direction through the campaign like Sudhir Kumar's and Titan. It could be because the strategy is not very clear, or it could be because a theme matching the strategy is not easy to identify. However, any company can make the campaign inspiring. Remember, motivating the elephant is an important aspect of running any innovation programme.

The campaign may be the first buzz creating activity in an innovation programme. However, it certainly is not the only one. We will look at more mechanisms for creating a buzz in the subsequent chapters.

Now, let's look at the last of the three key processes of an innovation programme: training and development.

INNOVATION SCHOOLS

By 2008, the innovation programme at Titan was four years old.[35] Close to 300 ideas had been implemented by this time. Several process improvements and automation ideas set benchmarks not only for the industry but for the world. And yet L.R. Natarajan realized that the ideas came from only 15 per cent of the employees. This is when he asked the question, 'Why should only a few people innovate? Why can't everybody innovate?'[36] And this thought resulted in setting up an innovation school of management with a goal that everyone in the organization should become an innovator by the year 2014–15.

Every participant in the innovation school first undergoes a three-day training course where an awareness of why innovation is needed is inculcated and some of the tools and techniques related to idea generation and implementation are taught. Subsequently, for the next six months, each participant is given four hours for working on an idea and two hours of guidance from a mentor. At the end there is a convocation ceremony where the managing director hands over a diploma to participants who have successfully completed the course. By mid-2011, the programme had created 187 innovators.[37]

Can innovation be taught? Can those moments of epiphany— 'Newton's apple' moments—be really systematically reproduced? To be sure, there are certain things which are really hard to teach: to be empathetic, how to develop insights or how to develop passion or even an itch for solving a particular problem. However, there are many areas where more awareness and techniques help develop skills.

The first thing innovation training sessions or workshops do is to create awareness about what innovation means in the context of an organization. Innovation, in fact, means different things to different people—for some it is only about invention, for others it means the iPod and Nano kind of ideas. Innovation workshops use examples from within and outside the organization to define the scope of innovation.

Sukumar Rajgopal, head of the Innovation Programme at Cognizant Technology Solutions, says one of the primary objectives of these sessions is to bring about 'creative confidence'.[38] He feels that we often don't speak up in meetings, especially when the boss is around. In this environment of non-confrontational passive resistance, how do we create confidence that an idea may be worthy of others' attention? Innovation workshops create such a space where through an idea generation session, people get confidence that 'I can innovate' and 'My ideas count'. Cognizant, for example, has a 3,000-people-strong team of innovation evangelists that facilitate sessions where creative confidence is built.

The following table summarizes some popular techniques that can be taught to sharpen creativity skills:

TABLE 2.1: THREE SCHOOLS OF CREATIVE THINKING

Focus area	Techniques
Design thinking[39],[40]	Immersive research, rapid prototyping, brainstorming
Systems thinking	TRIZ[41],[42] Systems archetypes[43] Theory of constraints (TOC)[44]
Lateral thinking	Edward de Bono's six thinking hats[45]

A design thinking approach begins with empathy and advocates spending time with people, observing their behaviour, emotions, anxieties and aspirations. It is based on the belief that prototyping is a great form of thinking. This notion is sometimes referred to as 'act your way into thinking or building to think'.[46] It promotes rapid iterative improvements and collaboration through cross-functional teams. Schools such as the Institute of Design at Stanford, US, or the School of Design Thinking in Potsdam, Germany, specialize in teaching design thinking.[47]

The systems thinking approach, in contrast, tries to create a model of the larger system. Then the next step is to identify a point of leverage where a small change can produce a large impact. The popular metaphor of a 'silver bullet' signifies a point of leverage. However, identifying the 'silver bullet' is one of the most difficult parts in systems thinking. Donella Meadows has created a list of nine places where one can find the point of leverage.[48] Peter Senge in his seminal book *The Fifth Discipline* highlights commonly found patterns or what is called nature's templates and a point of leverage in each template.[49] The approach based on the Theory of Constraints (TOC) popularized by Eliyahu Goldratt is another form of systems thinking.[50]

Lateral thinking techniques popularized by Edward de Bono helps a person to move from one known idea to creating new ideas.[51] Tools designed for lateral thinking help break the current thinking patterns. For example, 'Six Thinking Hats' is a tool for solving problems through a group process.[52] If you are wearing a 'white hat', you need to focus purely on information, while if you are wearing a 'black one', then you are supposed to identify flaws or barriers. While the diffusion of tools and techniques does not guarantee innovation, it helps build a common language for innovation, and to demystify innovation as a process.

In this chapter we looked at three key processes of an innovation programme—the idea management process, the buzz creation process and the training and development process. So far we assumed that if we roll out an idea management system, ideas will come in. What if ideas don't come? What do we do? That is what we will look at in the next chapter.

Key Takeaways

→ Innovation programmes are an effective way of making the innovation process more systematic and predictable. Different types of triggers can lead to the initiation of such innovation programmes. But you don't need to wait for that crisis or 'a-ha' moment to start an innovation programme!

→ Though it's natural to worry about the quality of ideas, the Toyota experience shows that a focus on quantity may be more rewarding. Quotas, incentives, managerial involvement, and even the vocabulary used to respond to ideas influence the number of ideas generated.

→ The three important elements of an innovation programme are the idea management process, the buzz created around the programme, and the training and development that goes into the programme.

→ A well-designed idea management process pays attention to the source of ideas, their scope, the number of stages an idea will go through, the back-end technology to be used, the idea selection process, and how ideas will be supported and sponsored.

→ Though it's tempting to emphasize big ideas, the cumulative impact of small ideas can be considerable. Encouraging small ideas helps make the ideation process more broad-based and creates an innovation culture in the organization.

→ Ideation is a creative and divergent process. It is more likely to be encouraged by positive rather than negative emotions. A positive 'buzz' will work better than fear in generating new ideas.

- → A succinct tagline that not only relates to the problems at hand but also gives a clear direction to innovation efforts—like Sudhir Kumar's 'Heavier, longer, faster'—creates the right 'buzz' for an innovation programme.
- → Innovation tools and techniques, and even the design of innovation spaces, help spread the message that anyone can innovate, and help build creative confidence.
- → An effective innovation process supports visualization and communication of ideas, and builds a community around innovation.

Things to measure

- → The number of ideas in the pipeline in your organization (team, BU, company).
- → Percentage of employees who gave ideas over the last year.
- → Rhythm of the innovation programme review. How frequently do people meet? Who attends the programme? What decisions are taken?
- → Consider the tagline of your innovation campaign: Does it direct the rider? Does it motivate the elephant?

Things to do

- → Have you defined goal(s) for your innovation programme?
- → Have you defined an idea management process?
- → Did you roll-out a campaign? Did it engage the rider and the elephant?

→ Have you formed an innovation programme committee?

→ Have you rolled out any training/awareness programme?

Experiment

→ Find out what is working regarding the idea management system in your team/organization. How can you do more of it?

chapter two

STEP 2
Create a Challenge Book

'The mobile petition box was like a mirror which reflected the goings-on within the jail'[1]

–Dr Kiran Bedi

MAHATMA GANDHI'S PROBATION PERIOD

In Richard Attenborough's film *Gandhi*, the scene of M.K. Gandhi's arrival in Bombay in 1915 begins with an army band welcoming the new military governor of the Northern Frontier Province who is on the same ship as Gandhi.[2] A British gentleman watching this from the deck observes a gathering at the back of the ship where the passengers in third class are exiting. He asks, 'What's going on back there?' Another gentleman next to him replies, 'Must be the Indian who led a fast back in Africa. My cabin boy tells me he is on board.' As he is saying this, Gandhi (played by Ben Kingsley) is exiting the ship dressed in a white kathiawadi cloak, turban and dhoti. The second one says, 'There he is!' To that the first one says, 'God! He is dressed like a coolie!'

A huge crowd has gathered to welcome Gandhi, including the Congress partymen represented by the young Nehru (Roshan Seth) and Sardar Patel (Saeed Jaffrey). Both are dressed in three-piece suits strikingly dissimilar to Gandhi's dress. Gandhi's one-line speech, 'I am glad to be home and thank you for your greeting', disappoints both Nehru and Patel. Gandhi and Patel start their journey in a horse-drawn buggy towards a welcome party arranged for Gandhi.

The second scene starts with the buggy moving in a crowded street. Gandhi's head is lowered as he watches the sheer number of poor people milling around the buggy, which is stark evidence of poverty. Patel, however, is oblivious to the surroundings, and is happily explaining what is happening on the political front to Gandhi.

The third scene is at a party organized in a garden at magnate Jehangir Petit's place where Gandhi is introduced to the who's who of the Congress party. Gandhi recalls in his autobiography, 'In those palatial surroundings of dazzling splendour I, who had lived my best life among indentured labourers, felt myself a complete rustic.'[3] As the introductions are going on, G.K. Gokhale (Shriram Lagoo) arrives on the scene and pulls Gandhi away to a quiet corner for a one-on-one discussion. Gokhale had already spent a month in Africa with Gandhi, when he managed to persuade Gandhi to return to India. The conversation between Gandhi and Gokhale goes as follows:

> Gokhale: We are trying to make a nation. But the British are trying to break us up into religions, provinces etc. . . . what you were writing in South Africa? That's what we need here.

Gandhi: There is so much to learn about India. I will have to begin my practice again. One needs money to run a journal.

Gokhale: You forget about your practice. You have other things to do. India has many men with too much wealth. And it is their privilege to nourish the effort of the few who can raise India from servitude and apathy.

Gandhi: India is an alien country to me.

Gokhale: Change that. Go and find India. Not what you see here. *Real* India. You will see what needs to be said, what we need to hear. When I saw you in that tunic, I knew. I knew I could die in peace. (Pause) Make India proud of herself.

How much of this conversation actually happened is anybody's guess. However, a few things are certain. Gandhi did meet Gokhale, not in Bombay as depicted in the movie, but in Poona where Gandhi went later. What is also certain is that Gokhale took a promise from Gandhi during this meeting. What was this promise? Gandhi mentioned it later in his autobiography while narrating a discussion with his friend C.F. Andrews. From Poona, Gandhi travelled to Shantiniketan where he got a telegram informing him about Gokhale's death. The same day Gandhi left for Poona with Andrews and Kasturba, Gandhi's wife. Andrews asked Gandhi, 'Do you think that a time will come for satyagraha in India? And if so, have you any idea when it will come?'[4] To that Gandhi answered, 'It is difficult to say. For one year I am to do nothing. For Gokhale took from me a promise that I should travel in India for gaining experience, and express no opinion on public questions until I have finished the period of probation.'[5]

Perhaps Gandhi would have put himself on probation even without Gokhale's advice. But the question is why such a probationary period? After all, Gandhi was no novice in fighting with the British or writing a journal. He had led the movement for the Indians in South Africa since 1906 and had been writing in journals since 1903. In fact, Gandhi was complimented for his book *Hind Swaraj or Indian Home Rule* by none other than Leo Tolstoy.[6] The message Gokhale was giving Gandhi was that to serve India, he needed to know her real self. In 1915, Gandhi was a man with a hammer in the form of satyagraha in his hand. And we know that to a man with a hammer everything starts looking like a nail. You need to identify which nail to hit first. And for all you know, the most critical nail doesn't need a hammer but a different tool, say a screwdriver.

Managing innovation is no exception to this rule—identifying the right problem to solve is an extremely important step in innovation. G.V. Prasad, vice-chairman and managing director of Dr Reddy's Laboratories, one of the leading pharmaceutical companies in India, underlined this when he said, 'It [innovation] requires you to think of defining the problem you are trying to solve first.'[7] Similarly, when Ratan Tata, chairman of the Tata Group, was asked, 'What does it take for industrial operations like Tata Motors to innovate in a knowledge era?' he said, 'The truth is I think that if there are challenges and those challenges are difficult, then some interesting, innovative solutions will come. If you don't have those challenges, then, I think, the tendency is to go on to say that whatever will happen, will take place in small deltas.'[8]

A place where an organization lists its problems is what we call a challenge book. Unlike financial statements like a balance sheet or a profit and loss account, a challenge book doesn't have a prescribed format. A five-member team may have its own challenge book while a thousand-member business unit may have another one at a different level.

How do different organizations manage their challenge books? Let's look at two organizations, which are very different from each other in terms of culture and technology friendliness.

U&I PORTAL AT HCL

In his book, *Employees First, Customers Second*, Vineet Nayar, the newly appointed CEO of HCL Technologies, explains how he took on the challenging task of rejuvenating one of India's top IT services firms in 2005.[9] As Vineet started talking to employees at the company's offices spread over the globe, he realized there was a need of a forum where their questions could be collected and answered. A possible solution came up when Vineet met with a social networking group to develop an online forum where any employee could post a question and the top management would answer it. The questions and answers would be open to all the employees so that questions would not have to be repeated.

People were worried about the possible negative publicity and whether Vineet and his team would be able to answer all questions truthfully and transparently. When the portal was launched, it got flooded with queries, not all of which could be answered by Vineet and his team. However, people started discussing how to solve these problems in corridors and during coffee breaks. In short, the portal raised the problem consciousness of the entire organization.

Seeing how powerful this forum is, Vineet added another section to the portal called 'My Problems' in which he posted questions that were bothering him and sought ideas and answers from his colleagues across HCLT. One of the questions he asked was how HCLT could persuade analysts in the IT ecosystem to have a better view of HCLT. This was considered essential to change the perception of HCLT among influential buyers of IT services. Vineet was amazed by the response he got to this and other questions.

The U&I portal helped HCLT show the advantage of bringing out problems in the open and inviting suggestions. It also showed how individuals across the organization can even help in solving the knotty problems that CEOs face.

HCLT is a technology company and putting up and using a social networking site was easy. Can a challenge book work in an organization where a book would usually mean a register (physical book) and a petition box would mean a physical box? Let us look at how Dr Kiran Bedi catalysed Tihar Jail to create a challenge book.

PETITION BOX AT TIHAR JAIL

The account of a set of radical experiments to reform Tihar Jail is presented by Kiran Bedi in an autobiographical account *It's Always Possible*.[10] When Kiran became inspector general of Tihar Jail, the largest prison in India, in May 1993, an ex-IG (Prisons) told her that it was possible to do the job merely by sitting at home and clearing a couple of files every day and not going to the prison. Kiran, of course, chose a different path.

As she started taking rounds with the superintendents she would take notes on things that could be improved inside the jail. Actions would be initiated from these observations and followed up to completion. Perhaps the thought that the complaints could come directly from the inmates themselves led to the idea of a mobile petition box that was carried to the inmates in their barracks. The key to the box was in Kiran's custody.

During the first month, the mobile petition box collected several petitions, some on medical problems, some on staff corruption, some others on inmate corruption, and some on miscellaneous matters such as the need for police protection for families of inmates, welfare needs, transfer between prisons etc. In the first six months, the staff attended to as many as 2,279 petitions. Kiran personally acknowledged each petition before the respective superintendent followed it up. Gradually, the staff joined the prisoners in voicing their grievances through the petition box.

The petition box, along with the rounds, became the basis of reforms inside Tihar Jail. The petitions would be discussed in daily team meetings. Sometimes a single petition led to a collective problem-solving exercise with prisonwide implications.

HARRY POTTER AND THE MIRROR OF ERISED

HCLT and Tihar Jail have completely different organizational objectives and cultures. Yet the idea of a challenge book catalysed innovation in both places. Challenge books in these places were dressed in different attires—in HCLT it was part of a web-based portal while in Tihar it was a register maintained manually. However, both challenge books manifested the same thought.

What is the underlying principle behind a challenge book? A challenge book reflects curiosity and in turn, curiosity is the mother of innovation. Sometimes, curiosity is triggered by necessity. For example, a demand for electric cars may come about due to increasing petrol prices and depleting oil reserves. However, curiosity also comes from asking new questions that are not driven by necessity. For example, life may be just fine without e-book readers like Amazon's Kindle, or a mobile phone serves its purpose just fine without the touch screen as in Apple's iPhone. And yet Kindle and iPhone have become successful product innovations in the last few years.

Perhaps the best metaphor for the challenge book is a mirror. And we may well ask—what kind of mirror?

On the night of Christmas in his first year at Hogwarts School of Wizardry, Harry Potter stumbles upon the 'Mirror of Erised'.[11] It is in this mirror that he sees his dead parents and other family members standing around him. Harry tells his friend Ron Weasly, who looks into the mirror, expecting to see his family members too, but to his surprise, Ron sees himself standing alone as the captain of the Quidditch team. They both start wondering—what was this mirror actually showing them? Later, Principal Dumbledore explains to Harry the mystery behind this special mirror. The Mirror of Erised shows the person standing in front of it the deepest and most desperate desires of his hearts. Harry Potter lost his family when he was a baby, which is why he sees his parents in the mirror. Ron Weasly, on the other hand, was always dominated by his elder brothers. Hence, he saw his deepest desire reflected in the mirror—being better than all of them as the Quidditch team captain.

A challenge book is a poor man's version of the Mirror of Erised. For example, the man who carries his wife and two kids on his scooter would see himself as driving a car in this mirror. Similarly, an organization should see the desires of its employees, customers (current and future), partners and investors being reflected in the challenge book. Not all desires may be the 'deepest' ones as in the Harry Potter case. Providing toilets, benches and drinking water to the visitors of Tihar Jail may not be the deepest desire of Kiran Bedi. Nevertheless it is a desire she carried with her. And it got reflected in the challenge book maintained at Tihar Jail.

Okay, so you might agree that the challenge book is a useful thing. But in order to create one we need to start somewhere. Where?

HOW TO BUILD A CHALLENGE BOOK?

Can we build a challenge book systematically? To find out, we looked at several innovations, and asked a simple question, 'What was the source of curiosity in this story?' For example, when we came across the steam engine improvement by James Watt we asked, 'What is it that Watt was curious about that got him to begin experimenting with the steam engine?' or 'what was the curiosity trail that led Mark Zuckerberg to Facebook?' or 'what got Davasia, president of Mahindra's farm equipment sector (FES) to start a hybrid tractor project that eventually got launched as Shaan?' We pored through hundreds of innovations and looked at sources of curiosity.

We found three templates that dominate the curiosity world: pain, wave and waste.

Diabetics find it very inconvenient to inject themselves with insulin since it causes hypoglycemia. They prefer the tablet instead, which whips the pancreas to produce more insulin. Kiran Mazumdar-Shaw, MD of Biocon, a leading bio-pharma firm in India, feels this pain of diabetic patients is a potential source of opportunity. Feeling the pain of your current and future customers is perhaps the greatest source of curiosity for innovators. Even the early work on the steam engine at the turn of the seventeenth century was motivated by a need to avoid the flooding of coal mines in Britain.[12] We have seen earlier how the pain of customers triggered innovations at HMT (Rajappa's story) and at Mahindra (tubular chassis). We call this template 'Feel the pain'.

K. Ram Shriram runs a venture fund called Sherpalo Ventures. Shriram was one of the first investors in Google—he owns 900,000 shares of Google and continues to remain on its board.[13] Through Sherpalo, Shriram has been investing in Indian start-ups for the past seven years. The Sherpalo portfolio includes start-ups such as naukri.com, the leading job portal site, InMobi, which is into mobile advertising, Green Dust, a reverse logistics company, clean energy provider Kotak Urja and online travel services firm, Cleartrip. What is interesting is how Shriram selects the companies in which to invest. What he says is, 'We fundamentally believe in spotting underlying trends in an economy and backing companies that address these trends.'[14] The key phrase here is 'spotting underlying trends'. Sherpalo isn't unique; many venture capital firms do this systematically. For example, in 2007, when Sumir Chadha, MD of Sequoia Capital India, was asked about which wave he was trying to catch, he mentioned areas like microfinance, financial services and wireless.[15] Isn't it imperative that every organization spots trends relevant to its business? We call this template 'Sense the wave'.

Curiosity comes naturally to Srinivasan, who is a senior assistant at the Hosur plant of TVS Motor, a leading two-wheeler manufacturer in India.[16] While analysing the cost break-up of the StarR motorcycle model, he observed that the piston pin in the model cost Rs 15.08 while it cost only Rs 13.87 for the VictorGLX model. After doing a 'why-why' analysis, he found out that the cost was different due to the logistics overhead—the pin for the StarR came all the way from a place in Andhra Pradesh (500 kilometres), while the pin for the Victor came from a nearby place, which was only eight kilometres away. After a laboratory analysis, he found that the material properties of the two pins were the same. When Srinivasan was satisfied with his testing, he suggested that the piston pin coming from the nearby vendor be used for StarR, resulting in savings for TVS.

Guess how many such ideas Srinivasan has suggested that have been implemented? A whopping 5,792 ideas over the last six years, saving TVS Rs 4.86 crore![17] He has won the Best Suggestor award six times at TVS and has also travelled abroad twice to attend international conferences. TVS is one of those companies where the kaizen process has been implemented religiously. Kaizen involves systematically identifying the *muda* or waste and removing it. We call this template 'See the waste'.

FEEL THE PAIN

How do we find out customers' pain areas? Often, the broad customer pain areas are well known. For example, when Arimasa Naitoh, vice president of Lenovo, and also known as the Father of Thinkpad, was asked, 'What are the innovations to the notebook you are working on?' Naitoh replied, 'You need to eliminate some of the pain points. When you use notebooks you still have to worry about whether they have enough charge, if you are carrying an AC adapter, if there is a charging point etc.'[18] Every portable device, whether it is a laptop or a mobile phone, would benefit from lower weight and a higher charge capacity.

Customer complaints are a great way of understanding

customers' pain. Anil Khandelwal, ex-chairman and MD of the Bank of Baroda (BoB) narrates one such story in his autobiography, *Dare to Lead: The transformation of Bank of Baroda*.[19] On the eve of the centenary year celebrations in 2007–08, BoB used the slogan '100 years of banking with passion'. An unhappy lady customer challenged BoB by writing that the bank's tagline should be '100 years of banking with patience.' After probing further, it was found out that she could not get her registration for internet banking done even two months after making the request. Further investigations revealed that about 1,000 applications were pending for registration on account of internal problems. Khandelwal mentions in the book, 'I would have never known the real problem but for this complaint. Customer complaint is the most critical input in understanding the ground reality.'[20]

Many times, the pain is not expressed anywhere. It remains buried within the aspirations and anxieties that cannot be articulated. The person riding the scooter didn't tell Ratan Tata that he would like to have a four-wheeler. It had to be felt by the innovator. How does one feel the pain without it being articulated? That's where the technique recommended by Gokhale to Gandhi—of immersing oneself in the social context by keeping the eyes open and the mouth shut—comes handy. In the book *The Game-changer* written by the ex-CEO of Procter & Gamble A.G. Lafley and consultant Ram Charan, this technique is referred to as 'immersive research'.[21]

What is immersive research?

In 2002, P&G launched two programmes: 'Living It' and 'Working It'. 'Living It' involved employees spending several days with consumers, say in a lower-middle-class household. They would participate in some of the family activities, such as eating a meal together or shopping in a store. They would observe what the family members bought and how various brands fitted into their social context. This close look at a family led to unique insights, way beyond what conventional market research can generate. 'Working It' involved spending time behind the counter selling the product to the consumers. The employees would observe what type of consumers were buying the company's products, who was buying the competitors' products, and get a glimpse into how they might be making these decisions.

By 2007, 75 per cent of all P&G executives had at least one experience from either 'Living It' or 'Working It'. By spending time in lower-income Mexican households, P&G folks realized how difficult the hand-wash-rinse cycle was. With this insight, P&G came up with Downy Single Rinse, which reduced the six-step process to three: wash, add softener, rinse. Intuit's follow-me-home process that we described in the last chapter was also an example of immersive research.

Many consumer-centric businesses in India have realized the importance of immersive research. For example, Future Ideas, the innovation department of Kishore Biyani's Future Group, sends its teams to visit homes of all classes of consumers across the country. They check out all the rooms in the home, take photos and make notes to understand the usage of space, furniture, utensils etc. This has resulted in the launch of community-specific offerings. One of the insights achieved during such visits led to offering pulses and grains to stockpile for a year for Gujarati consumers in Big Bazaar, Kandivali.[22] Similar home visits by employees of Mirc Electronics/Onida helped them realize that working couples do not like returning to a hot house in summer. They introduced the Onida Pre-cool AC that can be turned on with an SMS. The company sold 75,000 pre-cool ACs in the first five months after the product's launch in January 2011.[23]

Hindustan Unilever, the leading fast moving consumer goods (FMCG) player in India, is also discovering the importance of immersive research. In May 2010, about 4,000 HUL employees cleaned and organized shelves at 20,000 kirana and chemist shops in seventy-two cities.[24] In fact, HUL has created a phone booth called 'Voices from the street' in its Andheri campus in Mumbai. The glassy booth has a telephone, a headset, a table, a chair and standing room for four. However, the room is used mostly by only one person at a time. It is a room where a HUL manager listens to consumers rave, rant, request, inquire and give suggestions about HUL products. Each of the 981 HUL managers has to spend fifteen minutes in the booth a week.[25]

Organizational structure and decision-making authority can sometimes come in the way of innovation that addresses user pain points. That's because the top management of the company makes important investment decisions (including new product launch decisions) and they are often too insulated and isolated to 'feel the pain'. Professor Huggy Rao of Stanford depicts this sharply when he explains employee progression in a large automobile company.[26] At first a manager gets a free company car for his use. As a result he is not much concerned about its reliability and maintenance—that's taken care of by the company. As the manager is promoted up the ranks, he starts getting free petrol. As a result, he is no longer worried about fuel economy. Once he reaches the CO level, he gets a chauffeur as well. By this time, the only contact of the manager with the car is the seat! Are you still surprised that auto companies might miss out on what the customers are looking for?

How do you overcome this? Professor Rao has some useful advice. Every senior manager should know the three top 'disgusters' and 'delighters' of every important segment of customers, and be able to distinguish these from annoyances and frills respectively. How does the senior management find these out? At Britain's largest retailer Tesco, even CEOs have to spend some time every year on the shop floor in customer-facing roles. For years, Tesco's customer service agents had been requesting the company to print bar codes on both sides of items sold in the store so as to make scanning and billing easier. But the final approval came through only after the company's chief financial officer (CFO) experienced the difficulty of billing items during one of his 'required' stints at the cash counter! [27]

Other companies adopt similar methods to make managers and employees sensitive to customer pain points. At financial services giant Vanguard, senior managers are required to spend a few days every year as call centre agents so that they listen to customer complaints and feedback first-hand. The Japanese consumer electronics giant Sony traditionally required all employees to work in sales, service or customer support before they could work in the company's R&D department.

SENSE THE WAVE

When we visited Vijay Ivaturi, then chief technology officer (CTO) of Wipro, in his office, he was just back from a visit to Lavasa, India's first smart city located fifty kilometres from Pune in the Western Ghats. It is planned in four phases and the first phase, known as Dasve town, consists of almost 1,000 villas and 500 apartments. Development of the other three phases will be carried out over the next decade. Lavasa may have been in the news recently for the wrong reasons, but this was Vijay's first visit there and he was impressed by the magnitude of effort, the vision and the opportunities it is likely to create. Is 'smart city' a new trend that is going to catch up in India? Vijay doesn't know, perhaps nobody does. But will Vijay watch this trend? Sure, he will. That's one of the important functions of the CTO's office in an IT services company: to spot and track trends relevant to the business and selectively invest in building technology platforms.

If 'smart city' is an interesting technology trend to watch for Vijay, 'stem cells' excite Kiran Mazumdar-Shaw, MD of Biocon. Stem cells are showing a promise that will make a non-functioning pancreas function after injecting a stem cell. However, the technology has a long way to go. She says, 'I am not going to do something right now, but I will watch this technology and see how it is progressing.'[28]

One person who epitomized spotting and exploiting waves was Steve Jobs. Apple under Steve's leadership identified and pursued three such technology trends successfully: personal computers (Apple II and Macintosh), digital music (iPod) and mobile phones (iPhone). Steve's relentless focus on tracking the next wave is apparent in the following incident narrated by Professor Rumelt of the University of California, Los Angeles (UCLA).[29] In 1998, Rumelt had a chance to talk to Steve Jobs after he had come back from his stints with NeXT and Pixar and turned Apple around. Rumelt was there to help Telecom Italia try to do a deal with Apple. After the business was completed, Rumelt got into a conversation with Jobs on Apple's long-term strategy. He expressed his concern that from where he saw things it looked as though Apple would always hold a niche position in the PC market. It looked almost impossible to break through the Wintel monopoly. Rumelt finally asked Jobs, 'So what are you trying to do? What's the longer term strategy?'[30] Steve didn't agree or disagree with Rumelt's assessment. He just smiled and said, 'I am going to wait for the next big thing.'[31] That big thing first turned out to be Pixar, and subsequently, the iPod.

What are the different types of waves? And how do we spot them? Perhaps the most talked about waves are related to technology. The internet has made the search for technology trends all the more easy. Every technology goes through a maturity cycle.

Gartner, the information technology research and advisory company, publishes a hype-cycle of emerging technologies every year.[32] It shows every technology going through five phases: technology trigger, peak of inflated expectations, trough of disillusionment, slope of enlightenment and plateau of productivity. For example, in 2010, it showed that computer-brain interface technology was in the first phase (technology trigger), cloud computing was just beginning to fall off the 'peak of inflated expectations', 'public virtual worlds' was at the 'trough of disillusionment', and 'mobile application stores' were on the 'slope of enlightenment'. 'Speech recognition' was at the 'plateau of productivity'.[33]

If all technologies go through this hype-cycle, shouldn't it be easy to decide which one to jump onto? Of course, there is a catch: one doesn't know the speed at which a technology moves along this curve. Some technologies, such as speech recognition, will take several decades to reach the plateau of productivity while some others like mobile application stores will take perhaps half a decade to get there. Some technologies may die a premature death.

Apart from technology, what are the other kinds of trends companies should be watching out for? One such powerful 'wave' is 'demographics'.[34] Sanjay Kapoor, Bharti Airtel's India and South Asia head, is confident that data traffic accessed through mobile phones is going to increase in India. In January 2011, data accounted for only 13 per cent of Bharti's revenue. Then what makes Sanjay so confident? He knows that there are 560 million young people in India and they love new gadgets. Sanjay said, 'The number of people who are trying to log on to the internet, or access our application store, from tier II, III, IV category cities is growing by the day.'[35]

One Indian company that exploited a demographic wave adroitly is Bajaj. The company launched Pulsar—a sporty, powerful bike with a distinctive brand and positioning for the young male—just as a new market segment of single men with sizeable disposable incomes, thanks to the software and BPO industries, came of age.

Disney is going to launch a theme park near Shanghai, its first in mainland China, by 2015. It was announced that Disney, along with partners in China, would spend $4.4 billion on the park. Disney CEO Robert Iger called the investment 'a defining moment'.[36] Why? About 330 million people live within a three-hour distance by car or train from the site and about 30 million Chinese enter the middle class segment every year. Disney is trying to exploit the changing demographic landscape of the Chinese suburbs.

The third category of waves is investment from government and regulatory approvals. For example, the auction of the 3G wireless spectrum has created an expanded bandwidth, which in turn is likely to spur a new set of applications containing video streaming on the mobile phone. Similarly, de-regulation of the education sector in India can have wide implications.

FIGURE 3.1: THREE SOURCES OF CURIOSITY

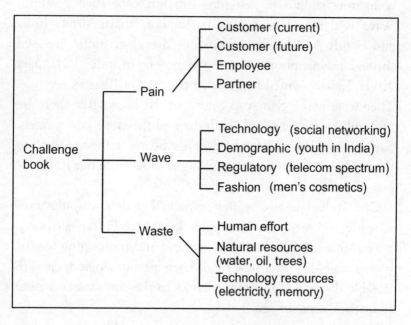

Infosys uses emerging waves as the themes for its innovation programmes. The company has aligned its innovation efforts around 'Building tomorrow's enterprise' with sub-themes of digital consumers, emerging economies, sustainable tomorrow, smarter organizations, new commerce, pervasive computing and the healthcare economy.[37]

We are familiar with two-minute noodles but not yet with three-minute idlis. And that is what the food industry in India—both global and Indian players—are today experimenting with.[38] Ready-to-eat meals and frozen foods are growing markets in India. Urban consumers, pressed for time and seeking convenience, are driving the demand. Consuming frozen food has not been part of traditional Indian culture—but the picture is changing. Social trends like these form an important category of waves. Some of the other changes visible in the Indian social milieu are the demand for men's cosmetics, health and fitness training, healthy food etc.

SEE THE WASTE

Would everybody in an organization be curious about the next technology trend or the implication of a demographic trend? No. But would everybody in the organization see waste of paper or electricity or material or time or money? The answer is a resounding 'yes'. V.R. Ferose, MD, SAP Labs India, narrated one such story in an innovation forum meeting in August 2010.[39] SAP Labs had organized a day-long event called SAP Genius. The mandate was clear: create products which have nothing to do with SAP's software products. An engineer observed that a lot of energy is wasted when people go for coffee breaks and don't switch their monitors off. 'Why not devise a mechanism that will switch the monitors off automatically when a person picks the coffee mug and goes for a break?' he wondered. He put a small micro controller underneath the mug, which sends a signal to the PC when the mug is lifted. A small piece of software detects the signal and switches the monitor off. The idea was so simple and easy to implement that SAP Labs implemented it throughout the organization.

Problems are easier to solve if they are clearly visible to everyone. This is particularly true of waste. For example, Toyota factories are laid out carefully and kept absolutely spic-and-span so that problems are easily visible. Since the factory floor is always scrubbed clean, any oil leakage is immediately visible, and the cause of the leak can be fixed immediately. If the problem persists, this becomes an issue for a 'Kaizen' or continuous improvement team to study and solve. Similarly, an accumulation of inventory at any stage of the assembly line becomes visible and the root cause can be identified. This underscores the importance of thinking of ways in which the processes in an organization can be modified so that any type of waste cannot be overlooked.

Does it mean that only incremental innovations come from noticing waste? A look at history shows us otherwise. Two of the greatest innovations in the last three centuries have come about when innovators tried to reduce waste. James Watt was a mathematical instrument maker at Glasgow University. In the winter of 1763–64, John Anderson, a professor of natural philosophy, brought a small model of the Newcomen engine to Watt for repair. By then, the Newcomen engine had been manufactured for more than half a century but it consumed far too much steam, which aroused Watt's curiosity.[40] He continued experimenting with this model for a year before coming to the conclusion that something else was needed to create a jump in its performance—and that's when he had the epiphany of adding a separate condenser. The dramatic invention of the modern steam engine, with its increased fuel-efficiency, therefore, started by observing the waste of steam in the Newcomen engine.

It was 1958, and within one year of its founding, semiconductor pioneer Fairchild Semiconductor had shipped one hundred transistors to a prestigious customer, IBM. Robert Noyce, who eventually co-founded Intel, was head of R&D at Fairchild. Silicon technology was moving from the not-so-old mesa to planar technology in producing transistors. The question was—what next? Robert Noyce remembers, 'Here we were in a factory that was making all these transistors in a perfect array on a single [silicon] wafer, and then we cut them apart into tiny pieces and had to hire thousands of women to use tweezers to pick them up and try to wire them together.'[41] Seeing that inefficient assembly process, Noyce asked the question, 'Why cut the wafer in the first place?' Explorations and experimentation on this question led to the invention of Integrated Circuits or what are called ICs. And it was IC technology that was to revolutionize the computer industry in the future.

In this chapter, we focused on the source of innovation—curiosity and its concrete avatar—a challenge book. Like the Mirror of Erised in the *Harry Potter* series, a challenge book reflects the anxieties and aspirations of various stakeholders of an organization: employees, customers and partners. In the previous chapter, we saw how we can build basic processes to manage an innovation programme. In the next chapter, let's look at how we can engage employees and bring them into this programme.

Key Takeaways

→ Innovation becomes more efficient when innovation efforts are focused on solving the right problems.

→ Problem consciousness—a degree of awareness of problems faced by different people across the company—feeds employees' curiosity and can enhance innovation in the process.

→ The challenge book is a place where the organization identifies and lists problems to be solved. By making problems transparent the organization can leverage the collective wisdom of its people to solve them.

→ The challenge book should reflect not only problems articulated by organizational members, but also future desires and needs.

→ There are three important sources for identifying problems for the challenge book: feel the pain, sense the wave, see the waste.

→ To feel the pain, track customer complaints, interact closely with your service department, or immerse yourself in the life of consumers.

→ Sensing waves involves tracking changes in technology, demographics, consumer behaviour, usage patterns, and regulation.

→ Waste is all around us, and we can see it if we are more sensitive to our surroundings.

Things to measure

→ Number of entries in your challenge book.
→ Number of entries corresponding to pain, wave and waste.
→ Number of entries in your challenge book based on customer inputs.
→ Number of people/managers who spend time on immersive research.
→ Number of insights from immersive research.

Things to do

→ Have you identified a challenge book at your team/business level?
→ Is there a process by which it gets populated?
→ Have you tapped the following sources: employees, customers, partners?
→ Do you track technology/fashion/regulatory/social trends?

Experiment

→ Discuss the top challenge in your challenge book in your team meeting. How many ideas did you get?

chapter three

STEP 3
Build Participation

'Without computer clubs there would probably be no Apple computers'[1]

–Stephen Wozniak,
Co-founder of Apple

CHANDRA'S MOTIVATION

In 1928, Nobel Laureate Subramaniam Chandrasekhar was a second-year student in the BA honours course at Presidency College in Madras and wrote a paper titled 'The Compton scattering and the new statistics'.[2] He wanted it to be published in a prestigious foreign journal like London's *Proceedings of the Royal Society*. However, to publish it there one either had to be a Fellow of the Royal Society or one's work had to be recommended by a Fellow. Fortunately, Chandra found a scientist named Ralph Fowler who was not only a Fellow of the Royal Society but was also familiar with the same mathematical techniques as those used by Chandra. When Chandra sent his paper to Fowler in January 1929, Fowler liked it and eventually recommended it to the Royal Society after a few corrections.

Meanwhile, Chandra got an opportunity to present his paper at the meeting of the Indian Science Congress held in Madras, following which one of Chandra's professors at Presidency College said that the author of the paper was a student in his second year of the BA honours course and that he had written the paper himself. The audience then greeted Chandra with thunderous applause. This is where, as Chandra's biographer Kameshwar C. Wali notes in *Chandra: A Biography of S. Chandrasekhar*, Chandra's career in science began.[3]

Even today, eighty years after Chandra's first paper, second-year students (especially in India) rarely do research. If they do, it is usually under the guidance of a professor. So where did Chandra's motivation and confidence come from? Let's look at another story in his life to get a clearer picture. We will have to go back twenty years, away from Madras, to Calcutta.

Eighteen-year-old C.V. Raman, a gold medallist from Presidency College in Madras, arrived in Calcutta in 1907 to begin his job as an assistant accountant general. One day he came across a signboard which read 'The Indian Association for Cultivation of Science (IACS)'.[4] Raman sought permission to perform experiments at IACS and began his work. Over the next few decades, IACS would play a big role in Raman's journey as a scientist.

In 1921, Raman travelled on a ship to Oxford as a delegate at the World Universities Congress. On the way, he was intrigued by the blueness of the sea and a germ of a discovery process was born. He wasn't convinced that the blueness was entirely due to the reflection of the sky, which was the prevalent scientific belief. He conducted a few experiments on the ship to validate his hunch. On his return, Raman initiated three research threads: (i) The scattering of light by liquids (ii) The scattering of X-rays by liquids and (iii) The viscosity of liquids. He pursued these areas with a single-minded focus along with his collaborators, K.R. Ramanathan and K.S. Krishnan.

The year 1928 turned out to be special for Raman. He, along with Krishnan, made a fundamental discovery in the molecular scattering of light, later known as the Raman Effect. Young Chandra, Raman's nephew, watched his uncle demonstrate his great discovery to visitors during Raman's Madras visit. Soon thereafter, Chandra went to Calcutta to spend the summer months working in Raman's IACS laboratory. The experience at IACS turned out to be a turning point for Chandra.

The second turning point arrived soon after Chandra returned to Madras. Arnold Sommerfeld, sometimes called the 'father of theoretical physics in Germany', was on a lecture tour in India and was to give a talk at Presidency College. Chandra had already read Sommerfeld's book, *Atomic Structure and Spectral Lines*. Chandra requested and got an appointment to meet Sommerfeld.

He told Sommerfeld he had read his book. Sommerfeld immediately told Chandra that physics had changed considerably after the book had been written and referred Chandra to the work on quantum mechanics, which was a new physics that was taking shape.[5] Sommerfeld also gave him the early draft of his paper on the electron theory of metals, which led Chandra to study Fermi statistics, a new form of statistics relevant for quantum mechanics.

With the dose of creative confidence imbibed at IACS, Chandra immediately launched into a study of the new developments in atomic theory. He knew enough mathematics by then to understand the new statistics of Enrico Fermi and

Paul Dirac. He began to look for a research problem where he could apply his new-found knowledge and wrote his first paper within a few months.

There are four critical elements in Chandra's story. First, the opportunity to see people whom you admire, whom we call 'role models', and feel 'If he can do it, why can't I?' Seeing Raman in action around the time he made the discovery of the Raman Effect was such an experience for Chandra. Second, being part of a community of practitioners where there is a common vision and everybody is excited about sharing knowledge. It is a network of people where energy is transmitted rapidly and a sense of identity is developed. IACS was such a place when Chandra visited Calcutta. Third, Chandra's meeting with Sommerfeld, which gave him valuable inputs on the direction he should pursue (as also what he should not pursue). Chandra himself refers to this meeting as 'the most crucial incident' in his scientific career.[6] Fourth, early recognition of Chandra's work in the form of the thunderous applause he received at the Indian Science Congress in Madras, and Fowler's recommendation of Chandra's paper to the Royal Society of London. Rewards and recognition play an important role in sustaining the motivation to pursue one's ideas.

Let's summarize the four elements:

Role model: People who inspire others, who then feel, 'If he can do it, why can't I?'

Community of practice: Places where practitioners 'hang out', learn from each other and together help others outside this community.

Innovation catalysts: People who encourage idea givers and offer constructive inputs.

Rewards and recognition: Mechanisms through which idea givers get appreciated.

The question is: How can we create these four elements in our organizations? Let's look at each of the four elements in more detail and explore the answers.

FIGURE 4.1:

FOUR ELEMENTS OF BUILDING PARTICIPATION

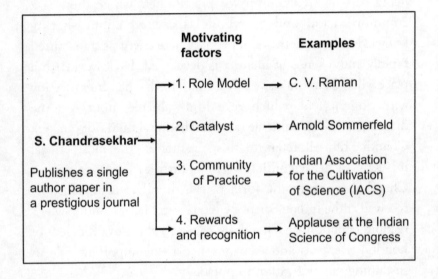

ROLE MODELS

Kishore Biyani used to occasionally visit a restaurant called Samarkand in Oberoi Hotel along with his friends when he was studying commerce at H.R. College, Mumbai. Why? It was to get a glimpse of his hero, textile tycoon Dhirubhai Ambani, who visited Oberoi's health club almost every other day. He recalls, 'Even if I could get a glimpse of him, I would be overjoyed.'[7] It was during this time that Kishore had started reading about business and Dhirubhai Ambani, founder of

Reliance Industries, became his first 'mental mentor'. Now, it is unlikely that getting a glimpse of Dhirubhai would have added anything to Kishore's knowledge of doing business. What exactly was it about Dhirubhai that inspired Kishore? It was the fact that Dhirubhai came from a modest background and had been able to create a large empire based on his own abilities.

Professor Edgar Schein of MIT Sloan School is an expert on organizational learning. In his seminal book, *Organizational Culture and Leadership*, Schein presents the two mechanisms through which we learn new concepts, new meanings of old concepts and new standards of evaluation.[8] Either we learn by imitating a role model and psychologically identifying with that person, or we keep inventing our own solutions typically through trial and error methods until something works. While the second mechanism, experimentation, plays a crucial role in innovation, we can't ignore the importance of role models. If you want to inspire people to be innovative, you need to demonstrate through a few individuals what an innovative person actually does.

Now, most organizations may not have legendary figures like C.V. Raman and Dhirubhai Ambani, but can occasionally invite role models from outside for a talk. And that helps. However, organizations don't need to have Ramans or Dhirubhais. Anyone exhibiting innovative behaviours can influence peers, juniors or even senior members. The following story from the book *40 Years, 20 Million Ideas* illustrates the point.

Takao Umezu was a shop-floor worker at Toyota's Kamigo factory's second machining division.[9] One day, his manager came up to him and said, 'Just a minute, Mr Umezu, do you have any free time later on today? If you don't mind, I'd like to see you for something.'[10] Umezu thought his boss was going to take him out for a drink. He got excited. Unfortunately, the place where the two went turned out to be different. The signboard at the hall read, 'Second Toyota GI Club Example Exchange Meeting'. Umezu was rather disappointed.

The 'Good Idea (GI) Club' was established in 1972 when six gold-medal winners of Toyota's idea management system began to meet regularly. What started as just a place for like-minded people to meet soon expanded in scope as a place to exchange creative ideas and give talks.[11] Umezu was in for a surprise when he entered the hall and looked at the front where presenters were seated.

One of the presenters had been one year junior to Umezu in high school. Umezu was impressed by the idea, the charts illustrating the idea and the delivery of his friend's presentation. He felt it would be worthwhile to be able to implement the kind of change his junior had talked about. That inspired Umezu to start looking for ideas, and within a few months, he ended up giving an idea himself. Within a couple of years, Umezu was submitting 200 ideas a year and he was awarded a bronze medal within three years of attending his first GI club meeting. Eventually, Umezu became the president of the GI club in 1985.

The important point to be noted in Umezu's story is that the person who inspired Umezu wasn't a well-known figure. In all likelihood, he was at the same or a lower position in the organization's hierarchy. However, through the platform of the GI club, his expertise got showcased to a larger audience. Similarly, every organization needs to identify behaviours that exemplify innovativeness in the organization's context: spot people like Umezu's junior who demonstrate such behaviour and give visibility to these ideas through channels or platforms such as the GI club.

Do you remember an Intel TV commercial shown in 2009 where Ajay Bhatt, co-inventor of the technology Universal Serial Bus (USB), is shown walking into the company cafeteria?[12] Everyone in the cafeteria, including the girls, start looking at Bhatt as though they are watching a rock star. Bhatt even winks at them. The ad tagline says, 'Our rock stars aren't like your rock stars.' Now, the real Ajay Bhatt may not be surrounded by people in the cafeteria for autographs. However, the commercial clearly brings out what is valued in the company. Organizations may not create internal videos presenting their 'rock stars' at work, but they use various platforms through which their innovation role models get visibility. One such platform is an alternate career path known as the technical career path created for technology and/or domain specialists. In contrast to a manager, a specialist may not have a team reporting to him. His primary contribution comes through innovations (all of which may not be innovations according to our definition!) in the form of new technology development, patents, papers, contribution to standards etc. For example, Ajay Bhatt is an Intel Fellow and holds thirty-one patents to his name, and probably has more in the pipeline.[13] This is remarkable because Intel will make someone a Fellow only when the person has made outstanding contributions to Intel's technology. In fact, positions like a Fellow's are usually peer elected and a Fellow will typically be considered at the same level as a senior vice president.

An explicit structure like a technical ladder is only one way to create role models. One of the popular mechanisms used by companies is to present 'Innovator of the Year' awards to individuals or teams, typically during an annual company day event. These are awards given by the CEO and send a strong message to everybody about the company values. In chapter one, we saw how the person with the highest number of suggestions would be invited to have lunch with the MD at Maruti. A monthly or quarterly newsletter highlighting the contributions of employees is also a popular channel to promote role models. No matter which mechanism you use, creating your own 'rock stars' is an organization imperative.

COMMUNITIES OF PRACTICE

The Indian Association for the Cultivation of Science (IACS) was started by Mahendra Lal Sircar way back in 1876.[14] Its goal was to create an institute equivalent to the Royal Society of London, but it never quite achieved the goal. However, it made a huge contribution in bringing the 'practice of science' closer to the common man. Scientists like Father Eugene Lafont, founder of the first scientific society in India, and Jagadish Chandra Bose used the IACS platform to perform lecture-cum-demonstrations on various scientific topics.[15] In the process it raised scientific consciousness, especially in Calcutta. In this way, the IACS created a successful community of practice.

A community of practice (CoP) is a group of people informally bound together by shared expertise and a passion for a joint enterprise. The group could comprise engineers writing open-source programmes, paediatric surgeons, drummers, long-distance runners etc.[16] A CoP has three characteristics: (1) members have a shared domain of interest; (2) members engage in joint activities and discussions, helping each other by sharing information and building relationships that enable learning; and (3) members develop a shared repertoire of resources such as experiences, stories and tools in order to enhance their capabilities. CoPs have been around for centuries. A case study published by the Harvard Business School depicts how MindTree a mid-tier IT services firm, developed and cultivated CoPs.[17]

In 2000, Raj Datta, whose job at that time was handling offshore delivery for US customers, initiated a study group focused on software design patterns. The study group was a hit, and Datta took on knowledge management (KM) as an additional responsibility. Within a couple of years, KM became a separate corporate function with Raj as its full-time leader. Today, MindTree has over fifty CoPs.

These communities cover a range of areas such as technical (for example, SAP, Mainframe), non-technical (for example, leadership, innovation) and role-based (for example, testing, business analysis). Some communities are focused on building domain knowledge.

How is a community formed? At MindTree, a group of people who share a common passion can form a community for learning and knowledge sharing. This group elects one or more champions. Any potential champion first attends a workshop with someone like Datta where his commitment is assessed and if required, is asked to do more homework and return.

Communities evolve over time. Initially, the activities revolve around knowledge sharing and seeking help for solving problems. Over a period, they start identifying areas where they can create a bigger impact on business through company processes and other organizational activities. For example, the J2EE (Java) community helped with MindTree's recruitment process by creating a question bank on J2EE projects.[18]

If the MindTree example gives a feeling that CoPs are relevant only in software firms, let us take an example from Kiran Bedi's book, *It's Always Possible*, of a different organization that leveraged the power of communities a decade before MindTree: Tihar Jail. Within the first three months of taking charge of Tihar Jail as IG, Prisons, Kiran Bedi had initiated a number of reforms, including adult education, yoga activities, daily morning prayers, sports and festivities. This was accomplished with the existing staff, and with the help of external organizations such as the Brahma Kumaris, National Open School, yoga teachers, storytellers etc. However, there was an acute shortage of internal staff for managing 7,200 inmates in a jail that had a sanctioned capacity of 2,273. With this realization came the idea of the Prisoners' Panchayat (Cooperative) System at a brainstorming session.[19]

The main objective of the panchayat system was to involve the inmates in solving the problems they were raising through petition boxes. The forum was also looked upon as a place where cultural and educational activities, and sports could take place. Some of the panchayats that were formed were involved in mess, education, medical and other areas. An orientation programme was organized where inmates were informed about the objectives of the communities and participation was solicited. Some inmates took up the lead responsibilities voluntarily.

The most significant community was the legal panchayat. Many inmates were not aware of the law relevant to their case. Moreover, almost 90 per cent of the inmates were undertrials. To meet the need, the legal panchayat, run mostly by 'inside' lawyers, educated the inmates about their rights and also provided help in exercising them. Kiran mentions the use of a 'case diary', an innovation that had a big impact on many undertrials. What it contained was an account of the court proceedings narrated by the undertrial after he returned from the court hearing as well as his opinion on whether it was effective or non-effective. Another boon was that several inmates obtained bail orders after petitions were filed by lawyers in the legal panchayat.

Similar to the legal community, inmates turned to teachers in the education community. With donations from various academic institutions, the number of libraries increased from three to twenty-five in a span of six months. The concept of a mobile library was introduced with the assistance of the Delhi Public Library. Kiran recalls, 'One of the most satisfying experiences for the inmates was their ability to sign their name while departing from the prison as opposed to merely affixing their thumb impression on entry.'[20] When such inmates were released from jail, they carried home their notebooks and other study material to prove to their family members that they had actually learnt how to read and write in jail.

Communities of practice evoke a sense of identity for the participants, be it Java programmers and test experts in MindTree or lawyers and teachers at Tihar Jail. Identifying oneself with a role makes it easy for the elephant to make decisions. When a teacher at Tihar Jail evokes the 'teacher' within, it acts as a powerful force that can overcome the resistance of the elephant because the participant is a helpless jail inmate. Communities of practice reinforce the identity and make it easy for people to grow into it.

INNOVATION CATALYSTS

In 1896, Henry Ford was working as a chief engineer with the Detroit Edison Company at a salary of $125 a month.[21] Ford's boss, Alex Dow, who did not like gasoline-related experiments, said, 'Electricity, yes, that's the coming thing. But gas, no.'[22] At that time electrical engineers took it as an established fact that nothing new and worthwhile functioned without electricity. It is in this context that Ford met Edison when Ford and Dow went to attend the annual convention of all Edison companies in one of the hotels on Manhattan beach.

During one of the sessions, a discussion on the emerging field of storage batteries and its various uses started. People present predicted that electric cabs and carriages would soon be on the streets by the thousands, and would require recharge batteries in large numbers. The talk continued at dinner when Dow, pointing towards Ford, said, 'There's a young fellow who has made a gas car.'[23] Then he narrated the story of how one day, he came across Ford and his family riding a carriage that was making a 'pop, pop, pop' noise. Ford began to explain how it worked, following which Edison and Ford got into a dialogue.

Edison asked if this type of vehicle was a four-cycle engine. Also, how would the ignition mechanism work, and was electricity used, or was the ignition on through a contact? Ford explained his current design to Edison and his idea of a spark plug. During the course of the discussion, Edison brought his fist down on the table with a bang and said:

> Young man, that's the thing; you have it. Keep at it. Electric cars must keep near to power stations. The storage battery is too heavy. Steam cars won't do either, for they have to have a boiler and fire. Your car is self-contained—carries its own power plant—no fire, no boiler, no smoke and no steam. You have the thing. Keep at it.[24]

Ford said 'That bang on the table was worth worlds to me. No man up till then had given me any encouragement. I had hoped that I was headed right, sometimes I knew that I was, sometimes I only wondered if I was, but here all at once and out of a clear sky the greatest inventive genius in the world had given me a complete approval.'[25]

Ford was offered a general manager's position at the Edison company on the condition that he give up the gas engine and focus only on an electric one. Instead, he quit his job three years after the Edison meeting on 15 August 1899 to pursue his idea—the gasoline car.

A typical idea author like Ford needs help on three areas in the early phase of idea development. First, you need a sounding board that helps you clarify your idea. Many times, your idea becomes clearer to you when you explain it to someone else. Edison's questions related to the spark plug and Ford's answers, for example, helped Ford validate his own assumptions about the idea. Second, you need help in communicating your idea better. You can be so much in love with your idea that you may feel that just the mention of it should make it clear how wonderful it is. But, most of the time, the reality is quite different. Even an idea such as Ford's gasoline car hadn't received much admiration until he met Edison. Third, an idea author needs to get introduced to the right people who may be interested in listening to the idea. The role Ford's boss Dow played was crucial in this regard. He might not have introduced Ford directly to Edison—but his loud narration of Ford's idea led to Edison getting interested in it.

CLARIFICATION, COMMUNICATION AND CONNECTION

Most idea authors are helped by three factors: clarification, communication and connection. How do organizations provide this help? At the India development centre of BMC Software, the pioneer of business service management, it works like this: BMC has set up an incubation team located in Pune and Israel under the leadership of Suhas Kelkar, CTO, Asia–Pacific. The charter of the team is to 'accelerate the rate of innovation'. The mission is not to replace the incremental innovation happening in the product teams, but to deliver radical innovation. The team takes up projects with a longer horizon (1–3 years), which are risky, and hence have a high probability (9/10) of failure.

The incubator team gets inputs from various sources such as the CTO's office, product/business groups, academia, partners etc. Ideas coming from the CTO's office or product management tend to be relatively mature because typically, they have already gone through an in-depth thought process. However, ideas submitted by engineers as a response to idea contests are not always completely thought out and require mentoring help.

The company's idea contest held in 2011 was based on the 'cloud' theme and 170 ideas came from an engineering base of 1,200 plus. A team of four judges narrowed them down to about thirty. Finally, ten ideas were declared as winners. At this stage, each idea author was expected to make a presentation. Presenting the use-case scenarios depicting the benefit was expected from the presentations. However, the business case proposition in monetary terms was not expected. A preparatory round of presentations was arranged and organizers gave a constructive feedback to the idea authors to improve the presentation. The quality of the final round of presentations was significantly better than the preliminary round. After the final round of presentations, a super-winner was identified and he was given the Top Innovator award. However, all ten ideas were considered for the execution phase, and two out of the ten ideas got sponsorship from business units (BUs). These, the BUs decided to execute internally.

However, the rest of the ideas needed help in being taken them further. Help was needed to find out the next steps to convert the idea into (1) a patent (2) a white paper/publishable paper (3) a proof of concept (PoC), or (4) a feature on the roadmap. Depending upon the domain/technology expertise required for the idea, experts were contacted and they readily volunteered to mentor the idea authors. In this process, BMC's incubator plays all the three roles of clarification, communication and connection.

In chapter two, we saw how Intuit has institutionalized the 'innovation catalyst' role. Cognizant Technologies Solutions calls them innovation champions. Consumer appliance major Whirlpool sowed the seed of innovation capabilities across the organization by putting seventy-five high-potential employees through a rigorous innovation training programme, and then diffusing these people across the company.[26] No matter what they are called, organizations need to create roles which help people nurture their half-baked ideas.

REWARDS AND RECOGNITION

Thunderous applause at the Indian Science Congress in Madras and Fowler's recommendation of Chandra's paper to the Royal Society of London must have been big morale boosters for Chandra. What is its equivalent in the corporate world? Since the corporate world revolves around profit, we might think that we should have monetary rewards. One of the obvious mechanisms is to reward each idea according to what it is worth. For example, many schemes offer a percentage—usually between 5 and 25 per cent—of the first year's savings or profit from each idea. However, Alan Robinson and Dean Schroeder, two professors and authors of the book *Ideas Are Free*, have discovered something completely different after studying idea management systems in 150 organizations from seventeen countries across twelve sectors, including financial services, retail, manufacturing, hospitality, healthcare, logistics, telecom etc.[27] They found out that the scheme of rewarding each idea based on its value wasn't working since it had three problems: measurement, fairness and corruption.

How does one calculate how much an idea is worth? If there were a formula, venture capital would be a commodity business. When Rajkumar Hirani bought the rights to adapt the book *Five Point Someone* from Chetan Bhagat, could he have predicted the success of the film (*3 Idiots*) he was yet to direct? The film budget was Rs 35 crore and the film ended up generating Rs 339 crore of revenue. Chetan Bhagat got paid Rs 11 lakh for selling the rights to adapt the story and many of Chetan's fans argue on his blog that he got cheated and was paid a pittance.[28] But hindsight is twenty-twenty and there could be several stories that are never made into movies. Now, imagine doing some calculation of this sort for each idea—small or big—that comes from employees. It is likely to be a messy affair. This is what Robinson and Schroeder refer to as a 'measurement problem', in their book *Ideas Are Free*.[29] There are some ideas that result in material saving or electricity savings of a department where measurement is easy. However, these are usually a small percentage of the total ideas. Many ideas improve quality and customer experience where value is difficult to measure.

The *3 Idiots* controversy came out a few days after the film, a box-office hit, was released. The primary conflict was between the contributions of two writers: Chetan Bhagat and Abhijat Joshi, who wrote the screenplay based on the novel. Abhijat and his colleagues, producer Vidhu Vinod Chopra and the director Rajkumar Hirani, felt that Chetan's contribution was 2 per cent to 5 per cent, while Chetan felt his contribution was 70 per cent. How does one decide the exact percentage? We don't know. In fact, nobody knows how to calculate exact percentages. Add to this the creative contributions from the director (Hirani), actors (like Aamir Khan), playback singers (like Sonu Nigam) and the measurement problem gets even more complex. When multiple ideas come together to create a product, it is difficult to do a 'fair job' in attributing credit. This is what Robinson and Schroeder refer to as a 'fairness problem'.[30]

The third problem relates to how the scheme can alter managers' behaviour. Robinson and Schroeder present an extreme form of this phenomenon in their book, which is that in Stalin's Russia, if a worker came up with an idea that saved ten tons of steel per year, the factory manager would be taken to task. There are several ways to interpret a process improvement idea like this. One way is to assume that the manager knew the improved process before it was implemented but did not bring it out earlier—on purpose. And why would he do that? In order to help the West by underperforming in the Russian industry. This was called economic sabotage in Russia and could result in execution.[31] Managers in most places don't have to worry about execution, as in this example. However, it makes them worry about what higher-ups might say when an idea that improves efficiency is rewarded by calculating how much saving it resulted in.

If rewarding each idea for what it is worth doesn't work in real life, then what does? Among the monetary rewards we have already seen in chapter two, one scheme that works is that of Toyota. In 1989, for each selected idea, Toyota awarded $40 to $300, depending upon how much it scores in the assessment. 'Superior' ideas get reviewed by division- or top-level idea committees. Many companies, especially technology companies, reward inventions in a similar fashion. An invention disclosure, which is a preliminary version of a potential patent, gets rewarded $100 to $250. And once the patent is granted, which could be two to four years from filing, the inventor gets anywhere between $1,000 and $5,000.[32]

Monetary rewards are just one part of the story. As Robinson and Schroeder found out, the non-monetary rewards and recognition play just as important a role, if not more. The most common way innovation gets recognized is by presenting awards such as the innovator of the year or the President's Innovation Award. The Tata Group Innovation Forum (TGIF) has institutionalized annual awards for innovations within the Tata group of companies.[33] 'Promising innovations' awards are given under four categories: process, product, new service and core operations. In 2011, a Jaguar Land Rover (JLR) team got the award in the process category for improving the efficiency in JLR's value chain, and a team in Tata Consultancy Services got it under the 'new service' category for creating a new technology, platform iON.[34]

When Tony Fadell came to Apple looking for sponsorship in the late 1990s, he wasn't sure if he would get a favourable response. Fadell was developing a portable music player at Philips when the project was shut down. Once out of Philips, Fadell thought of combining an MP3 music player with a Napster-like music sale service. He was rejected by at least one company he approached before he reached Apple, and Apple hired Fadell, first as a consultant, and subsequently as an employee.[35] As it turned out, Fadell's idea became a big game changer for Apple: the iPod-iTunes combination. Fadell went on to head the iPod division until he left Apple in 2009. Involving the idea author in the project either as a lead or a team member is a way to recognize him. SAP Labs has a similar policy where the author of an idea that enters the game-changer funnel (equivalent to the 'Imagination Breakthrough' pipeline of GE) gets to be a part of the team working on it either as a lead or a member.[36]

MANAGERIAL BEHAVIOUR INFLUENCES IDEA FLOW

It's Monday morning of a busy week ahead, and you are rushing to office. Your 'To Do' list already has thirty-five items on it. After a stressful ride through city traffic, you enter your office. As you get closer to your room, you see the juniormost member of your team waiting for you. Even before you reach your room, he comes forward and says, 'Boss, I had this great idea over the weekend about how we can transform our business. I would like to share this idea with you.'

How would you respond to this unexpected initiative? Please be truthful.

The likely responses? 'Can you meet me on Friday at 2.30 p.m.?' Or, 'Why don't you meet my secretary and fix an appointment?' Also possible: 'That's fine, but did you finish the project I assigned you last week?' or, 'I'll call you when I have time,' (whereupon you add him as item #36 on your 'To Do' list, and that's where he stays as more 'urgent' issues catapult into higher positions).

What you just did is give an unambiguous signal as to where

you really stand on innovation. How likely is it that a young colleague getting such a response will come back to you with fresh ideas? Though rewards and recognition are important, simple supervisory or managerial encouragement of ideas is the first step towards creating a supportive environment for innovation.[37]

Premature criticism or adverse evaluation of new ideas can destroy creative confidence—that's why brainstorming sessions separate idea generation from idea assessment. This principle applies equally well to your response to team members' ideas.

It's equally important that you (or your idea management system) respond quickly to ideas and suggestions. We know of a company that did an elaborate branding exercise to launch a new idea submission system. With all the hype surrounding its launch, hundreds of ideas poured in during the first week of the launch. But the company had underestimated both the number of ideas as well as the time it would take to assess each one; as a result, it took two or three months in some cases for the company to get back to those who submitted ideas. How enthusiastic would they be to go through this process again?

Key Takeaways

→ Broad participation makes an innovation programme vibrant. Motivating individuals to participate in an innovation programme is an important challenge.

→ Role models are an important source of inspiration for 'would be' innovators. Individuals are more likely to relate to role models who come from a similar background as themselves. Companies can identify and showcase role models to motivate employees to innovate.

→ Organizations can also encourage the formation of communities of practice—groups of people informally bound together by a shared expertise and passion—to create self-managed forums that encourage innovation.

→ Innovation catalysts help idea generators clarify, communicate and connect ideas. Catalysts can be trained through formal training programmes.

→ Carefully designed rewards and recognition systems can also shape the path for innovation.

→ Managerial behaviour can unwittingly put off people with ideas. Taking some simple precautions can help avoid such behaviour.

Things to Measure

→ Number of innovator 'role models' in your organization.
→ Number of active employee forums or communities of practice.
→ Number of innovation catalysts.
→ Number of people recognized for innovation per quarter/year.
→ Number of internal innovation stories published per year.

Things to do

→ Do you have a process by which 'innovators' get showcased?
→ Do you encourage the formation of active employee forums?
→ If an employee in your team has an idea, are there people whom he can approach to clarify it?

Experiment

→ Create an internal 'rock star' campaign like Intel has.

Part 2

IMPROVE IDEA VELOCITY

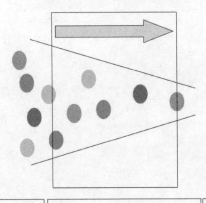

| Low-cost experimentation | Championing and communication | Business model exploration |

In June 1945, John von Neumann, regarded as one of the greatest mathematicians in modern history, circulated an article presenting the logical design of the computer he and his colleagues were building at the Moore School of Electrical Engineering.[1] 'The first draft', as the report was popularly called, influenced a number of computer design projects, including the one at Princeton University where von Neumann worked later and at the University of Illinois at Urbana Champaign. Even though the architecture wasn't conceived by von Neumann alone, the first draft popularized the term 'von Neumann architecture'.

Around this time, Homi Bhabha began work on the Tata Institute of Fundamental Research (TIFR) in India. He used to visit Princeton in the early 1950s and had discussions with von Neumann on several occasions.[2] He was convinced that to build a meaningful atomic energy programme the design and development of nuclear electronic equipment was essential. That is how the idea of designing a computer in India came about. The first computer built in TIFR was called TIFR Automatic Calculator (TIFRAC).

The TIFRAC development process began in 1955. The team consisted of a handful of fresh postgraduates in physics with specialization in electronics, supported by a few radio engineering diploma holders. The team had access to bits of information about the computer designed at the University of Illinois based on the von Neumann architecture. The pilot project for TIFRAC was completed in October 1956. The main project got an approval and a sanction of Rs 16 lakh after a successful demonstration of the pilot. TIFRAC had thousands of vacuum tubes, diodes and resistors.[3] It was commissioned in 1960 and its users included scientists of the Cosmic Ray section of the TIFR, the University of Madras and the Central Water and Power Research Institute. But one of the major drawbacks of TIFRAC was that it did not support a high-level language like Fortran.

According to R. Narasimhan, who led TIFRAC's development: 'The pilot machine, except for its size, was quite in pace with the state-of-the-art in 1954. The design of TIFRAC in 1957 was still not very much behind what was being attempted at that time elsewhere. But by the time it was officially commissioned in 1960, computer technology had surged ahead leaving our machine behind as an obsolete first-generation machine.[4]

What the TIFRAC team achieved in 1960 was highly commendable. The team had built its own memory system using the imported magnetic cores, designed a novel adder for fast addition of numbers, and had developed an electronic display of graphical information.[5] However, it was not sufficient to take the indigenous development forward. Experimentation capacity had to be much higher to keep pace with the latest developments. In 1962, TIFRAC was decommissioned and a CDC 3600 computer was imported from Control Data Corporation in the US.

In the last three chapters, we saw how we can generate a stream of ideas systematically. The TIFRAC story tells us that having ideas is necessary but not sufficient. How fast we are able to take the ideas forward is just as important, if not more. A few years can easily be too late, like it happened in the case of TIFRAC.

If you feel that TIFRAC was an isolated case, look at the Light Combat Aircraft (LCA) story. The LCA programme was launched in 1983 with the primary objective of replacing aging MiG-21 fighters.[6] LCA, which is now renamed Tejas, got Initial Operating Clearance (IOC) twenty-eight years later, on 10 January 2011. Contrast this with the early digital telecom switch development and deployment effort by the Centre for Development of Telematics (C-DoT) led by Sam Pitroda in the 1980s. Established in 1984, C-DoT deployed its first switch in thirty-six months.[7]

No matter whether you are dealing with a leading-edge technology such as microprocessor design or a consumer brand such as toothpaste, the rate at which you can take new ideas to customers matters.

In the next three chapters, we will explore the following questions: How do we improve the speed at which ideas move forward? Is it possible to organize ourselves better so that idea velocity can improve? Are there any competencies that can be built to facilitate this process?

chapter four

STEP 4

Experiment with Low Cost at High Speed

'Learn to fail with pride, comfort and pleasure'[1]
—Nassim Nicholas Taleb

DADASAHEB PHALKE'S PEA PLANT EXPERIMENT

It was Christmas Eve in 1910, a day remembered as one that witnessed the birth of an itch that would eventually lead to the development of the Indian film industry. On that Saturday evening, Dhundiraj (or Dadasaheb) Phalke watched the movie *The Life of Christ* and began visualizing making similar films with Indian mythological characters like Rama, Krishna etc.[2] By then forty-year-old Phalke had acquired various skills helpful for learning filmmaking: painting, printing, photography and magic shows. In fact, he had specialized in lithography and had done work for the famous painter, Raja Ravi Varma. However, none of his friends shared Phalke's sentiments.

For several months Phalke read all he could about filmmaking. He bought a camera for Rs 75 and performed several experiments. Then he raised money by mortgaging his life insurance and sailed to England to learn the tricks of the trade.[3] He got an opportunity to spend a week at Hepworth's Walton-on-Thames studio near London, one of the best-equipped studios in the world at that time. Phalke learnt trick photography too and returned to India two months later with a Williamson camera, a Williamson perforator, developing and printing equipment, raw material for several months of work and a collection of the latest film publications.

The next hurdle Phalke encountered was raising money for his cinema project. How would anyone believe that Phalke could produce a film all by himself? Besides, there was no market for Indian films. The local merchants probably hadn't seen any movie, so they were unlikely to believe that Phalke could produce one. This is also the most important point in our story: a situation most innovators encounter some time or the other. How do you communicate your idea with as little investment as possible so that it gives a glimpse of the future experience, and also demonstrates your capability as an innovator? Remember that Phalke had limited film and couldn't afford to waste too much of it before getting funding.

Phalke started with a project that would require no additional manpower and would use very little film. The idea was to shoot the birth and growth of a pea plant. He was shooting just one frame a day for a few days. Soon Phalke had a short film which was titled *Birth of a Pea Plant*.[4] He showed the film to his friends, relatives and prospective financiers. This created moments of truth for many, and Phalke began to gather the money he needed.

The *Economic Times* interviewed Guy Kawasaki, a Silicon Valley venture capitalist, when he visited Mumbai in November 2008.[5] He was asked, 'What are the few steps that an entrepreneur should get right?', to which Guy answered, 'Prototyping is the first thing. That's the first, second, third, fourth, and fifth thing. The sixth thing is to write a business plan.' Phalke had anticipated Kawasaki's advice by several decades!

What Phalke conducted wasn't just any kind of experiment. It was a low-cost one that created a tangible experience for the viewers. Such experimentation, which translates an abstract idea such as cinema to a tangible experience such as a pea plant film, is also referred to as prototyping.[6] The things Phalke needed for creating his prototype were a pea, a pot to grow the pea in and a few frames of his film. More importantly, the time he needed was perhaps a couple of weeks. Why is low cost so important? Because if you fail you don't lose much. You can get up and start running again. The principle is known as 'Fail early, fail often and fail inexpensively'. To use the elephant–rider model, a low-cost experiment directs the rider towards the next step that can be taken and also motivates the elephant by reducing the effort involved in the endeavour.

WHAT IS AN EXPERIMENT?

Professor Stefan Thomke of Harvard tells us that there are three ways to know whether an idea will work.[7] The first is to apply fundamental principles. For example, Newton's first law in physics can tell us where a bullet will land, given its mass, initial position and the force applied. Unfortunately, there are no fundamental laws in innovation which predict the future accurately. The second is to use experience, to see how somebody else has implemented the same idea and learn from it. Phalke did use this method when he went to London to learn from masters like Hepworth. In fact, Mr Cabourne, editor of the *Weekly Bioscope*, tried to dissuade Phalke by telling him how difficult it was to make money in this business.[8] Cabourne also pointed out several failed producers in England. However, once Phalke was back, he had only the third one left: experimention.

What is an experiment? When we think of experiments, we typically remember our science laboratory in school, the litmus test or the pendulum experiment in physics, or the first time we looked through a microscope. However, this is a narrow view of what an experiment is. An experiment is a planned activity to validate one or more assumptions of an idea. What kinds of assumptions? Let's go back to the Phalke story. Can you list some of the assumptions behind his intent to produce films?

Here are a few assumptions Phalke probably made when he imagined a movie production house:

1. Indian masses would enjoy movies depicting Indian mythological stories.
2. Phalke can master the know-how for operating the film equipment and the subsequent editing and processing in order to make films.
3. His production house can churn out movies and screen them in different places in India.
4. He can sell the tickets at an attractive price and make a profit.

Thomke divides the assumptions associated with every idea into four categories: need, technical, production and commercial.[9] The first assumption (Indian masses would enjoy movies) belongs to the 'need' category, which tries to answer: What does the customer need? The second assumption belongs to the 'technical' category, which tries to answer: How can we put together what we have (film, camera and actors) and create what we want (a movie)? The third assumption belongs to the 'production' category, which takes the idea from a prototype to the field and asks: How can we scale this idea without compromising quality? The fourth assumption belongs to the 'commercial' category, which asks: How can we make a profit in the end?

FIGURE 5.1: FOUR TYPES OF ASSUMPTIONS OF EVERY IDEA

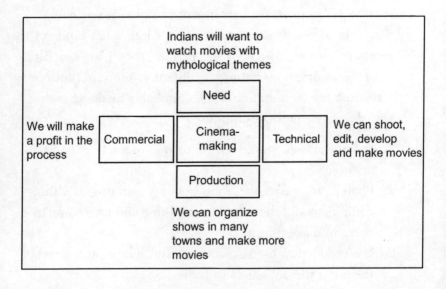

Phalke's pea plant experiment validated the technical assumption and demonstrated to his friends and financiers that he could create a movie. Mihir Bose points out two more experiments in Phalke's journey. As was customary during those times, no female was ready to act in Phalke's film.[10]

However, a breakthrough came when Phalke discovered Salunke, a young man with effeminate looks working in a restaurant. He was given Rs 5 more than his salary as an incentive and so, for a princely sum of Rs 15 a month, Salunke joined Phalke. This is how Phalke, for his first movie, made an assumption (out of frustration) that people will accept a male playing the female role. Luckily, it worked.

Raja Harishchandra, Phalke's first film, had a reel that was 3,700 feet long. The film was completed in 1912. It was first screened on 21 April 1913 at Bombay's Olympia Theatre with regular shows starting ten days later at the Coronation Cinema in the city. When he took the film to small towns, he was warned that the audiences there expected to go to a show and sit through a stage play for six hours, for which they paid just two annas. In contrast, Phalke's film would last a mere hour and a half for which they would be charged three annas. Phalke's advertisement proclaimed, 'A performance with 57,000 photographs. A picture 2 miles long. All for only 3 annas.'[11] With this tagline, Phalke was trying to validate assumptions along the fourth category: the commercial one.

What is the outcome of an experiment? This is perhaps the most misunderstood part about experimentation. Most of us believe that the outcome of an experiment is a 'success' or a 'failure' depending upon whether the assumption was validated successfully. Thomke points out that the real outcome of an experiment is 'learning'[12]; it tells us what works in what context and what doesn't work in what context, that is, knowing what doesn't work is also a successful outcome of an experiment. An experiment is a failure if we don't learn anything from it.

How does an idea move forward as various assumptions associated with the idea get validated? One way is to visualize this as a linear activity as we perform one experiment after another or perhaps some of them in parallel. However, we prefer to visualize the movement of the idea through two loops as depicted in the figure below.

FIGURE 5.2: TWO LOOPS OF EXPERIMENTATION

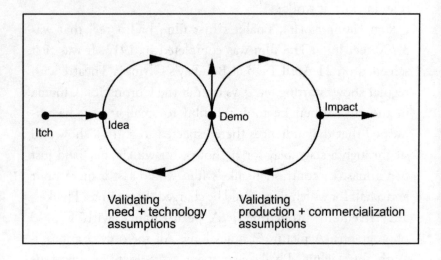

As mentioned in chapter three, the starting point of an idea is typically an itch to know or curiosity of some form. In Phalke's case the itch began in December 1911 when he went to see the movie on the life of Christ. An idea comes as a response to the itch. In the next phase, the need and technical assumptions that relate to the idea get validated. These involve multiple experiments, which is why we like to see this phase as a loop with a demonstration at the end of one or more experiments. A short film depicting the pea plant growth was one such demo. Some demos create turning points for the idea because the people watching the demo (such as senior management or customers) influence the project through feedback and funding and these are a nudge in the right direction for the project to become a committed activity. Remember the TIFRAC team got funding for the full-fledged development only after a successful demo. The next phase, depicted in the form of the second loop, involves a series of experiments validating assumptions related to production and commercialization. This phase is also called the business model exploration. Phalke's tagline of 'A picture 2 miles long. All for only 3 annas' was part of business model exploration. Revenue and profit are two commonly used proxies for the impact of for-profit innovations.

In this chapter we will focus on the experiments in the idea-to-demo phase. In the next chapter we will focus on the transition from the first phase to the second phase and in chapter seven we will look at the experimentation during the business model exploration phase.

EXPERIMENTATION IN SERVICES

We can visualize a product being prototyped. But what about services? Is low-cost experimentation equally relevant in services? We believe the answer is 'yes' and the following stories from Tesco, the Bank of Baroda (BoB) and the Bank of America illustrate the point.

Tesco is the third largest retailer and the largest e-grocer in the world. Sandeep Dhar, CEO of Tesco's Hindustan Service Centre (HSC) narrated how experimentation done by one of his teams improved the online shopping experience.[13] Tesco.com has a feature called 'Favourites'—the idea behind it is that if you are a regular customer and visit the site, you should be able to see your favourite list of shopping items. However, the way 'Favourites' was implemented made it seem more like the

'History' list because every item purchased was getting added to the list, which meant that the list was getting too long and not serving its purpose. A cross-functional team at HSC decided to work on this problem. How do you make the 'Favourites' list short and yet make it useful to the consumer? Through experiments undertaken in collaboration with the Indian Institute of Science (IISc), the team devised a predictive algorithm. The algorithm predicted the chance of an item getting purchased on that day before deciding whether to add it to the 'Favourites' list. For example, if you have purchased three gallons of milk on a Sunday, then milk won't show up in the list on Monday but will do so on Friday. The algorithm helped reduce the length of the list to one-third of the original size.

Anil Khandelwal, ex-chairman and MD of Bank of Baroda, narrates in the book *Dare to Lead* the following story of how the bank tested out a pilot before rolling out twenty-four-hour human banking.[14] It started with Khandelwal wondering how Mumbai, with a population of over 15 million, did not have a single branch of any bank that offered 24x7 service to customers. Services like ATMs and online banking existed and were useful. However, there was no service with twenty-four-hour face-to-face interaction. The idea got discussed in meetings and it was decided that a pilot one should be started at the Bandra branch.

Do people really need twenty-four-hour human banking in a city like Mumbai? Why would they need it at night? Would a few employees be ready to handle this? Would it be safe? Questions like these needed to be answered. However, unless you carry out an experiment, you wouldn't know the answers. As the Bandra branch started the service, customers began using it. Sometimes, it was a withdrawal for a medical emergency; at other times, it was a demand draft request, say, on the night before the last day of college admission. Looking at the encouraging customer response, the bank extended the service to eight other branches, in six centres, including Ahmedabad, Tirupati and Bengaluru.

Thomke explains how the Bank of America's innovation and development team went about systematically planning and executing experiments.[15] In one of the experiments the researchers at the bank found out that after about a gap of three minutes, the gap between the actual and perceived wait time rose exponentially. For example, you may have waited in the line for ten minutes, but it would feel as though you waited for twenty minutes. The team decided to experiment with an idea of installing TV monitors to entertain customers while they were waiting. The experiment demonstrated that the number of people who overestimated the perceived waiting time dropped from 32 per cent to 15 per cent at the branch with TVs while no such drop was observed in other branches. Encouraged by the result the subsequent studies focused on variations in TV programmes, advertising and sound–speaker parameters. For an organization that served 27 million households through 4,500 banking centres in the US, this was a systematic and a low-cost experiment.

Low-cost experiments like Phalke's pea plant, Tesco's 'Favourites' list and Bank of America's TV monitor experiments have a special place in systematic innovation because they help you crystallize various assumptions about your idea. They help you course-correct and also enable you to fail and learn from it.

HOW TO DESIGN A LOW-COST EXPERIMENT?

How do we design low-cost experiments? Let's apply the techniques we have discussed so far in the chapter to designing low-cost experiments. Let's imagine your corner grocery store's plans to become more innovative. The grocery store owner, Anna, starts asking his regular customers how he can improve things further. One of the customers tells him that she would like to send her orders through email. That way she can re-use a checklist every time she sends him the order.

Anna wants to try out this idea. What kind of low-cost experiments can Anna design?

Let's start by documenting the 'need' and 'technical' assumptions behind this idea:

Need:

1. It will be more convenient for many customers to send their order through email thereby re-using a checklist.

Technical requirements:

2. Anna can set up a computer and an email account in the store.
3. Anna can make sure either he or someone else is able to operate the email account.

To test assumption 1, Anna can call his friends who are in the same business and check if they have done this before. He can check with some more regular customers if they would be interested in sending their orders through email.

To test assumption 2, Anna can do any of the following: (1) Borrow a PC from a friend (2) rent a PC (3) buy a used PC (4) Use an existing smart-phone (5) Buy a used smart-phone with a GPRS connection. Depending upon his budget, and his friend, the set-up cost for this experiment may vary from Rs 2,000 to Rs 15,000. And this can be done in a couple of days' time.

Anna's bigger challenge could be validating assumption 3, that is, making sure that there is at least one person in the store who can operate it. Depending upon Anna's age and learning anxiety, this could take less or more time. However, Anna would never know the difficulty unless he gives this idea a shot. And that is the main point of this chapter. For any idea to move forward, you need to start validating your assumptions with as little time and money as you can spend.

As the complexity of the idea increases, the design of experiments has to become more sophisticated. For example, when the idea is to build a big jet such as the Boeing 777, the list of technical assumptions can be long and testing not so easy. Traditionally, any kind of testing would be done using physical mock-ups and also during final integration. These are expensive experiments, and mistakes uncovered during the final assembly can be costly. Now Boeing is using three-dimensional digital mock-ups with 3D computer-aided design (CAD) software to uncover the problems at an earlier stage. A test for twenty pieces of the 777 flap (wing section) involved the software making 207,601 checks which resulted in 251 problems.[16] It would have been much more expensive and time-consuming to fix these problems during the final assembly.[17]

The question we will explore next is: How will we make low-cost experimentation a systematic capability? That is, how can we make low-cost experimentation a discipline in the organization? Before we do that, let's understand who the villain in this story is.

FAILURE FALLACY

Let's revisit *3 Idiots*. The plot of the film revolves around the lives of three engineering students—Farhan Qureshi

(R. Madhavan), Raju Rastogi (Sharman Joshi) and Ranchhoddas 'Rancho' Shyamaldas Chanchad (Aamir Khan) at the Imperial College of Engineering, one of the best colleges in India. The most poignant moment in the film was surely when a final-year student, Joy Lobo (Ali Fazal), commits suicide in the hostel room by hanging himself.

In the beginning of the film, Joy Lobo selects a project which is ambitious—a chopper with a surveillance camera mounted atop. Joy's project has not been working out and as the deadline approaches, Joy asks Professor Viru Sahastrabudhhe, known as 'Virus' (Boman Irani) for an extension. Virus not only declines the extension, but also tells Joy and his father that he will not be graduating that year. Under pressure and highly frustrated, Joy commits suicide.

This whole episode highlights the chief villain in the experimentation: the failure fallacy. The real outcome of an experiment is learning, an understanding of what works in a particular context, and what does not work in that context. However, most people conducting the experiment (like Joy) as well as those reviewing the experiment (like Virus) feel that only when the experiment works, it is successful. Otherwise it is a failure. Ideally, Joy should have submitted the learning points from the experiment and Professor Virus should have judged them instead of the outcome.

There is a particularly important reason why we need to guard against the failure fallacy: the history of innovation shows us that several important and successful innovations arose from 'failure', and not from success. The best known of these is 3M Corporation's product, Post-it Notes. The distinguishing characteristic of this product is its ability to both stick to paper without falling off as well as being easily removable without leaving a mark. The key to this is obviously the adhesive or glue. The adhesive used in the Post-it Notes was never planned to have such properties; in fact, it is a 'failed' strong adhesive. And, the magic of the Post-it Notes is attributable not to the developer of this adhesive, but to Art Fry, a 3M employee who linked it to a user pain point.

Another prominent innovation that came out of a failed experiment is DuPont's Teflon, the material made from a variety of polymers, which is used in household products, such as the familiar 'non-stick' cookware. Closer to home, two-wheeler manufacturer TVS Motor launched a four-stroke scooter, Spectra, that didn't do well in the marketplace, but it used the knowledge and experience of four-stroke technology from the Spectra to launch Victor, a very successful motorcycle model. Similarly, Bajaj Auto had to wait for nearly fifteen years of flops and moderate successes in the motorcycle market before it had its first blockbuster bike, the Pulsar. Tata Motors' original launch of the Indica in 1998 faced several problems, which were tackled in the model's successful re-launch in 2001.

With this awareness let's turn to our original question: how do we build a capability for low-cost experimentation?

ORGANIZING FOR RAPID EXPERIMENTATION

Making one film is one thing and creating a factory that churns out films is another. After the first film, Phalke produced over a hundred films, ranging from short films to ambitious feature films over the following decade. Imagine the kind of travelling and expenses involved if you were to visit different places for shooting. But film producers had already discovered a new method—the film studio—something Phalke had seen when he visited London. Soon after the first film, Phalke moved his enterprise to Nasik and built a studio not far from where he was born. The plot of land had woods, hills, fields and caves—practically everything you need to make films with a mythological storyline.

Building a corporate studio is not exactly what Dennis Boyle had in mind when he created a 'Tech Box'.[18] Tom Kelley, general manager of IDEO, a leading design consulting firm, narrates this story in his book, *The Art of Innovation*. When Dennis became the studio head at IDEO he recommended that his colleagues create their own 'magic boxes', big cardboard boxes containing interesting objects and other things so that they could get ideas for new products they were developing.

Initially, people at IDEO thought the idea was weird. Many colleagues were afraid to contribute to the Tech Box because they thought they would lose valued things they had created. But the idea caught on as more people realized the utility of the concept. Over time, a special storage system was created to catalogue, store and display the items so that they could be referred to easily. The person managing the Tech Box is called a curator, a word borrowed from museum curators. Since its inception, hundreds of items have got added to the Tech Boxes and the concept itself has spread to other IDEO offices.

Tom calls the use of the Tech Box 'Making your junk sing'.[19] That's perhaps not very different from what Thomas Edison said more than a century ago, 'To invent, you need a good imagination and a pile of junk.' The laboratory in Edison's 'Invention Factory' founded in 1876 contained the followed 'junk': 'eight thousand kinds of chemicals, every kind of screw made, every size of needle, every kind of cord or wire, hair of humans, horses, hogs, cows, rabbits, goats, minx, camels . . . silk in every texture, cocoons, various kinds of hoofs, shark's teeth, deer horns, tortoise shell . . . cork, resin, varnish and oil, ostrich feathers, a peacock's tail, jet, amber, rubber, all ores . . .'[20] Why did Edison need all this 'junk'? Speed of experimentation was important to him as he and his team would perform several experiments every day. In a letter Edison has mentioned, 'A man will produce ten times as much as in a laboratory which has but little material.'[21]

Experimentation plays an important role in Kishore Biyani's Future Group. He writes in his autobiographical book *It Happened in India*, 'Prototyping has played an extremely crucial role in everything we have attempted.'[22] Future Group launches new stores and formats at a fast pace. However, Biyani feels that the two simple rules he and his team follow manage the risks involved in the process. They always keep a back-up plan ready. If things go wrong, they can cut the losses fast and move on to the back-up plan. The other rule is prototyping. Biyani writes, 'Every initiative, every concept or format we launched, always went through a prototype phase. We built it on a small scale and opened it to the customer interface. We then watched and learnt from how customers reacted to it, before we scaled it up. Any initiative at our organization, however big or small, must follow these two rules.'[23]

Organizations that are serious about building systematic experimentation capability also put an appropriate measurement system in place. Companies like Google and Intuit measure the speed of experimentation. For example, in 2010, Google performed 20,000 experiments to improve the search algorithm.[24] The result of each experiment first goes through a check by a few external trained experts to see if the improved search is working better. If it is working better, the new idea is put to test against live search traffic and checked for its consistency. In 2010, only one in forty experiments resulted in taking the idea to the users live.

Intuit measures the number of experiments performed involving customers in each of its product units. For example, in 2006, the TurboTax unit ran just one customer experiment while in 2010 it ran 600. Experiments in the QuickBooks unit went from a few each year to forty in 2010. Intuit also measures the time taken for performing the first experiment involving the customer. For example, for Mobile Bazaar, an idea developed in Intuit's Bengaluru development centre, the first trial was performed within seven weeks of the birth of the idea.[25] Scott Cook, the founder of Intuit, believes that an innovation leader should create an environment where high-speed, low-cost experiments can be performed. And then let the results of the experiment decide the course of an idea rather than politics and PowerPoint. Cook calls it 'Leadership by experimentation'.[26]

When we organize ourselves for experimentation by creating a laboratory, we are shaping the path for the elephant. We are making it easy for people to perform experiments. Whether it is Edison's Invention Lab or Google's search lab, a conducive environment goes a long way in making experimentation a part of the culture.

Can we always find a low-cost way of experimenting? Perhaps not. Sometimes the consequences of making a mistake are high. Perhaps we are playing with peoples' lives, such as in healthcare, in high hazard industries and in the transportation business. How do we go about experimenting? Let's look at one such experiment by the Indian Railways.

EXPERIMENTATION WHEN THE STAKES ARE HIGH

Do you remember the campaign launched in 2004 by Lalu Prasad, the then railway minister, and Sudhir Kumar, his officer on special duty, to turn the Indian Railways around? In chapter two, we saw that they launched a campaign to run 'Heavier, faster and longer' trains, as related in *Changing Tracks: Reinventing the Spirit of Indian Railways* by V. Nilakant and S. Ramnarayan.

Why 'heavier' trains? At that time, the Indian Railways was running trains carrying about 4,700 tonnes each. The comparable figures for other countries are 15,000 in the US, 30,000 in Brazil and 20,000 in China. What were these figures based on? A parameter called *axle load*: the maximum weight of a train per pair of wheels that is allowed for a given section of tracks.

In 2004, the permissible axle load on the Indian Railways was 20.32 tonnes. And this had remained unchanged for decades. Other countries like Brazil, US and China permitted up to 25 and 35 tonnes with rails of a similar quality. Increasing the permissible axle load offered the possibility of providing a major jump in freight revenues. Just a 6-tonne increase per wagon was estimated to add Rs 6,000 crore to the railways' topline.

In March 2005, R.R. Jaruhar, the new member (engineering) of the railway board, took up this challenge and placed the problem of the increasing axle load before his team.[27]

Jaruhar realized that the existing codes and provisions allowed him to conduct experiments. In consultation with the traffic department, he selected routes which had mainly freight traffic and very few passenger trains. This way Jaruhar ensured that there would be limited impact of a failed experiment. He increased the axle load on freight trains running on these routes. He contracted independent agencies such as the

Structural Engineering Research Centre, IIT Madras, and the Railways' own internal think tank, the Research, Design and Standards Organization (RDSO) in Lucknow, to measure the forces and stresses on rails.

The pilot began in May 2005 and continued for the next four months. Everything had worked out well but some unresolved questions still remained before freight trains could be loaded with more freight. Would maintenance schedules and protocols for tracks have to change? What would be the long-term impact on the rails? And, what if something went wrong?

What if there was an accident? Wouldn't the fact-finding committee set up by the government hold Jaruhar responsible? But Jaruhar's systematic experiments addressed most of the issues raised. They demonstrated how the axle load could be increased safely, thereby generating invaluable additional revenues for the railways. Lalu Prasad acknowledged this contribution in one of his speeches.

The Jaruhar story illustrates that experimentation plays an even bigger role when the stakes are high. In fact, systematic experimentation is the only way to respond to various challenges posed by changing situations. Are there at least some employees who can initiate experiments on their own? Are they defining and executing experiments? How fast? And at what cost? These are the important parameters that should be tracked.

The Jaruhar story also highlights the failure fallacy. His predecessors felt that failure of experiments meant failure in the job itself. This mindset could be a serious impediment in building a culture of experimentation. So how do we tackle this mindset?

FINDING KALAMS AND REWARDING FAILURES

India's ex-President Dr A.P.J. Abdul Kalam narrates the story of his first major failure in his book *Wings of Fire*.[28] In 1961, a team of four led by Kalam was given the responsibility to build an indigenous hovercraft prototype as a ground equipment machine (GEM). The team was given three years to launch the engineering model.

Although the project was completed ahead of schedule, it became a victim of controversies and was shelved. It was, for all practical purposes, a failure.

One day Dr Mediratta, Kalam's boss, asked him about the state of the hovercraft called Nandi. When Kalam told him that it was in a perfect condition to be flown, he asked Kalam to organize a demonstration for an important visitor the next day. The visitor took a ten-minute ride in the hovercraft, asked a few questions and left. He was Professor M.G.K. Menon, director of the Tata Institute of Fundamental Research (TIFR). A week after Menon's visit, Kalam received a call for an interview from the Indian Committee for Space Research (INCOSPAR) for the post of rocket engineer. The interview was at the TIFR campus where he would be interviewed by, among others, his mentor-to-be, Vikram Sarabhai. Kalam's entry into INCOSPAR, which was a precursor to ISRO, was clearly a turning point in his career.

For Kalam, the call for an interview was a message: experimentation matters. In fact, celebrating failures is one of the key indicators of the maturity of innovation programmes. Finding smart experimenters like Kalam may have been more a matter of luck than a systematic process at the Department of Defence. But can the celebration of smart failures be institutionalized?

The Tata Group Innovation Forum (TGIF) fosters a culture of innovation across all Tata companies. It consists of CEOs and CTOs of the Tata companies. TGIF has institutionalized an award called the 'Dare to Try' award to celebrate failure and to make risk-taking acceptable.[29] What kinds of teams earn the 'Dare to Try' award?

TACO-IPD is a division of Tata AutoComp and it produces plastic body panels for cars. Three employees of TACO-IPD— Anil George, Srinivas Devareddy and Gautam Pandit—saw an opportunity when the Nano project got started.[30] Why not design a low-cost plastic door for Nano? Team Nano hadn't asked for it, so Team TACO-IPD didn't have the specification. Unfortunately, the door developed by TACO-IPD didn't fit into Nano's cost budget. The team was disappointed, but they learnt the importance of co-development and phased review. Co-development would have helped the team understand end-user requirements better. Phased review would have warned them when they were veering off from the original parameters.

The TACO-IPD team was given a 'Dare to Try' award by TGIF. Dr Murali Sastry, a member of the TGIF said, 'The year the award was introduced, there were eight entries and all of them were from overseas Tata companies. There was not a single India-based company that sent its entry. However, there has been a big change in the scenario over the years and now we get a large number of entries from Indian companies as well.'[31]

While awards are one way of 'encouraging' honest failure, myths and legends in the informal organization play an important role as well. An innovative company like 3M is a storehouse of dozens of stories of inventors who dared to do something very different.[32] A newcomer hears these stories soon after entering 3M, and gets a message that awards and rewards will never be able to convey! At IBM, the story of a young man leading an important project that failed to achieve its objectives is often told. He walked into IBM founder Thomas Watson Sr's office with trepidation, expecting to be fired. 'Fired? I just spent hundreds of thousands of dollars educating you,' is what Watson is reported to have told him.[33] This story is so old now that one is not sure that this incident actually happened. But, what's more important is that it is told and re-told even today, conveying the importance of daring to try . . . and sometimes failing.

Kalam describes his experience while working on the Nandi hovercraft, 'I learned that once your mind stretches to a new level it never goes back to its original dimension.'[34] The question is: Are you rewarding the Kalams in your organization for stretching their experimentation muscles?

Key Takeaways

→ Every innovator faces the challenge of getting support for his ideas. Low-cost experimentation and demonstration helps overcome this challenge.

→ Though fundamental principles and experience or analogies can help support an idea, in the business context experimentation may often be the only option available.

→ An experiment is a planned activity to validate one or more assumptions of an idea.

→ The outcome of an experiment is not 'success' or 'failure' but 'learning'—it tells us what works in a specific context and what doesn't work in a context.

→ The key assumptions to be validated are need, technical feasibility, production and commercialization.

→ Effective experimentation involves overcoming the failure fallacy.

→ It also means being systematic, recording data properly, involving neutral agencies and different stakeholders, particularly if the stakes are high.

→ Remember that the outcome of experimentation is learning. It is, therefore, important to encourage people to keep experimenting. Companies use formal recognition mechanisms like 'Dare to Try' awards to encourage experimentation.

Things to Measure

→ Number of ideas that go through the experimentation phase.

→ Number of demonstrable prototypes/proof of concepts/pilots run in a quarter/year.

→ Number of experiments that gets customer feedback per quarter/year.

→ Number of laboratories.

→ Number of people rewarded for failure.

Things to do

→ Do you encourage low-cost experimentation?

→ Do you have a place where prototypes are showcased?

→ Do you measure speed of experimentation?

→ Do you have rewards for learning generated from failures?

Experiment

→ Hold a prototyping competition and throw a real challenge.

chapter five

STEP 5
Go Fast from Prototyping to Incubation

'The new idea either finds a champion or dies'[1]
—Professor Donald Schön, MIT

FACTORS THAT MOVE IDEAS FORWARD

The Bengaluru Innovation Forum is a platform created by the Confederation of Indian Industries (CII) under the leadership of Kris Gopalakrishnan, co-chairman of Infosys Technologies. The forum meets once in two months and listens to innovation stories from a couple of organizations, sometimes a global one like Siemens or sometimes a public sector organization like Bharat Electronics Limited (BEL). Siemens' presentation might be on scenario planning, while BEL might present its electronic voting machine story.

In September 2009, it was Ashish Khandpur, senior executive

director at the Technical Innovation Centre of 3M in Bengaluru who presented innovations such as the reflectors used on the New Airport Road in Bengaluru and dust absorbers used in auto garages that came from his laboratory. During the Q&A session, Raj Datta, then head of MindTree's knowledge management practice, asked Ashish what the typical time between an idea popping out and it becoming a formal project was, and whether it would take weeks, months or years.

Ashish said there was nothing like a typical time, and said two things were required to take the idea forward fast. One, how the idea was sold and two, how soon one found a champion. In fact, it took six years for the inventor Spenser Silver to find a champion, Art Fry, to use his 'weak glue', which after another six years was turned into Post-It.[2] In this chapter, we will look at the two levers: idea communication and idea championing, which help spread ideas faster. We will begin with the second one first. What is championing?

Let's look at an example. George Fernandes took over as railway minister on 5 December 1989. On 7 January 1990, he held a meeting at Raj Bhavan, Lucknow,[3] during which he spoke about two projects. One, a railway link crossing the mighty Gandak river between Chithoni and Bogha in Bihar, and two, the West Coast railway connecting Mumbai and Mangalore (later called the Konkan Railway). Dr E. Sreedharan attended the meeting as an engineering member from the railways. Fernandes told Sreedharan in the meeting, 'I will depend on you for the realization of these two projects.'[4]

The first one at Chithoni, a joint project between the railways, the state governments of Uttar Pradesh and Bihar, and the Ministry of Water Reserves, had already been sanctioned but was languishing for want of funds from all the four agencies. When Sreedharan met Fernandes a few days later he said getting the support of the two governments was a challenge but that it also presented a solution that would make the project more attractive. Sreedharan realized that the route wasn't a major revenue earner for the railways because of inadequate traffic, and suggested constructing a road-cum-rail instead of a rail bridge so that it could benefit the local poor people. This suggestion was in the interest of the state government. The road-cum-rail bridge project looked feasible since it would incur marginal additional costs. Fernandes liked the idea and approached Mulayam Singh Yadav, who was the chief minister of UP at that time, and Lalu Prasad Yadav, who was Bihar's chief minister then; both assured him of their help.

The second project, the Konkan Railway, was a tougher one. The idea itself was more than a hundred years old; it had been suggested in 1882 after a survey was conducted.[5] On the one hand, the project offered a great advantage by reducing the distance between Mangalore and Mumbai from 2,000 to 1,000 kilometres but on the other, it was an engineering nightmare with an estimated one hundred tunnels, some of them 3 kilometres or more in length, a few hundred major bridges and several thousand minor ones. Sreedharan estimated that it would take twenty to twenty-five years for this project if it was undertaken within the shoestring railway budget. Instead, he suggested that the funds be raised and the project executed with a public–private firm partnership.

Fernandes decided to take the matter to the prime minister, the Planning Commission and finance minister for clearance.'[6] He got the nod from Ramakrishna Hegde, deputy chairman of the Planning Commission, as well as the prime minister. Thus Sreedharan got clearance for what was to be one of the first successful public–private partnerships.

So what was George Fernandes doing? Was he generating ideas? No. The major ideas were old; in fact, one was more than a hundred years old. Many other ideas were presented by members like Sreedharan, but did Fernandes have the skill to technically assess the ideas? No. He had to rely on his partner Sreedharan. Did he have the required funds? No. Well, he had some funds as the railway minister but those were inadequate. He certainly had clout. Fernandes was trying to put all his weight behind this idea, pulling all the strings he could and clear the hurdles so that the project could move ahead smoothly. More importantly, he had an unwavering conviction in the ideas and the benefits they could create. What Fernandes was doing was 'idea championing'.

WHAT DO CHAMPIONS DO?

What exactly do champions do? 3M in, *3M: A Century of Innovation*, a book published during its centennial year, says: Champions have strong credibility within 3M and they are persuasive 'lobbyists' for company investments in new ideas or products. High rank is not mandatory for a champion, but the ability to listen, persuade and influence is.[7] Champions open new channels for the idea to move forward. To go back to the elephant-rider model, champions shape the path for the elephant.

George Fernandes had definitely built up credibility among a few chief ministers, members of the Planning Commission and cabinet ministers. And he was able to influence enough of them to move his project forward. In chapter two, we saw how Anand Mahindra championed Dahanukar's idea of the tubular chassis. Sometimes just the credibility that the champion lends is enough to move the idea forward. Satyendranath Bose, known today for developing the Bose–Einstein statistics and after whom the sub-atomic particle Boson is named, experienced this when he needed it most.

In 1924, Bose was a thirty-year-old reader in the Department of Physics in the newly started University of Dacca.[8] One day he was giving a lecture on the theory of radiation but made a mistake while explaining the mathematics behind the theory. However, to Bose's surprise, the mistaken formula was able to predict the experimental results—and he realized perhaps he had discovered a new and useful type of statistics for explaining radiation. Physics journals refused to publish Bose's paper, contending that he had presented a simple mistake, and Bose's findings were ignored. Discouraged, Bose sent his paper to Albert Einstein on 4 June, saying 'I have ventured to send you the accompanying article for your perusal and opinion. I am anxious to know what you think of it . . . If you think the paper worth publication I shall be grateful if you arrange for its publication in *Zeitschrift fur Physik*.'[9] On 2 July, Einstein sent Bose a postcard informing him that he had 'translated your work and communicated it to *Zeitschrift fur Physik* for publication', and told him that his work was 'an important step forward'.[10]

At age forty-five, Einstein was practically the God of Physics in 1924. It was also a crucial phase in the history of physics where a new type of physics—quantum physics—was taking shape. Einstein would certainly have been a busy man—yet he gave priority to a paper by a reader in the University of Dacca, translated it into German and sent it with his recommendation. It was indeed a turning point for Bose! That is known as 'championing an idea'.

To get an answer to the question of why champions are

required we need to understand how ideas spread in a social system like an organization or a market. Gabriel Tarde, a French sociologist, was the first to study this in 1898.[11] He studied the adoption of new ideas like how a chemist would study the interaction of molecules or how a physicist would study Brownian motion. He concluded that there are three distinct and yet inter-related forces that characterize human society—invention, imitation and opposition. Tarde observed that only 1 per cent of the people are truly inventive; the rest are imitators and copy what they see other people do. Opposition takes place when a new idea collides with another new idea or an old one. That is what happened when Bose sent his paper to a journal and his idea was rejected by people with old ideas. Tarde gathered data from crime rates, strikes, industrial production, church attendance, voting and other social acts to back up his theory.

A little over a decade after Tarde published his work, Joseph Schumpeter, the prophet of innovation, identified the chief villain in the diffusion of innovations: resistance to change. He wrote in his first major work on innovation published in 1911, *The Theory of Economic Development*, 'The resistance manifests itself first of all in the groups threatened by the innovations, then in the difficulty of finding the necessary cooperation, and finally the difficulty in winning over consumers.'[12] Half a century later, Everette Rogers synthesized and popularized work done on how ideas are adopted in his seminal book, *Diffusion of Innovations* (1962).[13]

Rogers grew up in Iowa, in the US. His father exhibited a peculiar bias when it came to adopting new ideas. He was open to using new electromechanical devices but resisted bio-chemical innovations. He refused to use hybrid corn seeds even though they had a significantly higher yield and were drought-resistant.

Eventually, he learnt a lesson the hard way during the 1936 drought when he lost his crop. It was only then that he started using hybrid seeds.

A study of how farmers like Roger's father adopted new ideas like the hybrid seeds led to the idea of the S-curve, a concept that literally gave a shape to the process of idea adoption.[14] Bryce Ryan and Neal C. Gross, scientists at Iowa State University, found out that a population can be classified into five adoption categories: innovators, early adopters, early majority, late majority and laggards. At first, a few innovators—about 2.5 per cent of the population—who are willing to take risks will adopt something new. They will be followed by the early adopters, a group that consists of about 13.5 per cent of the population. Then the first mainstream group, the early majority (34 per cent) will start to adopt the innovation, followed by the late majority (34 per cent). Finally, the laggards (16 per cent) will adopt the innovation. Roger's concept has stood the test of time across five editions of his book since 1962. In the early 1990s, Geoffrey Moore brought the model to the attention of technology markets by arguing that there was a chasm between the early adopters (who are interested in the technology) and the early majority, a mainstream group that is more pragmatic about technology.[15]

Now we begin to see how important champions are. People like Fernandes and Einstein using their credibility and sometimes lobbying, help overcome the resistance to new ideas. They are the bees who carry the ideas to flowers beyond reach.

WHEN A CUSTOMER BECOMES AN IDEA CHAMPION

In any industry where price alone becomes the basis of competition, the result is rapid commoditization. Tata Steel was determined to fight this aspect of industry in the late 1990s by launching an initiative called customer value management (CVM) under Vineet Singh. Professor D.V.R. Seshadri and his colleagues have presented the initiative in the case study, 'Customer Value Management at Tata Steel'.[16] The objective of the CVM initiative was to work jointly with customers to create customized solutions that delivered more value.

When Vineet took up the new role, it wasn't clear if the customer would trust the company enough to be willing to share the data about their operations. Similarly, there were doubts about customers co-operating for co-creation. It was decided to start the initiative with a few key customers based on parameters like revenue contribution, business potential, technological sophistication, cultural fit etc. The CVM consisted of five phases: preparation, study, brainstorming, idea evaluation and implementation planning as given below.

During the preparation phase, a cross-functional team is formed and led by the customer account manager (CAM). First, a champion has to be cultivated in the customer firm. This person is typically a plant manager who is able to influence other functional managers. During the formal kick-off meeting, both of the companies have to form a joint working team that will work together on the CVM initiative.

The study phase, which is of a three-week duration, is when the CVM team studies the deployment of steel in the customer organization. This involves checking how the steel is received and stored, where it gets rejected and so on, identifying various problems faced by the customer relating to Tata Steel's supplies. These include issues such as transportation, packaging, order progress reporting, complaints handling, furnishing samples and test certificates, billing and some related to invoices. The next phase, which is brainstorming, is of a one-week duration. It includes a whole-day brainstorming session at the customer premises, involving the senior management from both companies. Typically 150 to 200 ideas emerge, though not all are unique. The presence of the senior management helps get a buy-in in the implementation process as the work may be needed to be done by Tata Steel or by the customer, or by both.

The idea evaluation phase, which is the next phase, is for the next two weeks. Here each idea is examined for its impact and feasibility by joint teams. The short-listed ideas are grouped into 'mother ideas' and divided into three categories: hygiene ideas, taken up for immediate implementation on a top priority basis, operational improvement ideas, which require three to nine months for implementation, and finally, joint study ideas that require a year or more and necessitate significant joint working between the customer and Tata Steel.

During the next phase of two weeks, that is, the implementation planning phase, ideas are narrowed down to ten or twelve and each idea is assigned an idea owner who is either a customer representative or someone from Tata Steel. An implementation plan with the start and the end date for each selected idea is developed. In the final step, lasting for one to two weeks, the project is formally handed over to the implementation team led by the unit leader (CAM). From this point onwards, it becomes a formal project to be tracked by the CVM initiative.

One CVM project involved a construction company that was being supplied steel reinforcing bars of a fixed length. The CVM team identified several inefficiencies in sourcing, storing, cutting, bending and forming the rods to form the steel structures for columns in large constructions. The biggest delay occurred when unpredictable contract workers did not turn up for work during the festive season, which also resulted in penalties on account of delivery slippage. The CVM team came up with a proposal for a service centre where all these activities could be automated with the help of machines in the company's stockyards, using CAD drawings from the customer as inputs. The service centre helped save the customer significant costs and reduced the difficulties in appointing contractual labour at its various construction sites in the city.

This Tata Steel story highlights how customer involvement can play an important role in generating, selecting and executing ideas. At various stages, the process ensures that a champion is identified to take the initiative further. For example, it begins with the CAM leading the project, followed by a champion from the customer side. In the middle it is the idea owner who leads the project, and finally, it is the CAM's responsibility. The baton is passed on from one person to the next and the involvement of the senior management of both sides makes a difference too.

Now what happens when your customers are end consumers? Can you co-create with them? Lego, the company that focuses on developing the creativity of children through playing and learning, provides an illustration of how this can be done.

In 2004, Lego decided to develop the next version of the Lego Mindstorms, which was by then six-years-old and produced kits to create small robots.[17] It had a fan following visible through forums, blogs and community sites. They looked for users who were most referred to and linked to by other users. Initially, twenty people were shortlisted, out of which four enthusiasts were selected who became part of the development process of the Mindstorms NXT. Under strict confidentiality, these hobbyists helped outline the specifications for the motors, sensors and firmware of Mindstorms' new version.

In a second wave of this project, Lego added eleven other users who gave their inputs, and in an effort to finish the project, the company recruited one hundred additional Mindstorms enthusiasts to test the pre-release kits. In May 2006, about three months before the official launch, the 115 users were given the green signal to post online photos and videos of the new robots they created with Mindstorms NXT. This created a buzz among enthusiasts.

CAN WE MAKE IDEAS STICK?

So far, we have focused our attention on the bees that brought about a buzz. We assumed that the pollen would be sticky, but what if it is not? Or what if some grains of pollen are sticky, while others are not? Is it possible that some ideas are inherently easier to spread while others are not?

The concept that ideas can, in fact, be made 'sticky' was proposed by Malcolm Gladwell in his bestseller *The Tipping Point*.[18] Gladwell argued that for an idea to spread like an epidemic, three things matter: the message, the messenger and the context. We have already looked at 'the messenger' in the form of champions. What about the message?

Chip and Dan Heath, who popularized the elephant and rider metaphor, asked a question, 'How can we make an idea sticky?' They articulated a framework in their book *Made to Stick: Why Some Ideas Survive and Others Die*.[19] Applying the framework to an idea is like taking pollen and pouring some honey onto it to make it sticky. Let's see the framework with the help of one of the stickiest ideas generated from India in the last century—the salt march of Dandi.

The idea of satyagraha occurred to Mahatma Gandhi in 1906 while he was in South Africa. For Gandhi it was an abstract concept, something called 'passive resistance', but he soon found out that it was misconstrued. A lot of people suggested various names. Maganlal Gandhi, his second cousin suggested 'sadagraha' (meaning firmness in a good cause), which was then amended to 'satyagraha' by Mahatma Gandhi.[20]

At the beginning of 1930, satyagraha or 'civil disobedience' as it was called had been sharpened as a tool for over two decades. However, the need was to take it to several hundred millions, many of whom were illiterate, without diluting its essence. During a visit to Sabarmati on 18 January 1930, Rabindranath Tagore asked Gandhi what the plan of action was. Gandhi replied, 'I am furiously thinking night and day. I do not see any light coming out of the surrounding darkness.'[21] From 27 February, Gandhi started articulating his idea through the editorial of Young India magazine. The first one called 'When I am arrested', had Gandhi's views on the salt tax and the issues associated with it.

On 2 March, the viceroy was sent a letter in which it was written that civil disobedience would begin in nine days. Gandhi's biographer Louis Fischer notes, 'As 11 March neared, India bubbled with excitement and curiosity. Scores of foreign and domestic correspondents dogged Gandhi's footsteps in the ashram.'[22] In response, cables kept pouring into the Ahmedabad Post.

On 12 March, after prayers, Gandhi and seventy-eight male and female members of his ashram left Sabarmati for Dandi.

The journey spanned 200 miles and was to be covered over twenty-four days. 'Less than twelve miles a day in two stages with not much luggage, child's play,'[23] sixty-one-year-old Gandhi said. On 6 April, Gandhi dramatized the simple act of picking up salt left behind after the waves retreated into the sea. India got the cue and every villager on India's long sea coast went to the beach to make salt, even as the police initiated mass arrests. Journalists narrated the drama in India to the rest of the world.

Fischer says, 'Had Gandhi gone by train or motorcar to make salt, the effect would have been considerable. But to walk twenty-four days and rivet the attention of all India saying "Watch, I am about to give a signal to the nation" and then pick up a pinch of salt in publicized defiance of the mighty government . . . it appealed to the illiterate peasant and it appealed to the sophisticated critic.'[24]

The salt march story highlights several elements of the 'Made to Stick' framework.[25] The first feature to notice is that the salt march was very concrete, unlike an abstract concept like satyagraha. The salt march also created suspense. 'What will happen next?' is what people and even the government kept thinking. It was emotional because it charged people with patriotism. It generated several stories and even many myths that helped sustain the momentum. Credibility wasn't an issue for Gandhi as he had established a brand for himself and satyagraha. These are the elements—concreteness, unexpectedness (suspense), emotion, credibility and story—that make an idea sticky. To appreciate how these elements help us make our ideas sticky, let us understand who the chief villain of the story is. Why are good presentations so rare?

THE CURSE OF KNOWLEDGE

The post-lunch session in conferences is usually difficult since the audience tends to fall asleep. The first day of the Innovation Summit held at Bengaluru's Taj Residency Hotel in 2009 was no different. The session began with a presentation by the chief technology officer of a large Indian conglomerate. The speaker knew the challenge that lay ahead in keeping the audience awake. However, his first presentation slide came as a big surprise. It had sixteen lines of text elaborating what innovation was, according to the late founder of the group. When he put up the slide for half a minute so that the audience could read it, it felt as though the temperature in the hall suddenly dipped; there was a chill. The rest of the talk lived up to the expectation the first slide had created!

Is it true that the more highly educated you are, the more challenging it is for you to make an attention-grabbing presentation? Chip and Dan Heath bring this out in *Made to Stick* through the story of Elizabeth Newton's PhD thesis at Stanford. Elizabeth performed an experiment, which involved two roles: 'tappers' and 'listeners'. First, a tapper chooses a song from a list of twenty-five commonly known songs such as 'Happy Birthday to You'. The tapper taps the song on the table and the listener's job is to recognize it. Guess how many listeners identified the song correctly? Only about 2.5 to 5 per cent of 125 listeners. However, this wasn't the most surprising result in Elizabeth's research. Before the tappers started tapping, Elizabeth asked them what the chances were of the listeners getting it right. The answer was at least one in two listeners, showing an astounding difference between the tappers' guess (50 per cent) versus the actual correct guess (2.5 per cent). Why did the tappers get it so wrong? What was happening here?

According to the Heath brothers, once a tapper picks a song, it starts humming in his mind and it is almost impossible to imagine what it is like not to have the song humming. However, this is the state of the listener. He doesn't know the song and what he hears is like a bizarre Morse code being tapped. Once we know something, we find it hard to imagine what it was like not to know it. Our knowledge has 'cursed' us, and it becomes difficult for us to share it with others because we can't readily re-create our listeners' state of mind. The presenter at the innovation summit was suffering from this curse of knowledge.

Now we have an interesting problem. While organizations need experts to generate good ideas, they have the curse of knowledge that makes it difficult for them to communicate their ideas. So, how do we overcome the curse of knowledge?

USE CASES, CURIOSITY FLOW AND TESTABLE CREDENTIALS

The Gandhi story illustrates how the salt march was more concrete and hence easier to understand than satyagraha. How do you make your idea more concrete? We have already seen a powerful mechanism, which is the process of developing and showcasing a prototype. We saw it in Rajappa's case in chapter one as well as in Phalke's case in the previous chapter. Prototypes not only make the idea concrete, they also demonstrate the capability of the idea authors in implementing the idea.

What else can idea authors do to make the idea concrete? Another technique that is commonly used is the presentation of 'before-and-after' user scenarios. We all are familiar with 'before-and-after' advertisements of weight-loss and hair-gain programmes. Imagine applying the technique to your idea. Can you describe a scenario 'before' your idea is applied and then a scenario 'after' your idea is implemented? Well, if you do, then you have helped your idea become more concrete. The CTO at the innovation summit could have narrated one such story of a new product or a service or a business that came from his company to illustrate the spirit of innovation there. Toyota has created a template for idea communication in which 'before' and 'after' are two sections to be filled by the idea author.[26] Essentially, the template is an attempt to shape the path for the elephant in making the idea more concrete.

We saw how the twenty-four-day salt march created enormous curiosity. What will happen next? That is, how we would like our audience to keep thinking when they listen to an idea. How do we do it? One way is to build a curiosity flow in the presentation. Do you want to know how Steve Jobs did this? We suggest the following short exercise—watch the nine-minute video on YouTube where Jobs launched iPod for the first time in October 2001.[27] As you watch, please note down every time Jobs asks a question. Five seconds into the video and you hear the question, 'Why music?' followed by his explanation. Then comes 'What is iPod?', and so on. On an average, Jobs asks one question per minute in this video. He doesn't show the actual iPod until eight minutes and thirty seconds of the video are over, with only forty-five seconds remaining. Talk about building a climax! How about building a curiosity flow into every presentation? Let's go back to our CTO friend at the innovation summit. He could have introduced a few teasing curiosity questions before presenting his ideas.

Perhaps the most challenging aspect of the 'Made to Stick' framework is adding the 'credible' element in your communication. How do you make people believe your idea? In this chapter, we have seen one mechanism—that of finding a person with clout or credibility and getting your idea championed through him. Bose was able to do this through Einstein. Tata Steel did that systematically by finding champions within the customer organization. What if you are not that lucky? The Heath brothers suggest a technique called 'testable credentials' that can be useful to you.[28] In fact, we created a small illustration of testable credentials in the previous paragraph—through the Steve Jobs iPod launch exercise to illustrate the idea of the 'curiosity flow'. Through this exercise we created a way for anybody with access to the internet to experience what curiosity flow feels like and how Steve Jobs does it. It is like saying, 'Try before you buy'.[29] Another example of testable credentials we have seen in the book is the metric: an idea per person per year. Do you want to know how innovative you are as a company? How many ideas per person do you have in a year? Toyota is at forty-eight (chapter two) and Tata Motors is at twenty-five (chapter two). You may question the viability of this metric as a proxy for innovativeness. However, it is unlikely that you will not do a quick mental calculation to check where your organization stands.

Table 6.1 summarizes the techniques we discussed in this section.

Now, let's go back to the beginning of this chapter. We started with the question: 'How do we take ideas forward fast?' We have looked at two things that matter: one, how do you sell your idea, and two, how soon should you find a champion. In both cases, the responsibility rests primarily on the idea author. But, let's look at it from the other side—what can organizations do so that good ideas move forward fast? Let's look at two things: one, the key process in taking ideas forward—the innovation review process, and two, the structures organizations build to incubate selected ideas.

TABLE 6.1: TECHNIQUES OF MAKING YOUR IDEA STICKY

Characteristic of a Sticky Idea	Technique of Improvement
Concrete	Prototype (Rajappa, Phalke), 'Before and after' scenarios (Toyota template), Stories (Dandi salt march)
Curiosity	Curiosity flow (Steve Jobs, iPod launch)
Credible	Find a champion (Bose and Einstein), Testable credentials (idea per person per year)

HOW GOOGLE DISCOVERED ITS MOST IMPORTANT SOURCE OF REVENUE

'Some people can sell their ideas with a brilliant speech or a slick Power Point presentation. I can't.' That's how Paul Buchheit begins his blog titled 'Communicating with code'.[30] Paul was the key person behind Google products like Gmail and AdSense. And like many engineers he preferred to communicate his ideas through prototypes rather than through presentations. In the following story by Marissa Mayer, the then product manager and Paul's officemate, she narrates how she almost killed Paul's idea of AdSense, the primary source of revenue for Google today.[31]

In 2002, when Paul Buchheit was a tech lead of the Gmail project, the idea of finding relevant ads from the web pages had been floating around the company for a long time. It was considered 'obvious' and also an 'obviously bad' idea. Most people believed that it would require some kind of fancy artificial intelligence to understand the web content well enough to target ads, and even if that was accomplished, nobody would click on the ads.

And then one day, when Paul and Marissa were discussing how they would make money from Gmail, Marissa said, 'We will give small mailboxes for free, and upsell on the large mailboxes.' This was the prevalent business model at that time. Paul replied, 'I am not so sure. May be we should put ads there.' Marissa immediately said, 'Paul, Paul, Paul. Ads are not going to work. We won't be able to find relevant ads and then there will be privacy concerns.'

In the end, both of them decided against exploring the ad aspect. Nevertheless, Paul started experimenting by using a component called a 'content classifier' that selected keywords from the web content, used them to search the ads database, selected some ads and displayed them in a crude UI. Within a few hours he released this crude version of Gmail internally to hundred users of Google and left his office after finishing a throwaway prototype implementation.

At 9 a.m., Marissa went to the office and logged into Gmail—and that was when—she saw ads everywhere on the screen. Her first reaction was, 'Oh, my gosh! What has he done?' She felt like calling him immediately to take this feature off. However, she resisted the impulse because she felt Paul should sleep for at least a couple more hours before she disturbed him. Between 9 and 10 a.m. Marissa got two emails. One was from a friend about going hiking—and up popped an ad for hiking shoes. This was followed by another email containing information that Al Gore was visiting Stanford at which point another ad popped up, showing Al Gore's books. Slowly, Marissa was beginning to appreciate the ad factor. However, on the first day the general response from Googlers who used the new version of Gmail wasn't positive. In the next few days the response was tremendous as more and more Googlers began to appreciate the ad-based approach.

On seeing this interest, the Google management reviewed the project. Paul writes in his blog, 'Within a couple of weeks "content targeted ads" switched from being a lowest-priority (unstaffed, will not do) project to being a top priority project, and an extremely talented team was formed to build the project.'[32] Not only did the management decide to push this idea, they also decided to apply it to their flagship 'search' product first, before applying it to the Gmail product. A live beta of content-targeted ads was launched within six months and the revenue generated from ads accounted for more than 80 per cent of Google's $30 billion revenue in 2010.

Innovation review is only implicit in this story. And yet it illustrates three characteristics of an effective innovation review. First, it is a forum where decisions regarding which ideas should be developed further, and which ones should be put aside are taken. In this case, it was decided to take the AdSense idea further for development. Second, an innovation review influences resource allocation by changing the priority of projects. In this case, AdSense ended up getting top talent within the company. This must have meant lowering the priority of some other projects. Third, an innovation review checks the scope of the idea and changes it if appropriate. Paul's idea was suggested in the context of Gmail application. However, during the review someone must have asked, 'Why restrict this to only Gmail? Why not apply it to the search engine itself?' That is how the idea was launched for the search engine even before Gmail was introduced.

Any not-so-small idea can go only so far as a side project. There comes a time when it either becomes a formally funded full-time activity, typically with a small team, or it dies. Innovation review plays an important role in moving some 20 per cent projects to 100 per cent and de-prioritizing some others or perhaps killing them. What does an effective innovation programme review look like?

INNOVATION REVIEWS AND INCUBATION STRUCTURES

In his book *The Game-changer*, A.G. Lafley, ex-CEO of P&G, explains how innovation reviews took place at P&G.[33] According to Lafley, the priority was to ensure that all the critical players were present. For P&G that meant Lafley, the head of the business, the head of R&D, the head of design and the head of consumer understanding, all had to be present in the same room. The first thing that was discussed was the business goals and strategy and related innovation goals and innovation strategy. If the objective was to grow business by x per cent then the next question was to check if there were ideas in the pipeline that could potentially deliver it. The next question that was discussed was how the innovation programme stacked up against the competition. The last question was what would it take to move the stream of ideas through various stages like development, qualification, commercialization and a market-launch?

One unique factor about the methodology of review at P&G was that it was organized more like a school science fair, in the use of posters. Each poster articulated five elements: The key idea; relevant consumer data; business potential; the timeline; key milestones and key issues.[34] Apart from displaying the poster, the team was encouraged to 'show' the idea through prototypes and 'tell' the reviewers about it. Why posters? Lafley explains various advantages of this approach. First, the poster template helped scientists speak a language understandable to business leaders. Second, it brought focus—the presenter had a limited tool to tell the story. Third, it made the presentation simple. When the reviewers walked around the room, listening to potential innovations, they also started connecting the dots from seemingly distant projects. Over a period of a few hours, the group could go through a dozen or so innovation projects.

What kinds of questions were asked in each project review? Lafley gives some examples: Do we have a proprietary technology? Do we have a prototype? Do we have a few iterations with a few consumers so we know whether we have got something useful? If the idea is in the development phase, then the questions are: What are the critical milestones? What are the top two–three killer issues? And what are we doing to learn more about them?[35]

Nokia India CEO D. Shivakumar uses the following questions when reviewing innovations: Is it consistent with the company's strategy? Does it involve a big opportunity? How resource-intensive is it and will the resources invested be commensurate with the likely rewards? Will new competencies be needed to make this innovation work, and, if so, how difficult is it to develop these competencies? Finally, will the innovation give a sustainable competitive advantage?[36]

The innovation programme review in every organization might not resemble a science fair. However, we agree with Jeff Immelt of GE that unless there is rigour and rhythm to the review process it would be difficult to sustain the programme.[37]

Innovation reviews ensure that good, workable ideas get selected. How do we ensure that they get adequate resources and funding?

One way to ensure that good ideas get nurtured is to set aside a budget for them. Raghunath Mashelkar, former director general of the Council of Scientific and Industrial Research (CSIR), created a fund called the Kite Flying Fund in the National Chemical Laboratory, India's flagship research laboratory on chemical sciences, in the early 1990s.[38] Why did a research laboratory need a separate fund for implementing good ideas? The purpose of a research lab is to discover new things itself, as Mashelkar explains in his lecture at the Indian Institute of Metals in 2002.[39] He felt that scientists in the laboratory were not willing to try out risky ideas because they feared failure. The objective of the Kite Flying Fund was to encourage risk-taking.

FIGURE 6.1: WAYS OF GOING FAST FROM PROTOTYPE TO INCUBATION

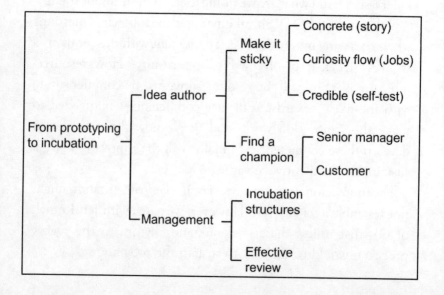

Organizations create a separate fund for ideas that are either considered very risky by the business units or don't fall directly within the scope of the businesses. For example, out of the ten ideas selected in an idea contest at BMC Software, only two were picked up by the businesses to be executed.[40] What happens to the other eight? Is it possible to incubate ideas which may not be interesting to the businesses? That is the reason BMC has formed an incubator team located in India and Israel where riskier ideas get adequately funded.

Cognizant Technology Solutions has created a fund called Cognizant Capital that funds promising employee ideas. The company's Cognizant 2.0, a knowledge management and web 2.0 platform with social computing characteristics, was incubated from an employee's idea. Cognizant has spent over 1000-person years in building and managing the platform, which would translate into over $10 million of expenditure on it.[41]

Key Takeaways

→ Ideas can move forward faster if they are 'sold' well, and if they have a champion.

→ An effective champion has credibility in the organization. The champion is effective when he believes strongly in the idea, and uses his influence to getting organizational support and helping to overcome hurdles such as the typical organizational resistance to new ideas that come in the way.

→ Customers can become idea champions, particularly when they are involved in the innovation process as co-creators.

→ How an idea is communicated influences its acceptance by others. Stories help in selling an idea. Good stories are concrete, have a curiosity flow, are rich in emotion and contain a ring of credibility.

→ Experts often face difficulties in selling ideas because they suffer from a curse of knowledge that prevents them from communicating their ideas effectively. Story-telling, prototyping, curiosity flow and testable credentials are ways of overcoming the curse of knowledge.

→ Organizations can help ideas move faster by holding effective innovation reviews, and by supporting the incubation of new ideas.

Things to Measure

→ Number of ideas being championed in the team/organization.

→ Number of ideas championed by a customer.

→ Number of ideas mentored for better communication.

→ Number of active champions in the organization.

→ Funds dedicated for sponsoring large impact ideas.

→ Regularity of the innovation programme review and regularity of its attendees.

Things to do

→ Do you encourage managers to champion ideas?

→ Do you approach customers for idea championing?

→ Do idea authors get help in communicating their ideas better?

→ Do you conduct training for communicating ideas better?

→ Do you have a template or guidelines for idea communicators?

→ Do you have a calendar for innovation programme reviews (say, once a month/quarter)?

Experiment

→ Next time you prepare a presentation, measure the percentage of time spent on stories.

chapter six

STEP 6

Iterate on the Business Model

The theory of business has to be tested constantly'[1]

—Peter Drucker

WHAT IS A BUSINESS MODEL?

'Twenty million miracles and counting!'[2] is how shaadi.com, one of the leading online matrimonial sites, boasts of its success. The site hosts a number of 'Thank you' notes from happily married couples. One note says, 'We are very grateful to shaadi.com for bringing us together.' If this gives an impression that it is a site where boy meets girl, here is a variant, 'Rashmi's parents liked my profile on shaadi.com and they got in touch with my parents to proceed further.' So, it looks like it is also a place where the boy's parents meet the girl's parents. So what's the story behind shaadi.com?

Anupam Mittal, the founder of shaadi.com, comes from a

family that ran a textile business.[3] He joined the family business with his father when he was in college. Subsequently, he formed a new company for manufacturing and export of cotton made-ups but lost a lot of money in the process. That was when he realized that he didn't want to pursue the textile business but needed to learn more about how to run a business, which is why he went to the US to do a MBA.

During his visit to India in 1997, he decided to experiment with the internet. But he soon realized that there was no easy way to make money from websites. Around this time, Anupam had a chance encounter with a pandit (matchmaker) and realized that the pandit considered himself to be in the business of connecting families, not individuals. He also discovered that the matchmaker had around fifty to sixty families in his network, but felt the number wasn't sufficient because it meant an awfully limited choice for the people whose profiles the matchmaker had. Anupam thought of creating a platform on the internet for connecting match-seekers. And shaadi.com came into being.

Initially, the revenue was subscription-based, that is, match-seekers paid for the number of profiles they wanted to receive. However, it didn't take Anupam much time to realize that this wasn't going to work as Indians are too thrifty and getting them to make online payments was going to be difficult. No one would pay until they actually realized the benefit. Keeping this in mind shaadi.com changed its approach. A marriage-seeker would look at profiles and send in proposals to the best suited candidates and only when someone accepted the proposal would they have to pay. After the payment, he or she could continue communicating with the interested parties.

Growth was slow in the initial four to five years, until in

2002, when Anupam decided to focus completely on shaadi.com. After analysing who was buying the services, the team realized that the internet users were young and technology-savvy people, in the age group of around twenty-one to thirty-five. They were the 'early adopters' we mentioned in the last chapter. But this age group constituted a small portion of the overall marriage search market. So shaadi.com decided to address the parents' market by launching Shaadi Point, a network of matrimonial centres across India. It offers services from matchmaking to wedding planning. It caters to parents and helped combine traditional practices and modern culture.

FIGURE 7.1: BUSINESS MODEL EXPLORATION AT SHAADI.COM ON FOUR DIMENSIONS

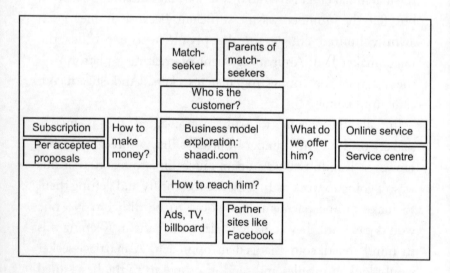

What is a business model? We like a simplified view of a business model that asks the following four questions:[4] (i) Who is my customer? (ii) What do I offer him? (iii) How do I reach him? (iv) How do I make money?

For example, when shaadi.com started, the target customer was a match-seeker. The service offered an easy way of finding suitable partners not limited by any location and at an affordable cost. The internet was the medium to reach the customers and money was made by charging the customer per profile.

As the shaadi.com team interacted with its paying customers, it started realizing the limitations of the original model. For example, their target customer was the young person seeking a match. However, such people formed a minority of match-seekers in India. For the majority of marriages in India, the parents or a relative constituted a larger market, and they were often not internet-savvy. That is how the idea of Shaadi Point, a forum where people could go and talk, and someone helped them find suitable candidates, was born. This redefined the process of reaching the customer.

This process of testing and tinkering with various assumptions of the business model is called business model exploration. And this is an essential part of every idea as it goes from a prototype to the customer. Many of us know that Johannes Gutenberg invented the printing press and produced the celebrated Bible in 1455. However, what many of us don't know is that the Gutenberg Bible was a ruinous project that put him out of business.[5] Why? It was because he failed to find a profitable business model. In fact, nine out of the twelve companies established by 1469 folded up because the printing industry couldn't find a profitable business model. Eventually, a successful one was found when the purchase of the Bible meant the buyer would be forgiven and no religious punishment would be meted out to him.

Let's explore answers to each of the four questions one by one: (1) Who is our customer? (2) What do we offer him? (3) How do we reach him? and (4) How do we make money?

WHO IS MY CUSTOMER?

The deceptively simple question, 'Who is my customer?' is perhaps the trickiest one as far as business model exploration is concerned. If you decide to own a taxi or an auto in an Indian town, this question may not bother you so much. Anyone on the road who is waving is your customer. Or if you are seasoned enough, you may be able to figure out who among those standing at a bus stop are potentially your customers. But what happens when you decide to run a helicopter taxi business? Who is your customer?

The question becomes even trickier when you know that there is nobody waking up saying, 'I want to go from Bengaluru to Kabini River Lodges, let me find a helicopter taxi.' Captain Gopinath, the pioneer of low-cost commercial flights in India and founder of Air Deccan, has narrated the story of how he figured out who the customer for his helicopter service would be in his autobiography Simply Fly.[6]

Several user scenarios came to Gopinath's mind—VIP visits, surveys for power and gas lines, tourism, surveys for land-use mapping, aerial photography etc. The service was launched after clearing hurdles, such as getting a licence from the government, putting a team together, financing the project, getting a hangar ready, leasing a helicopter etc. Creating a business plan on paper and having a customer willing to hire a helicopter taxi and pay Rs 35,000 per hour are two different things. One event made Captain Gopinath understand the customer better.

The CEO of a large multinational bank was to visit India and the local office of the bank wanted to arrange an outing for his wife during his visit.[7] The programme the Air Deccan team came up with included a visit to the royal palace in Mysore, followed by lunch; then a flight to a game sanctuary nearby; a barbeque on the Kaveri's banks and then a return flight to Bengaluru before dusk. The India head of the bank liked the proposal but was not so sure about its actual execution.

The bank's headquarters would not go by just the India head's approval so one team was flown in to do an audit of Air Deccan's systems and another one to carry out a security audit. Air Deccan passed both. In the event, the CEO's wife had a great experience as Jayanth, the Air Deccan pilot, was not only an excellent pilot but a capable tourist guide and conversationalist as well. In this way, over a period, Air Deccan came to understand the needs of global CEOs better. Subsequently, Air Deccan learnt that global CEOs were not the only type of VIP customers they were to get. One of Air Deccan's customers was Sai Baba of Puttaparthi.

Understanding who will look for the services or products you offer and why they will come to you instead of going to your competitor is an important aspect of the business model exploration. Sometimes you get lucky and a global CEO comes to your doorstep sooner than you expected and that defines who your customer is. As you start serving global CEOs you may end up asking, 'Why isn't any survey-related work coming our way?' And that exploration may lead you to a different customer. For example, within two years of its launch, Air Deccan built a diverse portfolio of contracts like aerial survey, aerial photography, support to oil rigs, geophysical survey for mining, logistics support and medical evacuation apart from, of course, heli-tourism.

What if Captain Gopinath wasn't so lucky and the global CEO hadn't turned up so soon? It was quite possible. However, it is important to note that Captain Gopinath had identified at least six different customer categories as possible use cases for his helicopter taxi idea. Thomas Edison did something similar when he invented and built his first prototype of the phonograph in 1877. He wrote ten possible uses of the phonograph in the *North American Review* in 1878.[8] They were: (i) Letter writing/ dictation (ii) Audio books (speaking to the blind) (iii) Teaching elocution (iv) Music reproduction (v) Family record—sayings from members of the family (vi) Music boxes/toys (vii) Clocks that time everyday activities (viii) Language preservation (ix) Education (x) Connection with telephones.[9] Only one of them—reproduction of music—became a commercially viable business model during the lifetime of Edison. The trick is to identify as many usage scenarios of your idea as you can and start testing them quickly and at a low cost.

WHAT TO OFFER? PRODUCT VS SERVICE

It was Diwali, October 2005, and Phanindra 'Phani' Sama wanted to visit his parents, but could not get a bus ticket to go home.[10] He was working at Texas Instruments, Bengaluru, and wanted to take a bus to Hyderabad. The travel agents he approached didn't have a ticket and directed him to other agents. Apparently, each travel agent had a limited quota of bus seats. By 2005, you could buy a ticket online for both air and rail travel, but not for a bus trip. The helplessness of not being able to reach home during the festival made Phani wonder, 'Why can't bus ticketing work more like airlines or trains?'

He thought of building a ticketing platform and ran his idea past a few travel agents, bus operators and friends who were frequent bus travellers. Their response was encouraging and Phani got together with four of his friends from his college, the Birla Institute of Technology and Science (BITS), Pilani, to start

RedBus. In the next six months, Phani and his team got version 1.0 of their ticketing platform ready. Phani thought of selling the software to bus operators, but after talking to them he realized that they were not comfortable with technology and many of them did not have computers. At this point, Phani got some advice from Sanjay Anandram, a mentor he met at The Indus Entrepreneurs (TiE), a professional network promoting entrepreneurship. Sanjay suggested that instead of selling a software product, Phani should sell tickets directly so that the bus operators could see the power of the technology. 'We ended up selling bus tickets online as travel agents, something we didn't at all plan to do initially,'[11] says Phani.

The RedBus service was started in August 2006 and broke even the same year. As of May 2011, it had 700 bus operators in its network, had 10,000 buses listed on it, was working in fifteen states and was selling 5,000 tickets every day.

What is interesting about Phani's journey with RedBus is how the business model changed over time. The original model was about selling a software product. However, eventually what worked was the online retailing model. In this model, RedBus earns revenue as a commission on every ticket, just like any other retailer earns money on every item sold—think Big Bazaar, Amazon and your local grocery store.

If the RedBus model went from selling a product to being a retailer, mobile-phone maker Micromax went in the other direction, from offering a service to selling products. Led by Vikas Jain, Micromax has been engaged in reselling hardware since 2000.[12] It also did software projects for big IT companies and later on graduated to become the back-end partner to Nokia and Airtel. Around this time, Vikas and his team realized that leading mobile-phone brands were not selling phones that fulfil the unique requirements of Indian consumers. The first such requirement that the Micromax team focused on was the battery power. In 2008, Micromax entered the market with a phone that boasted a month's battery power. After a slew of phones targeted specifically at the rural market, the company made a shift towards selling handsets that come with features appealing to urban consumers such as a dual SIM, music phones, a Qwerty keypad and the internet. In the financial year ending March 2010, the company sold 7 million mobile handsets, had a revenue of Rs 1,601 crore with a net profit of Rs 200 crore. Revenue had jumped 4.5 times over the previous year while the net profit had gone up 5.7 times.

Going from a distributor to a consumer electronics manufacturer may look like a big shift in what you offer. However, a closer look reveals that the shift is not as big as it appears. Think of making a mobile phone and you might start wondering how to make or at least integrate various complex technologies that go into its manufacture. Well, that's just one way to make the phone. The other way is to find a phone made by a contract manufacturer in China and focus on branding and marketing. In fact, Micromax made use of the zero import duty for cell phones and in the initial years, it invested very little in R&D. In the financial year ending March 2010, the company had an employee cost of Rs 7 crore and selling and distribution expenses of around Rs 75 crore.

The point is, if you offer products then don't rule out the possibility of creating a service offering like it happened in the case of RedBus. Similarly, if you offer services, consider making products as a possible option for your offerings in future. In fact, some innovations, particularly in the software domain, offer options as to how they can be commercialized. One option is to license the software as a product, while another is to follow a 'pay-by-use' model and offer it in the form of 'Software as a Service' (SaaS). Salesforce.com is perhaps the most successful software commercialized in this way, but today a number of enterprise resource planning (ERP) products are offered in this form, particularly for use by small companies and professionals. Tata Consultancy Services's new industry-customized ERP product iON hopes to revolutionize Indian small and medium businesses using a SaaS model through Cloud computing.[13]

Is it always an either-or between a product or service? Can't we create a business by combining both a product and a service? Yes, we can.

GOING FROM A PRODUCT/SERVICE TO A SOLUTION

A third model is to combine the product with an associated service and offer a solution. Solution selling, though seemingly an attractive proposition, is often difficult to do because it requires complementary skills such as consulting to understanding the user's needs well.

One of the classic transformations of a product mindset to a solution mindset is the story of Eastman Kodak and the way it changed its business model in the late 1880s. George Eastman began his dry plate film processing business in 1878 by focusing on three basic elements of photography: the film, the process of filmmaking and the roll holder.[14] Eastman and his team would file patents, pool patents from others and control the price. However, he soon realized that the rate of invention was just not enough to counter the competitive threats. The Sherman Antitrust Act in 1890 also made patent pools illegal.[15] It was no fun spending time in courts fighting the patent battles, so what did Eastman do? He added two new elements to the business model that would make it invincible for close to a century. The first element was a brand for the mass market and the second element was a complementary service.

By December 1887, Eastman launched a 'little roll holder breast camera' with a new brand name—Kodak. And what would the Kodak brand stand for? It stood not only as a product such as the camera but also for the service of developing the film and delivering the photos after the roll was finished. The $25 camera came loaded with a roll of one hundred frames of unexposed film.[16] Once the roll was used up, the photographer sent the camera back to Rochester where the Eastman Kodak company unloaded it, developed the pictures, reloaded the camera and sent the camera and the pictures back to the user. This service would cost $10.[17] Kodak later launched a mass market campaign that tells the essence of the story: 'You press the button, we do the rest.'[18] Steve Jobs was to achieve a similar feat for Apple more than a hundred years later with the launch of iPod and downloadable music from iTunes giving a fantastic combined effect.

Another company that successfully transformed itself from a products and services provider to a solutions provider is IBM. IBM did not build the solution capability overnight. In fact, when Louis Gerstner took over as the CEO of IBM, he realized that the existing capabilities were of a business model that had fallen widely out of place with marketplace realities. It meant that IBM had to develop competencies to integrate systems to solve customers' problems. It meant selling capabilities rather than products and also playing with new business models which supported open source development and putting some of IBM's IP in the public domain.[19]

IBM's solution-provisioning approach was demonstrated by the IT outsourcing deal between Bharti and IBM signed in 2004.[20] Bharti was growing at almost 100 per cent a year in 2003 and could see the same type of phenomenal growth in the foreseeable future. They needed help in managing the growing infrastructure requirements. However, they were not in a position to give precise specifications of what the technology requirements were going to be one or two years down the line. Rather, they wanted someone who could understand Bharti's growing needs and also predict where relevant technologies were going and marry the two.

The IBM–Bharti infrastructure transformation deal was originally worth $750 million over ten years. However, in 2009, when five years were completed, IBM had earned $2.5 billion. The business model involved sharing revenue. In 2004, Bharti's subscriber base was 10 million; by 2009, it had reached 94 million and was growing at 3 million a month.

Michael Cusumano and fellow researchers at the Sloan School of the Massachusetts Institute of Technology (MIT) have studied the dynamics of software product and service firms in *The Business of Software*.[21] They have found that product companies need to embrace services, particularly once their product matures. They similarly advocate service companies productizing some of their offerings so as to enhance efficiency and lower costs. With the advent of the Cloud, they see greater scope for SaaS models. But again, it's likely that a firm would have to experiment with different variants of a SaaS model before finding a sweet spot for its offering.

HOW TO REACH THE CUSTOMER

Imagine a small biotech company that has developed a wonder drug for a killer disease like cancer. While the company obviously has great R&D capabilities that allowed it to develop the drug, it may not have the knowledge of regulatory processes that are essential to navigate the complex regulatory terrain of drug approval. It may not have the financial resources to fund the multiple stages of trials that could extend for several years. It may not have the distribution capabilities to reach different markets and may lack the manufacturing set-up to produce the drug. While the company can, in theory, create the capabilities it lacks from scratch, this would cost a great deal of money and take a lot of time.

So, what does a company like this do? One obvious possibility is to sell or license its molecule to a more resourceful competitor or a large drug company. Another is to partner with a large drug company and piggyback on the complementary assets of this partner. A third is to bring in an investment from an outside investor (such as a private equity firm) and to build the capabilities required on its own. Many small biotech companies in the US have chosen the second option, which is a win-win situation for both the company and its partner—the former gets access to the market, and the latter gets a useful addition to its product portfolio.

Sometimes you may have the capability to produce a product but taking the product to the customer may be difficult. This would be especially true if you are trying to reach a non-urban population. For example, in 2007, four students of the Institute of Design at Stanford designed a low-cost infant incubator as part of the 'Entrepreneurial design for extreme affordability' course project.[22] The cross-functional team consisted of Jane Chen, an MBA student, Rahul Panicker, a PhD student working on artificial intelligence, Naganand Murty, a master's student of management science and engineering and Linus Liang, a master's student of computer science. They developed a device that would cost 1 per cent of the price of a traditional incubator, which costs between Rs 2 lakh and Rs 13 lakh. The final product consists of three main components: a snug sleeping bag in which the baby can be wrapped, a pouch containing a patented phase-change material and a heater (running on electricity) in which this pouch can be heated and then inserted into the sleeping bag unit.

The team won several prizes in design competitions. In 2009, they started a venture called Embrace to produce and sell low-cost infant warmers. They conducted clinical trials in Karnataka and rural areas of other states in India. When they visited some of the hospitals they saw donated incubators lying unused because people didn't have the technical know-how to use them. When Embrace launched the product in April 2011, its biggest challenge was to get a partner who could distribute this infant warmer, which is priced at Rs 11,000. They have forged a partnership with GE Healthcare to distribute the product in India and abroad. Now, it is not only the 8 million low birth-weight babies in India that their product might warm up but possibly many more in Peru, Bangladesh, the Philippines and perhaps also in the US. That's the power of partnership.

You may produce a product or service, reach the customer physically, and still face a problem of getting the customer interested in your product. Vaatsalya Healthcare Solutions Private Ltd realized this when they opened up hospitals in tier-two towns like Gadag and Hubli.[23] But they faced a problem, and it was that people in semi-urban areas have apprehensions about private hospitals. Moreover, they have faith in, and long-term relationships with, local medical practitioners. Hence, forming a partnership with local practitioners was imperative for Vaatsalya in order to reach out to people. These partners also acted as part-time consultants for specializations such as dentistry not available in Vaatsalya. However, Vaatsalya had to tackle the unholy nexus that exists between local practitioners, diagnostic laboratories and pharmacists. Many local doctors receive commissions for referrals to city hospitals and diagnostic labs that can range between 20 per cent and 25 per cent of the bill value, but Vaatsalya took a stand that it would not pay doctors referral fees, because of which, close to 70 per cent of the local doctors refused to get associated with Vaatsalya. However, this practice helped gain the community's trust.

Vaatsalya has still a long way to go before it can truly reach the bottom 30 per cent of the pyramid. For example, most of its customers don't have health insurance. Could it partner with micro-health insurance agencies to reach out to these folks? Vaatsalya is experimenting with such options in order to get closer to its mission.

Examples of the company developing a novel cancer drug, Embrace Infant Warmer and Vaatsalya show us that there are different reasons why reaching the customer directly may be difficult. It could be because we don't have the capability to produce the complete product (drug developer) or we may not have the resources to go close to the customer (Embrace) or we may not be in the psychological comfort zone of the customer (Vaatsalya). In such situations it makes sense to find a partner to reach the customer. But what if the partner grabs all the value the innovation creates? How do we ensure that the innovation does create value for the innovators?

HOW TO MAKE MONEY FROM AN INNOVATION

Hundreds of start-ups in India eye the large installed base of mobile phone users and develop a variety of applications or 'value-added services' (VAS) that they believe could add utility to the mobile phone user. Some recent applications help to access social media without internet access (GPRS) on a phone or give different types of SMS-based search capabilities. But mobile service providers zealously guard their subscriber base and are reluctant to share revenues with start-ups. So, new VAS ideas that require support from the service provider are difficult to monetize. Of course, the advent of the android and the downloading of new applications from online 'app stores' has changed this picture, but there is now the fresh problem of rising above the clutter of applications available on the internet.

The biggest threat companies face in getting value out of innovation is from imitation. Service industries like mobile services or financial services are particularly prone to such imitation. How do you prevent a better endowed or stronger player from copying your innovation? The first thing that comes to mind is the use of patents and other forms of intellectual property rights.

Managers at Sasken Communication Technologies, a leading Indian player in embedded software for the telecom industry, were excited when they built an efficient and easy-to-implement software to perform the functions of an asymmetric digital subscriber line (ADSL) modem. But that euphoria soon turned into a concern when they realized that the royalties they would have to pay out to other companies whose IP they were building on would negate the cost benefits of their own solution. And, without any IP of their own, they had no currency with which to negotiate. Eventually Sasken ended up building an IP portfolio around this product.[24] Through its chipset partners Sasken ADSL IP reached more than one million units.[25]

Patent protection can certainly help prevent imitation. Xerox Corporation defended its monopoly in the photocopying industry for close to twenty years using a thick wall of patents that protected its core technology as well as adjacent variants. Another legendary company that used patents effectively was Pilkington in the float glass business. The world's largest patent holder, IBM, is granted more than 5,000 patents a year by the US Patent Office alone. Patents have become an important aspect of corporate strategy in India as well—Bajaj Auto used its patent on its DTSi technology to successfully prevent TVS Motor from launching a new bike, Flame, a few years ago. We will see more about this in chapter nine.

However, the use of patents to defend innovation (or to be more technically correct, invention), is not without its challenges. The process of obtaining a patent and defending it costs a lot of money and takes time. You need to obtain a patent from every country where you want patent protection. The infringement of it is not always easy to prove, and involves long-drawn-out proceedings in courts. Robert Kearns invented the first intermittent wiper system for cars in the early 1960s and filed his first patent application in 1964. Though Kearns tried to license his technology to the leading US automobile makers, they did not take a licence, but started installing intermittent wiper systems in their cars five years later. Kearns filed patent infringement suits against Ford and Chrysler, but it was only in the 1990s that he finally won compensation from these companies. Kearns' story is portrayed in the 2008 film *Flash of Genius*.[26]

No company relies on patents alone to get value out of innovation.[27] Product market actions such as appropriate pricing and rapid penetration ensure availability ahead of competitors. Branding and promotion create better awareness among consumers and seek to associate an innovation with a particular company in the customer's mind. Every Bajaj Pulsar advertisement carries a prominent mention of its proprietary DTSi technology. Companies seek to create a whole range of switching costs that dissuade consumers from shifting to competitors with similar products or services.

Another way of getting value out of innovation is when your product becomes a de facto standard for the particular application. No government or industry body has decreed that Microsoft Windows is a standard for PC operating systems, or that the MS Office suite should be the default productivity tool, but both of these have been adopted by an overwhelming majority of users. Such potential for standards is enhanced in industries which have network economies, that is, when users find the product or service more valuable as an increasing number of users adopt the same product.

In high technology industries, continuous innovation is often the only way to keep ahead. While Intel has seen many competitors, including Motorola and AMD, in its core microprocessor business, it has always managed to stay ahead of the pack by coming out with new and more powerful chips at frequent intervals.

ENHANCING VALUE THROUGH COMPLEMENTARY ASSETS

Patents, switching costs and network effects make it more difficult for competitors to imitate products and reach our customers. However, imitation is only one part of the story. The other question we need to worry about is: How complete and customer-friendly is our product? A drug formula patent is neither complete nor customer-friendly. Only when someone manufactures the drug based on the formula and markets it, does it becomes complete and customer-friendly. A mobile phone may be complete but not customer-friendly until it reaches a nearby store with a known brand label.

A complementary asset is the set of other parts our product needs to become complete and customer-friendly. For example, if we offer an unbranded phone (white-labelled) then an existing mobile phone brand would become a complementary asset. If we intend to license patents then complementary assets would be manufacturing and marketing capabilities. If we offer primary healthcare service like Vaatsalya in tier-two and tier-three towns then existing relationships with customers become complementary assets. A service from a hospital like Vaatsalya may be complete but not customer-friendly until it creates a comfort feeling among its customers. In his book, *Business Models: A Strategic Management Approach*, Allan Afuah calls these factors—manufacturing and marketing capability of a drug maker, brand and retail outlet of a mobile phone maker and relationships of local doctors in a tier-two town complementary assets.[28] Without them our offering is not complete and will not appeal to customers.

Now, based on how easy it is to copy and how easily available the complementary assets are, we can represent a business model as follows, as proposed by Afuah in his book.

FIGURE 7.2: COMPLEMENTARY ASSETS FRAMEWORK

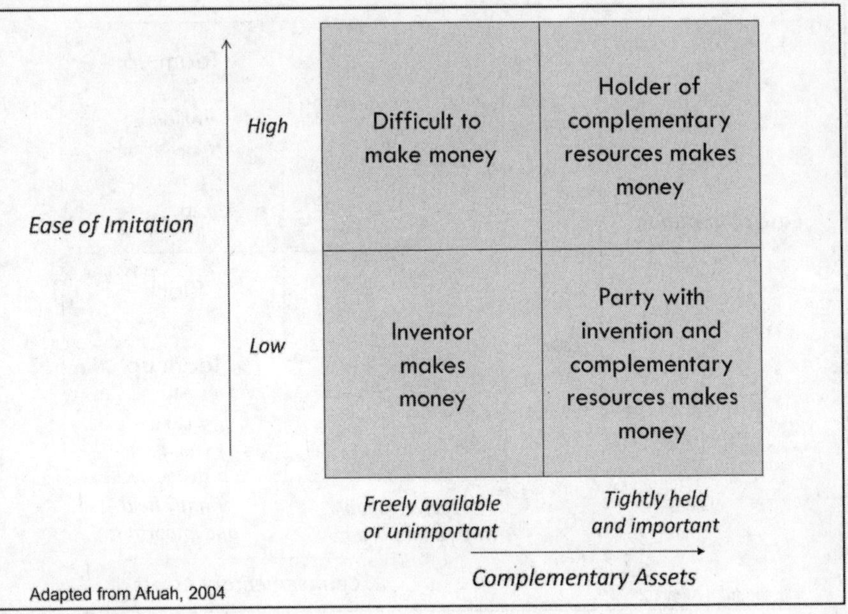

Ease of Imitation

High — Difficult to make money | Holder of complementary resources makes money

Low — Inventor makes money | Party with invention and complementary resources makes money

Freely available or unimportant — Tightly held and important

Complementary Assets

Adapted from Afuah, 2004

Figures 7.2 and 7.3 show how different combinations of inimitability and the importance of complementary assets lead to different degrees of challenge in monetizing an innovation. If the innovation is easy to copy (that is, inimitability is low) and complementary assets are easy to create or access, it's obviously going to be difficult to make money. If it's easy to copy, but complementary assets are tightly held and important, the holder of complementary resources holds the upper hand, which is the story of most of the value-added services on the mobile. When an innovation is difficult to copy and complementary resources are not critical, the inventor has a good chance of making money. In the last case where an innovation is difficult to copy, and complementary assets are critical, possession of both the

FIGURE 7.3: STRATEGIES TO MAKE MONEY

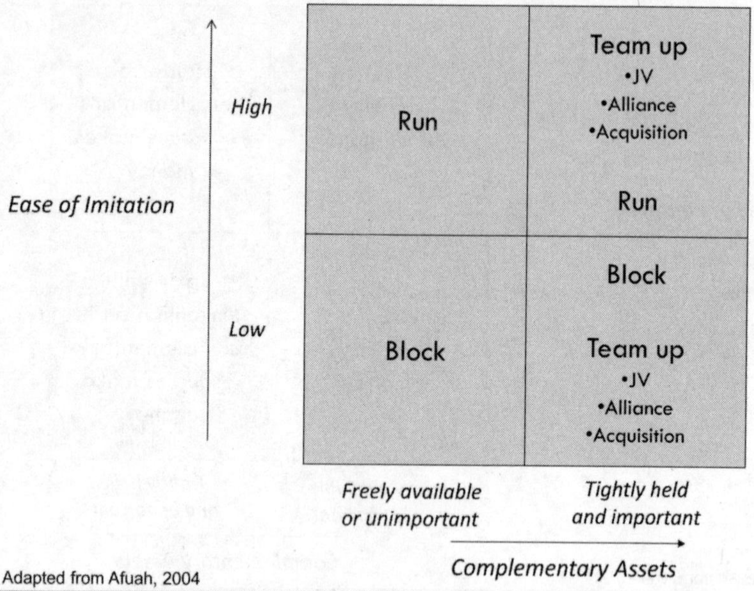

Adapted from Afuah, 2004

rights to the invention and complementary resources becomes important.

What are the strategic implications of this?

When imitation is easy and complementary assets are unimportant, the only option is to run fast, keep innovating and hope that the speed with which you innovate is faster than others' ability to catch up. If complementary assets become important, it may still be important to run fast, but now teaming up with others who own complementary assets becomes inevitable if you don't possess those capabilities yourself. When imitation is more difficult, blocking strategies (either through intellectual property protection or various forms of deterrence such as pre-emption, commitment or scale) become important.

When complementary assets become important, teaming up is once again a good option.

MONETIZING A BUSINESS MODEL IN RURAL INDIA: HUSK POWER SYSTEMS

Gyanesh Pandey came from a family in rural north Bihar. He was fortunate enough to be educated in a city boarding school followed by IIT Varanasi (then IT-BHU) and then a master's from the Rensselaer Polytechnic Institute in the US.[29] The journey to the US had made him acutely aware of the lack of basic amenities in the place he grew up.[30]

Gyanesh asked himself a question, 'How can I help people back home?'[31] The year was 2002, and he was working in a power management firm in Los Angeles at that time. He decided to partner Ratnesh Yadav, a childhood friend based in Patna. Based on their experience in rural Bihar, Gyanesh and Ratnesh narrowed down their challenge book to two pain areas: flood and energy. Given Gyanesh's background and experience in electrical engineering, both of them decided to focus on energy and more specifically, on rural electrification.

For the next four years, Gyanesh was the idea man working out of US, generating ideas and money, while Ratnesh was the on-the-ground executor. Gyanesh started from a premise that something like rural electrification is not being done because the right technology is not available. He started experimenting with new and promising technologies, spending the first two years on polymer solar cells until he was convinced that they wouldn't work. The next set of experiments were related to fuel cells until the same conclusion was reached.[32]

The third major technology Gyanesh turned to was jatropha-based biodiesel because it was a time when taxis running on biodiesel were launched in Los Angeles. Gyanesh studied the relevant literature and spoke to experts in India who were working on the same technology. Based on the analysis, Gyanesh and Ratnesh purchased land to cultivate jatropha. Around this time, Gyanesh happened to attend a course on Vipassana meditation, left his job in the US and returned to Bihar.

After visiting some of the jatropha-based biodiesel projects, Gyanesh realized that the data published in the literature he studied was not correct. After plugging in the revised numbers in his model, he realized that the project was unviable. At this point Gyanesh's idea pipeline dried up. Fortunately, around this time, Gyanesh was introduced to an agent supplying gasifiers used for generating electricity in Bihar. The gasifier was running on rice husks, using 40 per cent diesel and 60 per cent gas run on a mode called dual-fuel mode. Gyanesh started wondering, 'Why can't we use 100 per cent gas?'[33]

Gyanesh studied the existing gasifier-based generators in detail, identified possible areas where technology can be improved and created a 100 per cent gas-based generator. He collaborated with an engine-maker from Agra and modified the engine to suit his requirements. Within three to four months of the gasifier idea, Gyanesh and his team had a rice-husk-based system electrifying the first village, Tamkuha, in August 2007.[34] Thus Husk Power Systems (HPS) was born. Soon HPS put out two more systems, electrifying five villages. By then the team ran out of money.

Gyanesh collaborated with Manoj Sinha, a college-mate doing an MBA in Darden Business School, to raise money. The HPS team in Bihar created a video presentation of the electrification experiment and sent it to Manoj, who participated in various business plan competitions with his friends and won multiple awards for the HPS business. Gyanesh says, 'I could have never done it.'[35] This brought in more than $500,000 to take HPS forward. Moreover, Gyanesh, Manoj and HPS got good media coverage in the US including in the *New York Times*, which created interest among people in India who started enquiring more about HPS.

In the beginning, HPS did not stipulate any minimum power load for each household. Consumers could even ask for a single bulb connection of ten to fifteen watts and pay Rs 30 per CFL per month.[36] But, with such a low usage, HPS found it was wasting a lot of energy in transporting the electricity through wires. Nine or ten months into the operation, HPS realized that it would need to generate around Rs 35,000 to 40,000 per month to be financially sustainable. The challenge was to create an attractive price structure and, at the same time, not waste too much of energy.

How did HPS arrive at their pricing structure? The initial pricing was based on how much a kerosene-based lamp cost a villager in a month.[37] It was assumed that villagers use six hours of lighting and the kerosene price of both the regular as well as the black market was taken into account. The amount a household was spending per lamp per month was calculated to be Rs 500. After observation and interaction with customers, the team realized a basic flaw in the calculation because the average household didn't use six hours of lighting—they used it for only two hours. This is how HPS arrived at a price of Rs 50–60 per CFL lamp per month.

To expand the scale of operation, HPS initiated three models. In the first one, mini plants are built, owned, operated and maintained by the company. In the second one, the plant is built, owned and maintained by HPS, but in partnership with a local entrepreneur who operates the plant and invests 10 per cent of the project costs. The third model consists of HPS building and maintaining the plant. However, the entire investment is done by the local partner, who owns and operates the plant.

By mid-2011, HPS operated seventy mini-plants in 125 villages impacting 1.5 lakh households. And it was installing two new systems per week.

The HPS story summarizes many of the principles and practices we studied in this and the previous chapters. It reinforces the importance of a challenge book. Let's go back to the two loop models we introduced in chapter five. For Gyanesh, the first loop—the idea to demo loop—lasted for five years. Wasn't it rather long? Well, we need to understand that the challenge wasn't simple either. In no other story in this book is the primary customer of a for-profit venture a person living in an off-grid village in India. Also, an assumption such as 'something hasn't happened because the right technology is not available' could be a deep-rooted assumption for a technologist. It took Gyanesh several years of experimentation with new technologies to realize that an old technology could perhaps be a better candidate.

The story also identifies the point at which the idea moved from the idea-to-demo loop to the demo-to-cash loop. It is the point where the HPS idea gets presented in business plan competitions, wins awards and brings much needed money as well. It reinforces the principle that how you communicate your idea matters.

The HPS story involved experimentation along three of the

four dimensions of business model exploration we saw in this chapter: what to offer, how to reach the customer and how to make money. The HPS story is still evolving and we hope it becomes a role model for many such innovations to come.

In this chapter, we looked at how business model exploration happens along four dimensions: (1) Who is the customer? (2) What do we offer him? (3) How to reach him? and (4) How to make money? Often, a successful innovation involves tinkering along all four dimensions. iPod, for example, redefined Apple's customers—from publishers and students to all music enthusiasts, it offered the iPod and iTunes 'app store', it created a new way to be in touch with the customer—by downloading more music onto the iPod, and it monetized money not only through the iPod but also from the music downloads.

You can explode the dimensions even further. For example, a leading innovation consulting firm—Doblin—has studied innovations on ten dimensions and has found that successful innovations involve tweaking at least six of these.[38] The point is that business model exploration involves exploring multiple aspects of your innovation and finally making sure you make money in the process.

Key Takeaways

→ A business model exploration involves experimentation in order to answer four questions: (1) Who is the customer? (2) What do we offer him? (3) How to reach him? (4) How to make money?

→ A list of usage scenarios gives us a starting point for understanding who our customer could be.

→ A product offering may need a service supplement and vice versa.

→ Offering a solution instead of a product or a service needs a deeper understanding of customer needs and investment in creating strategic assets (think what IBM offered to Bharti).

→ Most innovations need complementary assets to become complete and customer-friendly. Hence, forming right partnerships is important.

→ One may not be able to get value from an innovation due to imitation.

→ Patents, higher switching costs (lack of number portability), and the network effect (Microsoft, Facebook) make imitation more difficult.

→ Ease of imitation and ease of finding complementary assets decide your competitive position.

→ The easier it is to copy your innovation, the faster you have to keep innovating.

→ The easier it is to find a complementary asset, the stronger is your position.

Things to Measure

→ Number of experiments in defining new products/ offerings.

→ Number of experiments in validating who the customer is.

→ Number of experiments in validating how to reach the customer (channels).

→ Number of experiments in validating the pricing model.

→ Number of patents filed last year (if relevant for the business).

Things to do

→ Do you check an unexpected inquiry about a new service or a product for a possible new type of customer?

→ Do you evaluate your business models for a possible commoditization?

→ Do you actively look for new channels?

→ Do you explore if your offerings can be sold as products/services /solutions?

Experiment

→ Identify the dominant business models in your industry and explore dimensions in which you can tinker with them.

Part 3

INCREASE THE BATTING AVERAGE

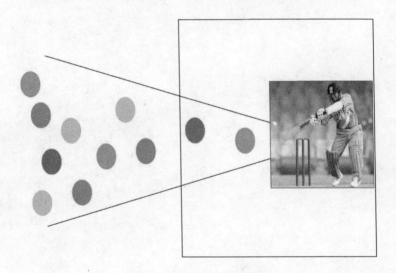

Innovation sandbox	Margin of safety

→ In October 1939, Walchand Hirachand Doshi, an Indian industrialist and founder of the Walchand Group of Companies, was on board a China Clipper seaplane from San Francisco to Calcutta via Manila, Hong Kong and Singapore.[1] While reading the newspapers, Walchand got intrigued by an interview of William Powley, head of the Harlow Aircraft Manufacturing Company. As luck would have it, Powley was on the same plane. Walchand got into a discussion with Powley on what it would take to start manufacturing military aircraft in India. By the time the seaplane reached Manila, Walchand had worked out a rough memorandum of understanding (MoU) and business plan with Powley to create an aircraft manufacturing factory in India. The two got provisional approval for the factory, and a $10-million order from the government of India (still under British rule) on 4 July 1940.

Thanks to the investment of Rs 20 lakh from the maharaja of Mysore and the donated site 10 kilometres east of Bengaluru, the Hindustan Aircraft Company was registered on 23 December 1940. Work on the plant began on Christmas Eve. With a team of twenty-two American technicians, 300 Indian engineers and 2,000 skilled workers, the company delivered its first Harlow, a four-seater monoplane, to the government on 29 August 1941.

→ By 1992, Sunil Bharti Mittal, founder and group CEO of Bharti Airtel, was thirty-four years old and had been running businesses for sixteen years.[2] From making crankshafts for local bicycle manufacturers in 1976, Mittal had ventured into various businesses like the import and distribution of stainless steel, brass, plastics, zip fasteners, electric power generators and touch tone phones. In 1992, the government invited bids for licences to operate India's first mobile phone network. Mittal didn't know much about the technology. Handing over the phone manufacturing business to his brothers, Mittal moved to London to educate himself on the workings of the mobile phone industry. He hired a number of experts, and submitted a tender offer. Mittal managed to win licences for India's four largest cities. However, the legal challenges in the next two years brought it down to just one: Delhi. And that's where the journey of Airtel, India's largest mobile services player, began.

What's common between these two stories? Both demonstrate the ability of the innovator to perceive a potentially big opportunity and a willingness to act on it. In short, both stories involved taking big bets. In fact, Mittal remembers it as 'the bet of a lifetime.'[3]

Big bets form important milestones in the history of every organization. Whether it is G.D. Birla buying a jute mill in 1920, or J.R.D. Tata starting an airline business in 1932, or

Dhirubhai Ambani building a synthetic textile mill in 1966, bets are inflection points. Take away the big bets and you will wonder in what form the company would exist today. Big bets are like the sixers in a T20 game. Winning the game without them is almost impossible.

Big bets, however, come with big risks. Trying to hit every ball for a sixer is never a good strategy. In the case of Walchand Hirachand, the absence of groundwork before taking the plunge into aircraft manufacturing, showed up pretty soon. He realized that manufacturing a 20,000-component car is very different from a 200,000-component military aircraft.[4] Within a year of operation, lack of funds began to hamper the company's working. With a perceived danger of the plant getting bombed by the Japanese, the promoters bailed out quickly, and on 2 April 1942, the government nationalized the Hindustan Aircraft Company.

Even in the case of Mittal, the actual expenditure for putting a wireless network in Delhi turned out to be $100 million instead of the estimated $25 million. Mittal recalls, 'People told me this was a business for companies with deep pockets. Had we known how deep, we'd never have tried it.'[5]

In the first two parts of this book, we looked at how organizations can build a sustainable idea pipeline, and then how they can improve idea velocity. In this final part we look at how to improve the batting average especially by managing sixers well. In the next chapter we will look at: How do we manage the big bets? And in the subsequent chapter, we address the question: How do we avoid getting permanently crippled in the process? As the saying in Hindi goes—Sarr salaamat toh pagdi pachaas (Keep your head intact; you can always get fifty caps).

chapter seven

STEP 7
Build an Innovation Sandbox

'*Managers who want breakthrough innovation need to build a new capability for it in themselves*'[1]

—C.K. Prahalad

TRANSFORMING TRANSPORTATION

In early 2003, a four-member team at Tata Motors was called for a meeting and given the mandate of building a 'four-wheel low-cost transportation'.[2] The team was asked to meet Ratan Tata, the chairman the next day. The story of how the design and roll-out of Nano evolved from here is narrated by Jackie-Kevin Freiberg and Dain Dunston in their book *Nanovation*.[3]

The team had a challenging job ahead of them: getting down from Rs 2 lakh, the price of the Maruti 800, to half the price was a steep target.

As they analysed various past attempts at making low-cost

small cars and car-like vehicles they began to see possible reference points. The team started questioning everything that is usually taken for granted in a car. Are doors necessary? Can plastic be used instead of metal? Can we have a cloth roof? What parts can be cut in the interiors? They realized that the customer was not going to settle for anything less than a complete car.

Two years after the first meeting with the chairman, in April 2005, the team gathered in Pune to test drive the first prototype. The frame and body were hand-tooled sheet metal on a borrowed suspension. There were four seats but no doors. The engine was a twenty-horsepower, single-cylinder marine engine made by another division of Tata. When Ratan Tata drove the prototype, he was disappointed and said he should not have driven it.[4]

Experimentation on every parameter was carried out. Plastic body option was explored for several months in collaboration with GE Technology Centre in Bengaluru. However, it didn't fit into the cost budget eventually and had to be abandoned. On the engine front, the first version was made in December 2005 with a 543cc engine but it failed to deliver the required power. The next version was with a 586cc engine. Still, there was not enough power. Subsequently, the transmission was changed from gearless (a transmission that is continuously variable) to a four-speed manual one by August 2006. Finally, after multiple experiments, Team Nano settled on a 624cc engine by early 2007.

The Nano story is a series of rapid experiments—perhaps with more failures than successes—all carried out within a given set of constraints.

C.K. Prahalad used the metaphor of a sandbox to depict what we just described about the Nano project.[5] Why a sandbox? Imagine a bunch of kids playing in a sandpit. A few are making castles, perhaps some of them are digging tunnels through the castles. Another set may be busy making a train and yet another just picking up sand from one side and throwing it on the other. One thing would be common among all. Each of them would be engrossed in their work or play while the mothers are having a conversation with each other or speaking on their mobile phones.

The innovation process can be subjected to a fixed set of constraints analogous to the walls of the sandbox. In the case of the Nano, these constraints from 2005 were: the Rs 1-lakh price point, meeting the minimum expectations of what a first-time buyer sees in a car, and meeting all standard quality and emission standards. The environment is similar to sand where experimentation and exploration can be done. And, there are tools like the bucket and the hand plough in the sandpit that help expedite the experimentation process. Most importantly, there's a bunch of enthusiastic kids who really enjoy playing within these constraints.

FIGURE 8.1: EVOLUTION OF THE TATA NANO SANDBOX

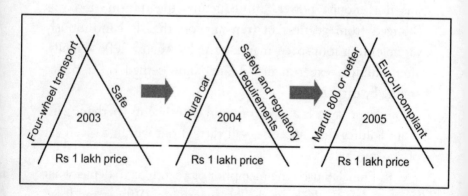

The sandbox process starts with a really stiff challenge that comes out of the challenge book. A small set of aggressive constraints that represent market realities or unquestionable customer needs form the sides of the sandbox. The sandbox helps the team question assumptions, and come up with breakthrough concepts that challenge the status quo. This process is very powerful for innovations that involve big bets such as new products addressing the bottom of the pyramid.

Apart from being passionate about playing in the sandbox, the kids are exhibiting another important characteristic: they are helping each other in creating their dream castles or trains. In the case of the Nano, the sandbox team consisted of engine, styling and body system experts. Moreover, they collaborated with scientists from GE in evaluating plastic as a body material. Diversity in terms of functional expertise, ethnicity, age, gender and culture is known to increase the chance of creating unique ideas.[6]

Where do the constraints of the sandbox come from? In Tata Nano's case, they came from their understanding of where the market opportunity was. In some cases they come from clarity of vision and the value system. Aurolab was created out of a sandbox because the value system at Aravind Eye Hospital got challenged.

AUROLAB

Dr Venkatswamy, or Dr V as he is popularly known, established the Aravind Eye Hospital (AEH) in Madurai in 1976 with eleven beds. His mission was to eradicate needless blindness.[7] Out of eleven beds, five were for patients who would pay to get treatment, and six were reserved for those who would be offered free or subsidized treatment. In 1984, a new 350-bed hospital was opened to cater exclusively to the patients who were given free treatment.

Dr V's focus was on the most prevalent cause of curable blindness—cataract. In the early 1990s, the preferred surgical technique in private clinics in India was extra-capsular surgery with an intra-ocular lens (ECCE).[8] This surgery was performed with an operating microscope and used an intra-ocular lens (IOL). However, Aravind didn't have skilled surgeons and the IOLs were very expensive, each lens costing $100, making it unaffordable for the poor.

Dr V's team strongly felt that the poor needed the IOLs even more than the rich.[9] This was because the poor man worked in harsher conditions and the thick 'soda bottle' glasses made conditions worse.

Dr V and his team decided to manufacture the IOLs in India. The creation of Aurolab, a three-year project, was started as a collaboration between Aravind, the Seva Foundation and Sight Savers International.[10] The team involved people like David Green, a social entrepreneur, and Dr Balakrishnan, an engineering research scientist in the US, and it visited many of the factories. The cost of production was found to be high because the companies were trying to develop a niche market. It was also to do with the shape and colour rather than the functionality of the lens. Since these two aspects—market size and fanciness of the lens—were not an issue for Aravind, they could focus on just the functionality.

In 1992, the team set up a small manufacturing unit in the basement of one of the hospitals and started making plastic lenses.[11] That is how Aurolab, the not-for-profit organization for manufacturing IOL, was born. They found a production partner in IOL International, a US company to enhance their manufacturing capacity.[12] IOL International provided the technology, the training and the initial supply of raw materials.

Aurolab now manufactures around 1.2 million lenses a year. Non-profit organizations get the lenses at $4 a lens, and for-profit ones get them at $8.[13] Since its inception in 1992, Aurolab has supplied more than 6 million lenses to non-profit users in India and 120 other countries. Today Aurolab has a 8 per cent market share of the world IOL market. How did Aurolab manage to reduce the price of IOL so drastically?

In some areas like raw material acquisition and manufacturing equipment Aurolab costs may be higher than its competitors.[14] Instead, the cost advantage comes from the cost of people, R&D, marketing and operating expenses. On whether the price of the lens will be lowered further, Aurolab's manager for regulatory affairs, Krishnakumar, said, 'If Aurolab reduces the price further, doctors will be afraid of purchasing [the] product.'[15]

Aurolab has added newer products to its portfolio, starting with medical sutures.

The Aurolab experience reiterates the power of the sandbox approach. Table 8.1 places the Aurolab development in the sandbox context:

TABLE 8.1: AN EXAMPLE OF THE SANDBOX THROUGH AUROLAB

Sandbox element	Aurolab element
Fixed walls	Constraints such as low cost, IOL, quality and scalability
Sand	Environment for experimentation like making no-frills IOLs (without shape and colour) in the basement of a hospital
Tools	Equipment
Kids	A cross-functional team like David Green and Balakrishnan

Does building an innovation sandbox always mean a large upfront investment? What if that is perceived as too risky? Does it mean we can't build a sandbox at all? Well, there is good news. Sandbox development can begin in a small way and slowly build confidence for a larger investment as the following Biocon story shows us.

AFFORDABLE LOSS HEURISTIC

Biocon, led by Kiran Mazumdar-Shaw, was originally a bio-enzyme company. It entered the biopharmaceutical industry in 1998 with the intent of leveraging its expertise in fermentation technology.[16] Lovastin, used in anti-cholesterol treatment, was the first such drug that Biocon developed. Around 2000, Biocon started R&D on recombinant human insulin and within two years kicked off a new drug development programme to create a differentiation in the future.

In 2002, Anand Khedkar, a member of the R&D team, became curious about oral insulin.[17] He spoke to the then head of R&D, Dr Shrikumar Suryanarayan and asked him if he would let him study the delivery mechanisms of oral insulin in animal models. Within a year, Khedkar developed evidence to show that glucose could come down when oral insulin is administered with the right technology.

In 2004, Kiran attended a presentation by a research team from Nobex, a North Carolina-based biotech firm, which had promising data on one oral insulin, HIM-2. With an investment of $6 million Biocon decided to collaborate with Nobex and co-develop two experimental drugs, one of which was an insulin pill. Subsequently, Nobex filed for bankruptcy in 2005, and Biocon acquired the company's intellectual property for $3.5 million and started a formal oral insulin research programme.

A new drug like oral insulin takes ten to fifteen years to develop before it reaches its users and may cost several hundred millions of dollars. Traditionally, the success rate of drug development programmes is 10 per cent. The jury is still out on whether Biocon's oral insulin will be a successful product. However, for now, let's focus on the process Biocon used to develop the oral insulin sandbox.

By the time Khedkar got interested in oral insulin, Biocon was already manufacturing generic versions of insulin. Hence, it wasn't a completely new territory—and yet, there were a number of unknowns associated with oral insulin. With India being the diabetes capital of the world—with one-fourth of the world's diabetics—any breakthrough product would be addressing a large unmet need. However, work on oral insulin didn't start with a big bang. The initial investment was Khedkar spending a year studying the idea and developing a proof of concept. The decision to allow Khedkar to go ahead with the study wasn't a big bet for Biocon. Comparatively, putting in $6 million two years later was a much bigger decision. However, with Rs 300 crore of cash in the bank, Biocon wasn't betting itself on this innovation.

The Nano and oral insulin sandboxes have two features in common, but differ in two ways. Both stories started with 'affordability' as an important constraint, although in the Nano case, the constraint was more concrete because of the Rs 1 lakh price tag. The second common feature is that both ideas intended to address huge markets in India and abroad.

The first difference between the Nano and oral insulin stories is in the idea's source. In the case of Nano, the idea came from the chairman of the Tata Group. In contrast, in the case of oral insulin, the idea came from Khedkar, a member of the R&D team. The second difference is related to the nature of the initial commitment of the senior management. In the case of the Nano, Ratan Tata had made a public announcement of a low-cost car in Geneva in 2003. For some it looked like a 'chairman's folly' but for the team inside the sandbox, commitment from the senior management was never an issue. However, the initial commitment for the oral insulin was tentative: it was for a one-year study.

Professor Saras Sarasvathy of the Darden School of Business has been studying the decision-making of entrepreneurs for over a decade. Her research has led to the discovery of a simple and useful heuristic prevalent among expert entrepreneurs. It is called the 'affordable loss' heuristic.[18] Instead of asking the question, 'What do we need to make this idea work?' we ask, 'What can we afford to lose today to learn more about this idea?' Similar questions in the oral insulin case would be like,

'To produce an oral insulin drug may need $500 million. Do we have that kind of money? If not, should we enter into this?' Affordable loss wisdom, on the other hand, asks a question like, 'For a company like Biocon, which is trying to develop innovative products related to diabetes and oncology, is oral insulin a relevant opportunity? If so, to find out more about this opportunity, what can we afford to lose today? For starters, can we support a study phase?'

We have already seen the affordable loss heuristic in action in the book earlier. Here are a few cases.

TABLE 8.2: EXAMPLES OF AFFORDABLE LOSS HEURISTIC

Story	What Could the Innovator Afford to Lose?
Jamsetji Tata supporting Brooksby's idea of a ring spindle in Empress Mills (chapter one)	Two ring spindle frames and an experiment with perhaps a couple of people lasting a few weeks
Phalke's short film on the birth of a pea plant	Film roll worth half a minute of film and a couple of weeks
Paul Buchheit developing a crude prototype of content targeted ads in Gmail	Six hours (half a night) of Paul's time

In chapter one, we looked at two villains in the story of systematic innovation. One was 'resistance to change' like how the government reacted to Aravind's move towards IOL production. The other was 'prediction disability': our inability to predict whether oral insulin will be a commercially successful product. The 'affordable loss' heuristic addresses both these villains neatly. Let's imagine one of your team members comes to you with an idea like that of Khedkar's and asks for time or money or both. Now, if you apply 'affordable loss' wisdom, you will say, 'I will give you two days, what can you show me?' The two days could be two weeks or two months, depending upon your position, the flexibility it offers you and how excited you are with the idea. In either case the question 'shrinks the change'.[19] This makes it psychologically easy to accept the change. Moreover, the 'affordable loss' heuristic doesn't get into the business of predicting the future. It says, 'I am doing what is in my control— which is protecting the downside. The upside is always welcome.'

When a strategic intent such as 'eradicating needless blindness' marries with constraints such as a 'lack of affordable intra-ocular lens', an innovation sandbox is born. However, the intent may look daunting to the people inside the sandbox. Affordable loss 'shrinks the change' and motivates the elephant to inch forward. But what if the new product or service doesn't work? Sometimes it helps to think beyond products, about building platforms.

PLATFORM THINKING

Professor Vijay Chandru belongs to the rare species of Indian professors who have turned entrepreneurs. Vijay is a co-founder and CEO of a leading bioinformatics company, Strand Life Sciences, headquartered in Bengaluru.[20]

For the first few years, Vijay and his team did consulting work and built computational models for their clients. Through this process, they were exposed to what Vijay calls the 'Data deluge problem'. Data was doubling every six months in the life sciences. For example, when a human genome is sequenced, it generates two tera bytes of data. How many biologists can meaningfully use such data by themselves? That is when the idea of creating a technology platform for sense-making of the huge and ever-increasing raw data in life sciences was born. Strand was lucky to get funding in 2001 even though the dot-com bust loomed large.

Over the next four years, the Strand team built the Avadis platform that enables its users to access, visualize, analyse and interpret underlying data. It involved a few hundred person years of effort from thirty to forty computer scientists from many top engineering institutes like the IITs. The initial set of customers came from Japan where Strand captured 20–30 per cent of the market share and subsequently, US distributors opened up. And today it has 2,000 licensees and 10,000 users. The platform is being leveraged across multiple products focused in areas such as diagnostics of breast cancer, oral cancer and rat liver modelling etc. Strand has created a number of partnerships with health research institutes within India and abroad where the platform is put to use in a focused manner. For example, Strand has partnered with the Mazumdar-Shaw Cancer Centre of Narayana Hrudalaya on joint research and training work for early detection, cure and prolonging the lives of cancer patients and providing affordable solutions.[21]

What is a technology platform? Similar to a railway platform, which provides access to different types of trains, a technology platform creates easier and faster access to underlying technology and data. It typically provides tools so that new applications can be developed. For example, the Microsoft Windows platform provides access to the PC hardware and the data stored in the hard drive. In fact, Bill Gates is considered the pioneer of developing and exploiting technology platforms.

In the case of Strand, the innovation began with the development of a platform. However, that is not how all platforms are born. Sometimes, a product is developed first and then someone asks, 'Why can't the underlying technology be used for some other purpose?' In fact, sometimes the product manager goes one step beyond and asks, 'Why can't we give access of the underlying technology to the rest of the world? Perhaps they might develop new applications we can't think of.' Bill Gates exploited this approach by creating the Windows operating system as a PC platform. The most familiar recent example of this approach is the famous social networking application—Facebook—created by Mark Zuckerberg, described in the book, *The Facebook Effect*.[22]

Zuckerberg launched Facebook at the Harvard University campus on 4 February 2004 and subsequently took it to other colleges. One interesting thing everyone noticed was that students were using one feature quite often, that is, the profile photo. Since users were allowed only one photo, they were changing this photo frequently, sometimes more than once a day. It was obvious they wanted to share more photos with their friends.

Should Facebook get into photo hosting? Zuckerberg was paranoid about the simplicity Facebook offered and worried that by adding a photo feature the simplicity would get jeopardized. In the end, Sean Parker, Zuckerberg's partner, and others convinced him it was worth a try. And a low-cost experiment was born. It was decided to add the tagging feature in the photo application but with a twist—you could tag only one way, with the names of the people in the photo. Also it was decided to compress photos into smaller files so that when they appeared on Facebook they were lower in resolution than the original. The objective was to make sure Facebook remained fast-moving.

As the feature went live tagging started happening on uploaded photos. Within a short time, the photos feature became the most popular photo site on the internet and the most popular feature of Facebook.

The success of the photos feature was a moment of epiphany for Zuckerberg. He started wondering why it was so popular. It wasn't the most sophisticated photo application; it wasn't storing high-resolution photos; and was missing some of the basic features such as changing the order of the photos in an album. And yet somehow, this application was the most trafficked photo site on the internet until then. Zuckerberg said, 'We did some thinking and we decided that the core value of Facebook is in the set of friend connections.'[23] Zuckerberg decided that the social network is a powerful distribution mechanism and that is where Facebook would focus. Let others build applications like photo sharing, he rightly thought, and in effect, Facebook was turned into a platform. Since social plug-ins were launched in April 2010, an average of 10,000 new websites integrate with Facebook every day.

By February 2011, the Goldman Sachs Group made an investment in Facebook, valuing it at $50 billion. Around the same time Zynga, the biggest maker of games on Facebook, was raising funds at a $9 billion valuation.[24] Will the Zynga games popular today be around ten years from now? We don't know. However, chances of Facebook's social graph being around are high. Platforms can live longer than the products from which they were created. The following 3M story illustrates this point.

PLATFORMS OUTLIVE PRODUCTS: 3M'S MICRO-REPLICATION

3M's corporate presentation on innovation describes what 3M calls the 'periodic table'. 3M's table has six rows, ten columns and forty-five elements (many empty spaces in between).[25] Each element corresponds to a technology platform that is accessible to any engineer working in 3M across its global offices. Each platform is used in multiple businesses. For example, the adhesives platform is used in twenty-four out of forty, filtration is used in eight and micro-replication is used in sixteen businesses.[26] How did the platform development for micro-replication begin?

In the late 1950s, 3M decided to develop an improved overhead projector internally to replace an older model sourced from an external vendor[27] but the new model turned out to be too big, heavy and expensive.

Roger Appeldorn, a young physicist in 3M's Copying Products laboratory, worked with his colleagues to design a projector that would be aligned with customer needs.[28] The target cost could not be met, and the project was almost scrapped.

A technical breakthrough helped Appeldorn's team replace the expensive cut-glass lens in the projector by a Fresnel lens made with a structured surface plastic that was superior to other plastic lenses.

The new projector was a big success, and the Fresnel lens was used in several other new applications. For his contribution Appeldorn was made the first director of 3M's Optics Technology Centre in 1983.

The original product for which micro-replication was developed, overhead projectors, is almost obsolete. However, the technology platform has continued to live far beyond the product, fuelling the growth of multiple 3M businesses.

PLATFORMS IN INDIAN COMPANIES

Chetan Maini, CEO of Reva Electric Car, presented the evolution of Reva at the Innovation Summit in Bengaluru in 2010. Chetan mentioned how the energy management technology, which is at the heart of the product, has come a long way since he and his team began work in 1994. During the Q&A session, one of the participants who also happened to be a Reva owner asked Chetan why he had sold his business to Mahindra. Chetan replied, 'In the last fifteen years, this is first time I am seeing everything coming together, the technology, government policies and consumer perception. If we can't scale up at this point, we may miss the bus.' Chetan referred to the Geneva exhibition where he saw forty electric car models on display and also mentioned the investment of Warren Buffett in a Chinese electric car company, BYD Auto Company Ltd.

Scale is certainly an important reason why Chetan needed to look for a partner like Mahindra. However, from Mahindra's point of view, scope is an equally important reason. When Anand Mahindra, chairman of M&M, was asked why they acquired Reva, he said, 'If you add our tractors into this [other types of vehicles] then we are a company which is already over half-million vehicles without even counting two-wheelers, which is growing. Any automotive company that does not have either the competence for sustainable transportation solutions or access to it is going to find that its risk is greatly increased.'[29] The hope is that the Reva technology leads to a platform that is re-used across different types of vehicles. Whether Reva as a car will exist a decade from now is anybody's guess. However, chances are high that the technology platform will live on in some Mahindra vehicles.

A platform can also be created out of a unique capability rather than a technology. Thanks to its long experience as an enzyme company, Biocon had strong fermentation-based manufacturing capabilities.[30] These capabilities allowed Biocon to enter the production of statins and immunosuppressants. Fermentation technology is also at the heart of recombinant human insulin, and Biocon came up with a new process to produce this important biosimilar drug. Fermentation technologies came in handy again as Biocon entered into a collaboration with a Cuban research institute to develop monoclonal antibodies that cut off the blood supply to cancer cells and thereby slow down their growth. This is an example of a capability platform that allowed Biocon to transform itself from an enzyme company into India's leading biopharmaceutical company.

In October 2011, Tata Motors celebrated the silver jubilee of one of its most successful platforms: the Tata 407 Light Commercial Vehicle (LCV). Originally designed to take on Indo-Japanese joint ventures in the LCV market, Tata 407 product applications included trucks, tippers, pick-ups and buses. More than 500,000 vehicles had been built on the 407 platform by 2011.[31]

We saw in chapter three how Infosys decided to focus its innovation on seven themes based on emerging technologies and the needs of tomorrow's enterprise. Building and leveraging technology platforms is an important part of Infosys's strategy to address these themes. The company's WalletEdge platform was recently chosen by India's leading mobile services company, Airtel, to power Airtel Money, India's first mobile wallet service.[32] This is expected to provide a big boost to mobile commerce in India, and also transform financial inclusion possibilities.

Another Indian mobile services company, Aircel, uses Flypp, the App management platform created by Infosys, for its popular 'PocketApps' service. The use of Flypp provides easy access to the ecosystem of Independent Software Vendors (ISVs) developed by the company.[33]

Platforms facilitate re-use. They make it easier to create product and service variants that are tuned to the needs of different market segments. They allow different products to interface with each other, sometimes as conveniently as 'plug and play'. Thinking in terms of innovation platforms rather than individual innovations makes the innovation process more efficient and effective.

So far, we have looked at two approaches to managing big bets: (1) creation of an innovation sandbox; and (2) development of an innovation platform. Both approaches assume that we have the core idea or the capability to develop the idea with us. What if we know which problem to solve but are not sure if the best solution can come from within the organization? Many organizations are throwing the challenge open to the world outside the organization boundary.

THE POWER OF OPEN INNOVATION

On 17 November 2010, the *Economic Times* carried a full-page advertisement from GE congratulating the winners of the Ecomagination challenge posed in July the same year. Twenty-two-year old Manohar Kota from KL University, Vijaywada, created a cost-effective, maintenance-free electrical micro-grid that can be installed virtually wherever self-generated power is required. Five students from IIT Kharagpur came up with the second winning idea. Nineteen-year-old Prateek Battsamant and his fellow students invented BioPyramid, a closed bioreactor system that encourages rapid micro-algae growth, substantially reducing the time and costs of producing bio-diesel fuel. At the end, the GE advertisement said, 'We are proud to support game-changing ideas no matter where in the world they originate.'

This was GE's first experiment in opening the front-end of the idea funnel on a global scale.[34] The first phase of the competition, launched at a large event on 13 July 2010, invited 'Powering the grid'-backed ideas and technologies for making electric grids smarter, cleaner and more efficient. Together with four venture capital firms—Emerald Technology Ventures, Foundation Capital, Kleiner Perkins Caufield & Byers, and Rockport Capital—GE committed $200 million to help entrepreneurs from anywhere in the world develop their ideas and bring them to market. $100,000 awards were offered for each of five winning ideas along with the potential to partner with GE or its VC partners.[35]

At the end of the ten-week challenge, the Ecomagination site gathered 70,000 users from over 150 countries, contributing 3,844 ideas and 80,000 comments and casting over 120,000 votes.[36] In a press event on 16 November, GE announced the winners of the Ecomagination challenge. Twelve projects were selected to partner with GE and receive funds totalling $55 million. As 15 per cent of the submissions came from students, GE promised to invest a million a year in academic partnerships to promote technological advancement through education. That is how Manohar Kota and Prateek Battsamant became the beneficiaries.

GE's Ecomagination approach is quite different from that of its founder Thomas Edison even though the broad problem area remained the same. Instead of creating water-tight compartments in the early phase of innovation, when ideas are proactively exchanged between companies and/or academia, it is referred to as 'Open innovation'. Throwing open a challenge to people outside the organization is one form of open innovation. In fact, Gandhi used this method to create an improved charkha or spinning wheel.

In 1916, Vinoba Bhave carried out an experiment in Nalwadi, Wardha.[37] After a year's experiment he found out that the maximum a person could earn from the khadi produced in a day was two annas. To Gandhi this was unacceptable. He felt: 'It has to be four times!' This was perhaps the reason for his announcing a prize of Rs 1 lakh or £7,700 on 24 July 1929 for an improved charkha at a cost not exceeding Rs 150 (about Rs 1.8 lakh today) that could produce 16,000 yards of yarn of twelve to twenty counts in eight hours. Several ideas came, however, the only meaningful one—Amber charkha—came only in 1954 after Gandhi's death.

There are several factors that have given a push to open innovation in the past few years.[38] The first and the biggest factor is the emergence of social networking platforms. It has become easy and cost-effective to reach out to millions worldwide in a short time. For example, the leading open innovation platform InnoCentive has 250,000 registered solvers from 250 countries. Second, much of the scientific work can be done in-silico, that is, the information content of material objects is extracted and modelled and further developed on computers. Computer simulations provide good first approximations of the viability of proposed solutions. Third, it is less expensive to own physical tools needed to generate solutions. And, last but certainly not the least, there has been an explosion of knowledge all across the world. Organizations have realized that the best ideas can be available in geographies very different from the ones in which they traditionally operate. Finding people who have good ideas wherever they are brings down costs and cuts time for marketing.

But, is open innovation useful only for high-tech problems? Certainly not.

Ideaken is a Bengaluru-based company offering an open innovation platform to leading MNCs as well as not-for-profit organizations. Ideaken collaborated with FINISH, a Finnish NGO focusing on financial inclusion, sanitation and health, in attacking the rural sanitation problem in India. Research by FINISH revealed that a family in rural India might have more than one mobile but not a single toilet. Surprisingly, affordability did not figure in the top reasons for not having a toilet. It was also found out that one of the main reasons girls dropped out of schools was non-availability of toilets in or near the school. In light of this research, FINISH decided to provide one million safe sanitation systems.

However, there was another problem. FINISH found that when NGOs get funding and backing from big organizations, they go berserk. They build toilet after toilet and in this case there was no point in building one more when the previously built ones were not being used. In short, building new toilets was not the only solution. So, FINISH decided they had to get the problem formulation right.

A two-day workshop was held in Ooty with experts primarily from NGOs working in sanitation and water from various states of India, and representatives of sponsors from Netherlands and France attending it. This workshop focused on refining the problem statement. It was clear that the solutions should address four areas: (1) environmental diversity (2) cost of maintenance

(3) water consumption (less than 1.5 litre) (4) cost of the unit (not exceeding 190 euros). Solvers were given an option to contribute to a specific challenge area such as the toilet slab, everything except for the toilet slab (walls, floor, complementary installations inside or outside the toilet for promotion of privacy or hygiene), collection and treatment of waste etc.

The challenge went live on 18 November 2010 and a four-month period was given for solvers to provide a solution—109 solvers signed up; innovators from twenty-six countries participated in this open innovation for sanitation contest and 2,500 unique innovators/SMEs showed interest; 3 (+3 consolations) innovators from four different countries were identified for the rewards. A total of 10,000 euros was given away to the winners.

Open innovation runs into both cultural and business challenges. When I throw open my problem, won't my competitor know what I am working on? This makes many companies uncomfortable. It is also admitting that we cannot solve our problems inhouse and need help. For the legal team it poses an even bigger challenge because when ideas start flowing in from outside, questions of sharing and ownership become important.

The jury is still out as to whether open innovation will become a mainstream paradigm. As Professor Henry Chesbrough, the leading advocate of open innovation observes, for a concept to become popular, various tools and methodologies for day-to-day activities need to get built and become part of a curriculum.[39] That is what happened to Six Sigma over the past couple of decades. Open innovation doesn't have those yet. But experiences like the Open Source development of Linux, and the success of Procter & Gamble in its Connect and Develop programme (in chapter one) have made companies across the world look much more closely at open innovation.

The broad principles governing the management of open innovation are not much different from the principles we presented in the rest of this book; most importantly, open innovation efforts need to be aligned with the strategy and priorities of the company. Open innovation is no magic bullet, but is another approach to complement the existing models of innovation.

Key Takeaways

→ It is useful to think of the innovation process as a sandbox: there are constraints or boundaries within which experimentation takes place.

→ Given the low odds of success, and barriers to innovation like resistance to change and prediction disability, entrepreneurs often adopt an 'affordable loss' heuristic or rule of thumb to find out more about the potential of an innovation, how much one can afford to lose today, and whether one can use that investment to find out more that will help one move to the next stage.

→ Another powerful way to think of innovation is in terms of platforms. A platform is a configuration of technologies and interfaces that allows customization to meet the needs of different user groups or the construction of new applications. Platforms have a longer life than products or processes, and provide a useful way to extract value out of innovation because they offer longer and more stable revenue streams. Platforms also facilitate economies of scale, and larger volumes over which innovation investments can be recovered.

→ Open innovation is a means of accessing ideas from a wider set of sources thereby drawing on a much larger base of expertise and experience. The innovation sandbox approach, a platform perspective on innovation, and appropriate use of open innovation are all means of managing 'big bets' and improving the company's innovation batting average.

Things to Measure

→ Number of active innovation sandboxes.
→ Average number of experiments per sandbox per year.
→ Number of technology platforms (if applicable).
→ Number of challenges for which ideas are invited from outside the organization.

Things to do

→ Do you measure the speed of experimentation in a sandbox?
→ Do you build an infrastructure that makes it easy and less expensive to experiment within a sandbox?
→ Do you look for possible external collaborations for some of the innovation sandboxes?

Experiment

→ If you were to build a new innovation sandbox, what would it be? Have a brainstorm or write your reflections down.

chapter eight

STEP 8

Create a Margin of Safety

'I can calculate the motions of the heavenly bodies, but not the madness of people'[1]
—Sir Isaac Newton after losing £20,000 in the 1720 South Sea stock crash

THE DAY AIR DECCAN SWITCHED ITS IT SYSTEM

On 28 September 2011, Vijay Mallya, chairman of Kingfisher Airlines, announced that they were doing away with Kingfisher Red, the low-cost airline service.[2] Mallya had entered the low-cost segment four years ago with a $300-million acquisition of Air Deccan. Among the non-negotiable points Air Deccan founder Captain Gopinath had listed, point number one was that the business model would not be diluted. Why did he have to sell his much-coveted business? What went wrong? Captain Gopinath presents this story in his autobiography *Simply Fly*.[3]

Air Deccan needed an online ticket reservation system that would perform all the essential steps the customer has to go through to buy a ticket. It was a big deal in 2003. At that time, Citibank was the only bank that supported internet banking.

Deccan wanted an experienced reservation system vendor so it chose Navitaire, a specialist provider of IT systems to low-cost carriers (the cost differential could be as much as a factor of 8:1). But, on the day of signing the final agreement, an incompatibility was discovered between the Navitaire system and the Citibank software. Gopinath was in a hurry as the announced launch was just six months away and the Navitaire team needed more time to sort out the issue. Finally, he went ahead with an upcoming and inexperienced Delhi-based company—Interglobe Technologies (IGT).

The IT system worked well in the initial days. After its launch in September 2003, Air Deccan expanded rapidly. In three years it went from two to forty-five aircraft, from flying 2,000 to 25,000 passengers a day and from flying daily from two airports to flying from sixty-seven airports across India. This expansion put a huge pressure on the IT system and it began to crumble. As if this were not enough, new business issues began to surface.

The owner of IGT, Rahul Bhatia, started a competing low-cost airline, IndiGo. The new airline had decided to go with Navitaire for its IT system instead of using its own platform from IGT, and that wasn't good news for Air Deccan. Its attempts to get Navitaire failed as IGT issued a legal notice to Navitaire to refrain from working with Air Deccan as long as IGT's contract was in force. Feeling trapped, Air Deccan decided to shift its IT system to Radix, another US-based IT company. In three months, Radix was ready to go live. On 27 February

2007, thirteen months after Air Deccan went public, it switched its IT system but the system crashed the very next day. It took three months to sort out the mess. Air Deccan was running out of cash fast and with 4,000 employees on the rolls, Gopinath needed capital. He had no choice but to look for a buyer, which is why he had meetings with Anil Ambani of Reliance and Vijay Mallya. Finally, Gopinath went ahead with Mallya.

Did Gopinath take enough precautions to guard his business against the potential system breakdown? We don't know. Remember how in chapter seven we saw how Bharti outsourced its IT in 2004 to IBM when it was growing at 100 per cent? That partnership has worked very well. As Warren Buffett said once, 'You only have to have your head ten minutes under water once in your life and it's all over.'[4] An event such as the IT system collapse can put your head under water for a long enough time. Such events and how we can prepare ourselves so that the head doesn't remain under water for too long is the topic of discussion in this chapter.

Every idea, especially every big bet, takes off on wings of hope and certain assumptions. Hope could be based on the success of the clinical trials of a new drug or an assumption such as that android will do better than symbian as a smartphone operating system or vice versa. Whatever be the assumptions, every innovation carries risks with it. Sometimes, one or more of the assumptions go awry—like the IT system collapse at Air Deccan. And it impacts the innovation in a big way.

Why don't people foresee the risks an idea might expose them to? To understand, let's see the psychology of decision-making under uncertainty illustrated by two stories.

HOW EXPERT INNOVATORS ARE TRICKED

By 1979, Steve Jobs and his partner Steve Wozniak had a hugely successful run in the market with their personal computer, Apple II. Following this success, Jobs set his sights on a new machine that would revolutionize the industry. The book, *iCon: Steve Jobs*, talks about how he created a plan for a $2,000 system that would be based around a 16-bit structure and was to be a high-end office computer.[5] The project was named Lisa.

Around this time, Jobs managed to get access to the Xerox Palo Alto Research Centre (PARC), considered one of the most advanced research centres on computing. What Jobs and his five friends saw in PARC was beyond their imagination. Seeing the graphical user interface (GUI), mouse, networking and a document editor, Jobs started jumping around the room shouting in the air, saying, 'Why aren't you doing anything with this? This is the greatest thing! This is revolutionary.'[6]

The experience at PARC had a direct impact on the Lisa project. The team wanted to implement everything they saw at PARC in the project and the original estimate of implementing these features was six months. In reality, it took four years to finish. The Lisa team improved the original PARC design in multiple ways.[7] It re-designed the mouse so that it could move in any direction instead of just up and down and sideways. Windows could overlap with each other. Eventually, Jobs was forced to move out of the Lisa project because of his clashes with the programme manager. All this bloated Lisa's cost and when it was launched in the market four years later, it was priced at $10,000 instead of the original $2,000. It was a 'no show' compared to the $3,000 IBM PC, which was significantly more affordable. Within two years, Lisa was discontinued.

Steve Jobs and the Lisa team exhibited what Nobel Laureate Daniel Kahneman calls an 'optimistic bias' in his book *Thinking, Fast and Slow*.[8] In fact, Kahneman calls it 'the most significant cognitive bias'. Due to the optimistic bias, we exaggerate our ability to predict the future and it makes us unduly overconfident. We have seen this bias in action earlier in the book when innovators took huge risks—Walchand Hirachand Doshi while starting an aeronautical company and Sanjay Lalbhai of Arvind Mills while carrying out a massive expansion of denim production. In some cases the optimism resulted in success; in other cases it failed.

Kahneman presents statistics on how the optimistic bias fools many entrepreneurs. In the US, research has shown that the chance of any small business surviving for five years is 35 per cent.[9] However, when asked a question, 81 per cent of the entrepreneurs put the chance of success of their enterprise at 70 per cent, that is, double the actual base rate. Neglecting the base rate is one of the most common forms in which the optimistic bias manifests itself. It is like the elephant side becoming euphoric by the idea of success and the rider failing to alert it with available base rate data.

One of the by-products of the optimistic bias is the persistence exhibited by innovators. How long do innovators persist in spite of really bad prospects? Kahneman presents an interesting research finding based on data provided by a Canadian not-for-profit organization, Canadian Innovation Centre.[10] This organization offers a service to inventors through the inventor's assistance programme (IAP) by providing an objective assessment of their invention's potential to become a commercial success. This assessment is based on rating each idea on thirty-seven criteria, which include differentiation with respect to an existing product, market readiness, whether the first customer has been secured and so on.[11] A final grade between A and E summarizes the verdict: A being a high chance of success down to E, which means a low chance of success. The total number of ideas rated D or E constitute 70 per cent of the ideas reviewed. The IAP model is accurate in predicting failures—only five out of 411 ideas that got the E grade were commercialized and none was successful. Also, half the inventors who got a bottom grade quit. However, surprisingly, the other half persisted enough to double their losses before calling it quits, because optimism goes hand in hand with persistence.

Now we are not surprised that the Lisa project persisted in spite of overshooting the price target of $2,000 by a wide margin. The Lisa story depicts another form in which the optimistic bias manifests itself—in competition neglect. By the time Lisa hit the market, 1.3 million IBM PCs and clones had been sold at $3,000. And yet, Apple was still to take IBM seriously as a competitor.

Lisa may have been a failure. However, it didn't put Apple on the ventilator. Apple was generating enough cash from Apple II to sail through at least for some more time. Tulsi Tanti, chairman and managing director of Suzlon Energy, wasn't so lucky in 2008. The company is yet to recover four years after it suffered the first big blow.

By 2008, Suzlon Energy had become the world's third largest maker of wind energy equipment. It had raised $340 million in a successful IPO in 2005 and in the next two years acquired two European equipment makers—Hansen Transmissions and REpower. Suzlon had borrowed heavily to finance the two acquisitions totalling about 1.8 billion euros.

In 2008, Suzlon suffered two unexpected setbacks.[12] First, customers reported that Suzlon's turbine blades cracked under the weight of ice. As a result, orders were cancelled or held back. Second, the credit crisis hit the US and the European markets. The order book dried up, and within fifteen months of the blade issue coming up, Suzlon wasn't generating enough cash to service the Rs 14,870 crore of debt. The crisis moment was saved by restructuring the debt, an exercise that involved twenty-four banks. It gave Suzlon two years of a breather before it needs to start servicing the loan again. Hopefully, Suzlon will turn around, and become a world leader in wind energy. But it was a close call. Only time will tell whether or not it will come out of this crisis.

Jobs and Tanti are not average risk-takers because they are experts in their respective fields. And yet these incidents show us the vulnerability of our ability to estimate risks and to take the appropriate action to protect ventures against the worst. It looks like the elephant can be easily tricked into believing that the future will always be as bright as the present. The question is: Is there any way the rider can alert the elephant?

THREE WAYS THE RIDER CAN ALERT THE ELEPHANT

Baseline alert: During the IT crisis days at Air Deccan, Captain Gopinath got an opportunity to meet Azim Premji, the chairman of Wipro and a doyen of the Indian IT industry.[13] Gopinath was curious to understand why companies like Wipro or Infosys hadn't ventured into building reservation systems for airlines. There were a handful of companies like Galileo and Navitaire that were ruling the multi-billion dollar market. Premji explained to Gopinath that developing mission-critical platforms needs several years of substantial investment and those people who have worked with airlines for a couple of decades have the domain depth to build such platforms since a platform takes several years to mature. Gopinath mentions in his autobiography, 'A cold shudder ran down my spine when I realized my vulnerability.'[14]

Now, how long it takes for an IT company to help its airline reservation platform gain maturity is known to experts such as Azim Premji. Statistically, such an average rate is called the baseline rate. Whenever one is trying to make a risky decision, one way the rider can help the elephant is by pausing and checking the baseline rate and then seeing how much of a deviation the current situation creates. Even if one goes ahead with the risky step, at least one is more aware of the risk at hand.

Look at zoomed-out history: Steve Job's Lisa story or Tulsi Tanti's Suzlon story tell us that extrapolating history into the future can be dangerous. It may give us a false sense of control. If we have done very well for the past few years, we may feel the same way about the future. However, the history our mind remembers is usually of the recent past. When we stretch it long enough, such as over a century, it can become a good guide.

John Weinberg was the chairman of Goldman Sachs from 1976 to 1990. When he was about to graduate from Harvard in 1950, his father, Sidney Weinberg, the then chairman of Goldman Sachs, sent him to see the heads of a few prominent banks such as J.P. Morgan, Morgan Stanley etc.[15] One such figure was Floyd Odlum, who told John that he was going to give him a book. However, John was to promise Odlum that he would read it once and refer to the book's table of contents from time to time. John took the advice very seriously and kept a copy of the book in each of his offices, referring to it religiously. This book was *Popular Delusions and the Madness of Crowds* by Charles McKay,[16] originally published in 1841, and is a historical account of crowd frenzy and its ill effects. The first three chapters have stories of the economic bubbles in the seventeenth and eighteenth centuries such as the South Sea bubble, which occurred in 1711 and 1720. In a matter of nine months, in 1720, the stock price of South Sea Company went from £128 to £1,000 and then back to £150. One of the major causes of the frenzy was the rumour about the trading potential of South Sea Company in South America where it had monopoly.

Before risky decisions, the rider can prompt the elephant to look at a similar book. Even a war story like that of Zorawar Singh who lost many of his soldiers due to frostbite in high-altitude Tibet during the winter of 1841 could teach a useful lesson.[17]

Premortem: How about making the articulation of future failure scenarios a legitimate agenda of the meeting? Gary Klein, an expert on intuition-led decision-making, and the author of *The Power of Intuition* presents a simple and useful technique for this called premortem.[18] A postmortem is performed after the patient is no more and is useful for the people who perform it so that they can discover the cause of death. However, it doesn't help the central figure in the drama: the patient. Instead of waiting for the patient to die or the idea to fail, why not start an investigation into what could be potentially fatal to the plan at the very beginning? In a premortem exercise, the facilitator looks into a crystal ball and sees that the project has been an utter and devastating failure. He then articulates what he sees in gory details to the team and then asks, 'What could have caused this?' Each team member then writes down all the reasons she believes the failure occurred. At the end the team knows where to avoid, or at least minimize, damage.

In premortem exercises we facilitated at the beginning of an innovation programme, the first issue which came up was the programme failed because it was perceived to be an initiative by the management for itself. The programme committee became aware of this potential bias, and started emphasizing the need for participation from early on. A campaign welcoming small ideas was launched and other forums such as blogs where employees of all levels participated were started.

How is a premortem different from risk planning? A risk-planning exercise can remain biased towards the success of the idea. It may look at the probability of failure for each event and focus on only those events that are more likely to happen. This may undermine the importance of rare, but potentially high-impact events. In premortems, you have to visualize the situation as if failure has already happened. It gives legitimacy to the failure scenarios and in fact can facilitate a healthy competition among team members to come up with new reasons why the project failed.

Let's say the rider has alerted the elephant on the possible risky scenarios associated with an innovation. Is there anything that can be done next?

DOING THE LAST EXPERIMENT FIRST

Nick Swinmurn founded Zappos.com, an online shoe retailer in 1999. When it was acquired by Amazon for $1.2 billion in 2009 it was the largest online shoe retailer in the world.[19] It all began when Nick went looking for a pair of brown Airwalks in a local mall. He found the brand but not the right size and style so he checked with a couple more stores in the mall and didn't find them there either. Nick came home and looked it up on the internet. That's when he realized that there is no single place selling shoes online. Thus developed the idea of selling shoes online.[20]

What did Nick do next? Think of major online retailers like Amazon and Flipkart and you start thinking of technology for managing supply chain and warehousing, development of partnerships, courier services etc. Nick did nothing of these. He went to a few shoe stores and asked them if he could take pictures of their inventory. He said he would put them up on his website. And if anyone bought a pair of shoes online, Nick would come to the store to purchase the shoes at full price. The stores didn't mind because they weren't losing anything. To Nick's surprise, he got a couple of orders within a few days. As he promised he went to the stores, bought the shoes and shipped them to the customers.

This was a successful low-cost high-speed experiment, like many of the experiments we have seen in the book. However, there was something special about it. Among the four types of assumptions we saw in chapter five: need, technology, production and commercialization, it validated a commercialization-related assumption. Will people pay to buy shoes online? Nick didn't know the answer before the experiment, nor did anyone else; he carried out the experiment as one of the last experiments in a new venture. A.G. Lafley calls this approach, 'Doing the last experiment first'.[21]

Throughout this book we have emphasized the importance low-cost high-speed experimentation. However, one of the questions we haven't answered is, 'Which experiment to perform first?' Lafley's 'last experiment first' principle gives us a clue. How do we identify which is the last experiment?

John Mullins and Randy Komisar present a method in their book *Getting to Plan B*, which we find useful.[22] Mullins and Komisar call the 'People will buy shoes online' kind of assumptions 'leap-of-faith assumptions'. They have two characteristics: (1) They are crucial for the success of the idea; and (2) There is no evidence to substantiate the claim because these assumptions come from the gut. For example, Sony's Walkman idea had a leap-of-faith assumption, 'People would want to carry music with them and listen to it.' Mullins and Komisar suggest that innovators need to identify leap-of-faith assumptions and validate them as soon as possible—for if the assumption is flawed, it helps to kill the project sooner than later. If innovators don't identify leap-of-faith assumptions at first then it is the job of the reviewers to nudge them to find out. That is what Lafley and the team did at P&G.

Let's look at some of the leap-of-faith assumptions we have encountered in the book so far.

TABLE 9.1: EXAMPLES OF LEAP-OF-FAITH ASSUMPTIONS

Idea	Leap-of-faith assumption
Pringles chips to carry images to make eating them more fun (P&G, chapter one)	We can print images/text on Pringles chips.
Make a cinema with Indian mythological stories in cities and villages (Phalke, chapter five)	Indians in cities and in villages will pay to watch the cinema.
Start a helicopter taxi service in Bengaluru (Air Deccan, chapter seven)	There will be people who will pay Rs 35,000 per hour and hire the helicopter taxi.
Start an online portal for matchmaking (shaadi.com, chapter seven)	People will pay per bio-data submitted to this site.

Through the experimentation process, some of the assumptions will turn out to be false. For example, Anupam Mittal found out that Indians were not willing to pay for each bio-data submitted at shaadi.com. So he had to figure out another revenue model.

Not all leap-of-faith assumptions are related to commercialization. In a drug development process, the most crucial assumptions relate to the clinical promise. For example, will the oral insulin be effective enough in treating diabetes? Will it have any undesirable side effects? Answers to questions like these can make or break the project's prospects. In 2001, Eli Lilly started Chorus, a separate unit that specialized in designing the right experiments that address the drug efficacy issues as soon as possible.[23] Chorus delivers molecules ready for phase II trials at almost twice the speed and less than a third of the cost of the normal process.

Can you always do the last experiment first? Perhaps not. However, the approach highlights the importance of (1) Finding the leap-of-faith assumptions and (2) Designing experiments to validate them at high speed and at low-cost. Will the approach always succeed in avoiding failures? Certainly not. No amount of experimentation can protect the innovation against an unexpected tsunami or an economic downturn. What do we do? Perhaps we can learn something from two of the most famous investors of the twentieth century—Warren Buffett and his guru Benjamin Graham.

MARGIN OF SAFETY AND THE BUFFETT TEST

The concept of 'Margin of safety' was introduced by Warren Buffett's guru Benjamin Graham in the classic textbook *Security*

Analysis first published in 1934.[24] By the time Graham began
writing the book in 1932 he had been on Wall Street, managing
funds for eighteen years. He had already seen what it meant to
lose badly three times. The first time was in 1903 when eight-
year-old Graham lost his father, and the Grahams saw their
furniture being sold to pawn shops to make both ends meet.
The second was during the market panic in 1907 when his
mother's margin account was wiped out, and her bank closed
down. The situation had become steadily better until 1929
when the market crashed, marking the beginning of the Great
Depression. That was the third high-impact event. Did the
market crash hit Graham really hard? Well, the fund cumulatively
lost 70 per cent of its value in 1930, 1931 and 1932. However,
it recovered much faster than others.

What hit Graham the most was the rent he was paying for the
duplex apartment on the eighteenth and nineteenth floors in
the heart of New York City. The Grahams had moved into the
ten-bedroom apartment in 1928 paying $11,000 as rent per
year with a ten-year lease. Graham regretted not keeping their
living expenses under control for that is what creates the cushion
in bad times. The Grahams moved out of the apartment as
soon as they could find another tenant.

The margin of safety became the core principle of the
investment philosophy of Graham's most famous disciple,
Warren Buffett. It helps to understand how Buffett analyses
situations because we can apply it in innovation management.
Let's look at the Buffett Test presented by Dan Senor and Saul
Singer in their book *Start-up Nation*.[25] The book beautifully
narrates how a culture of innovation pervades Israel, the country
that has been breathing war ever since it was born. In 2006,
Buffett invested in a tool-making company named Iscar in

Israel. It was Buffett's first investment in a non-US company. Iscar's main factory and the R&D facility is located in the northern part of Israel. Just two months after Buffett's investment in Iscar, 4,228 missiles landed in Israel's north, not far from Iscar's factory.

Doesn't the threat of missile attacks make Buffett's investment risky? Well, to pass the Buffett Test one needs to ask the question, 'What kind of catastrophic risk is there? And can I live with it?' In this specific case, the worst that can happen is that the missiles destroy the factories. However, that doesn't represent a catastrophic risk because they can be re-built. We saw in the Singur controversy how Tata Motors moved the factory from West Bengal to Sanand in Gujarat. This did affect Tata Motors, but it was not a catastrophe. A catastrophic risk for a technology business could occur by missing out on an emerging technology or business model that makes your business irrelevant. For example, for a Netscape a Microsoft giving Internet Explorer for free is a catastrophic risk. Similarly, for a bank a catastrophic risk could be heavy investments in risky financial instruments such as derivatives becoming worthless over a short period.

Buffett's catastrophe insurance lens gives a clear look at how different kinds of cushion can be provided to an innovation. Here are some ways of creating a margin of safety:

1. Liability insurance: Rao Bahadur Ranchhodlal Chhotalal, one of the pioneers of the Indian textile industry, learnt the importance of insurance early in the game. Ranchhodlal laid the foundation of a textile mill, the first in Ahmedabad, in 1859. The next step was to get all the machinery from Britain and get the mill constructed. Back then the Suez Canal had not

been opened up yet and ships had to go all around Africa to reach India. The ship carrying the machinery for Ranchhodlal's mill caught fire and was lost at sea.[26] Fortunately, the machinery had been insured and Ranchhodlal could order fresh machinery. We saw earlier in the Air Deccan-IGT case how a system upgrade can potentially result in loss of customer data. When the data is as sensitive as salary or credit card details, the damages could be high. This is when it makes sense to have liability insurance.

2. Portfolio: TVS Motor entered the 125cc two-wheeler segment with the launch of Flame on 30 August 2007.[27] Flame used a new technology licensed from a partner AVL—an Austrian engine technology house. The engine used controlled combustion–variable timing intelligent (CC-VTi) technology for which the US patent office had granted a patent to AVL in February 2003. CC-VTi used twin spark plugs, and controlled the richness of air-fuel mixture according to the rider's speed. To protect their technology, TVS filed a patent on 23 August 2007 in the Indian Patent Office at Chennai. However, on 1 September, Bajaj threatened to file a suit against TVS for infringement of its patent on DTSi technology.

In October 2007, TVS filed a suit in the Madras High Court alleging that the statements made by Bajaj on 1 and 3 September 2007 constituted baseless threats, and sought the intervention of the court to restrain Bajaj from interfering with the launch of Flame. As a response, Bajaj filed a suit for a permanent injunction to restrain TVS from using the twin spark-plug technology. On 18 February 2008, the Madras High Court issued an order to TVS to stop launching Flame and using the technology under contention.

Eventually, in 2009, TVS won its right to sell but the damage was already done. By early 2010, Flame was selling only 2,000 bikes a month, much less than what TVS hoped to achieve. When Venu Srinivasan, chairman and MD of TVS Motor, was asked whether consumers really care about whether they are buying a single spark plug or twin spark plug, he said, 'I don't think consumers are really concerned about that. But because the product did have a launch and a setback, I think that upset the rhythm and therefore we are selling lower than what we expected to sell.'[28]

Did the setback of Flame mean all was lost for TVS? Not at all. It is trying to balance its innovation risks along multiple products and segments over a portfolio of innovations. For example, Apache and its variants cater to the young, TVS King is a three-wheeler competing with the Bajaj autorickshaw, Jive is a clutchless two-wheeler meant for the city. Some of these new products will succeed, some may not. The assumption is that not all will fail. Its competitors Bajaj and Hero would do the same. Managing a portfolio of innovations is a way to balance your risks.

3. Innovation engine: Most of us know that Edison did pioneering work in electricity generation, distribution and developing a practical electric lamp, carried out from the late 1870s till 1890. Some of us would remember Edison's business in phonograph and movie cameras in the first two decades of the twentieth century. But how many of us know what Edison did in the decade of the 1890s? During this period Edison entered into a venture that would leave him deeply in debt, an attempt that historians would refer to as 'Edison's Folly'.[29]

By 1887, Edison had grown increasingly bored with his

electricity business as the business model was proven, competition intensified and legal battles became a norm. Around this time, Edison developed an interest in the ore separation process as he saw the high price he had to pay for high-grade steel while building big electric generators and dynamos. The high-grade ore on the East Coast was depleting, and transporting ore from the West meant high costs.

Edison's early experiments on ore separation began in 1879 when he and his team spent considerable time looking for the right material for the filament in the electric lamp.[30] This is when Edison turned to iron processing and he devised and patented a magnetic ore separation process in 1880. By 1887 he had filed for five patents covering improved processes of making high-grade iron ore from low-grade ore.[31]

Edison started a factory for iron ore separation in the northern part of New Jersey in 1891. It took him seven years to get the process working dependably. This involved doing continuous improvement as well as process inventions. By 1899, he was able to produce high-grade ore at $4.75 per tonne as against $7 per tonne of competition.[32] However, around this time two brothers had stumbled onto the great Mesabi Range in the northern Minnesota wilderness, with its hundreds of square miles of the purest iron ore in the world. It needed only to be scooped from the ground and sent directly to the furnaces. By 1899, Mesabi started to deliver high-grade ore at $2.75 per tonne. Edison's factory closed soon after.

It took a decade of effort for Edison. Most of what he got after selling his General Electric stock was invested in this venture—but it was rendered worthless in no time. However, Edison was back in action with the phonograph. By 1904, Edison's National Phonograph Company had sold over 113,000 machines and

7 million records.[33] How did he manage this? Edison had created an innovation engine that never stopped firing even as he was working on the iron ore business. When one venture failed, the engine had already created other opportunities by then. In fact, an innovation engine is a great form of insurance against failures.

Most of us are not Edisons. However, this book has shown that to build an innovation engine you don't need to be one. You can do it too. We don't mean to say that all kinds of crisis situations can be tackled. But even though some seem insurmountable, by definition they bring an element of surprise and create a forceful impact, which in turn means they can be dealt with proactively, as we have shown. To quote Intel co-founder Andrew Grove—'Only the paranoid survive.'[34]

FIGURE 9.1: WAYS OF CREATING A MARGIN OF SAFETY

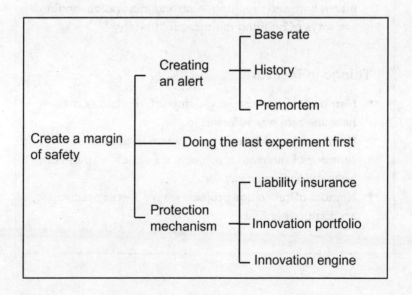

Key Takeaways

→ Every innovation carries a risk with it. But, if we are going to encounter failure, how do we guard against falling hard so that we can get up and run again?

→ Optimistic bias is a tendency to exaggerate our ability to forecast the future and even expert innovators like Steve Jobs get tricked by it.

→ There are three ways in which the rider can alert the elephant against potential danger: (1) By referring to the baseline rate (2) Looking at historical events over a century (3) Doing a premortem where the depiction of failure scenarios is encouraged.

→ 'Doing the last experiment first' involves first identifying the leap-of-faith assumptions associated with the idea, and then performing experiments to validate them.

→ Taking liability insurance, maintaining a portfolio of innovation and building a strong innovation engine are ways of building the margin of safety.

Things to Measure

→ Number of key or large-impact decisions where baseline rate was referred to.

→ Number of premortems on innovation projects.

→ Number of innovation projects for which leap-of-faith assumptions are identified.

→ Number of innovation projects where 'last experiments' are happening first.

Things to do

→ Do you have a list of useful baseline rates relevant to your business?

→ Do you have your own version of a 'Popular delusions' history book?

→ Do you have anyone championing premortems in your organization?

→ Do you focus on leap-of-faith assumptions during an innovation review?

→ Do you assess IPR protection/violations before formally funding any innovation?

→ Do you assess the catastrophic risks associated with innovation projects?

Experiment

→ Conduct a premortem of one of your innovation projects.

chapter nine

CONCLUSION
From an Innovation Programme to Innovative Culture

'A journey of thousand miles begins with a single step'[1]
— Lao Tzu

ANY ORGANIZATION CAN BECOME MORE INNOVATIVE

On a Wednesday morning in September 2009, Tihar Jail had a special visitor. It was Union minister P. Chidambaram, who was touring the high security prison. At the end of the three-hour visit, Chidambaram suggested a new vision for the prison: making Tihar self-sustainable. In 2009, 'Made in Tihar' products generated a revenue of Rs 6 crore and a profit of Rs 60 lakh.[2] By 2010, the revenue had gone up to Rs 10 crore.[3] The products came from various units, such as carpentry, weaving, tailoring, pottery and baking. In 2011 it received an order from the

Directorate of Education, Government of NCT of Delhi, for the supply of 60,000 dual desks to be used in all the government schools. The total value of the order was Rs 12 crore. Tihar Jail has five exclusive outlets under the brand name 'TJ's' in Delhi, with more in the pipeline. Moreover, Tihar products are being sold through the Delhi Khadi and Village Industries Board. Chidambaram wasn't creating a dream out of nowhere. Tihar certainly has the potential to be self-sustainable—and business isn't the only thing that has changed in Tihar.

For the past five years, inmates from all the jails in the Tihar campus participate in an annual winter sports event called the 'Tihar Olympics'. Similarly, inter-ward and inter-jail cultural meets called 'Ethnic Tihar' are held during spring, when competitions in music, dance, poetry, qawwali, painting, quizzes etc., are organized for inmates.

As for education, it is being pursued through formal and informal channels; ninety-six students have enrolled at the National Institute of Open Schooling and 215 at the Indira Gandhi National Open University. Five inmates are studying for an MBA and six are studying for the civil services examination. Literate inmates are continuing to educate the illiterate and helping them to read and write.

In 2011, a campus placement drive was initiated and nine companies including Aggarwal Packers and Movers, Vedanta Foundation and Good House Keeping participated in the initiative in which forty-three inmates were shortlisted by the prison administration and fourteen were given offered jobs with monthly pay packages ranging from Rs 7,000 to Rs 25,000.[4]

We aren't saying that Tihar has turned from a hell into a heaven. The place is still overcrowded—12,000 occupy an area with a capacity for 6,000 inmates. With 200 new inmates entering and 200 leaving every day, Tihar can perhaps never become free of drug abuse. However, it has come a long way from the time Kiran Bedi entered Tihar in 1993. What is more important is that many experiments that were conducted in the early 1990s have become part of the regular practice at Tihar today.

Culture can change. Looking at the rate at which Tihar is implementing new ideas, it is apparent that the Tihar culture is now more innovative than it was a decade or two ago. If Tihar, with all its constraints and baggage, can become more innovative, we believe any organization can. This book was our attempt to present one such way—a systematic way of becoming more innovative. We did not make assumptions about the existing culture of a specific organization. Chances are high that your organization culture lies somewhere between Tihar in the early 1990s (filthy, corrupt, hierarchical and with low trust) and Google in the early 2000s (open, flat, innovative). We did not assume a charismatic leadership. Tihar was lucky to get Kiran Bedi from 1993 till 1995. However, to the best of our knowledge, none of the subsequent DG (Prisons) has been as charismatic. But many of them must have contributed to fostering the culture.

What did we assume then? We assumed your *intent* to make your organization more innovative. The fact that you have come all the way to the end of the book, implies you are serious about this subject. And we presented various ways in which one can go about making a difference.

HOW INNOVATIVE ARE WE? A SIMPLE DASHBOARD

For most people, fitness programmes start with a weighing scale. Unless you find out where you stand, how do you set any goal? We believe that an innovation programme should be no different. In the earlier chapters we looked at the following four core questions that give an indication of how innovative you are:

1. How many ideas do you have in the pipeline?
2. At what rate do these ideas move forward?
3. What is your batting average?
4. How many people participate in your innovation programme?

We can create a dashboard that measures the lead and lag indicators for these questions. A lead indicator is an early indicator during the change process, which may last several years. A lag indicator shows results after implementing some of the initiatives.

TABLE 10.1: INNOVATION MANAGEMENT DASHBOARD

No.	Parameter	Lead indicator	Lag indicator
1	Pipeline	Number of challenges in the challenge book	Number of ideas in the pipeline; number of ideas per person per year.
2	Idea velocity	Average time to give relevant feedback on the idea of the author; Number of experiments/prototypes,	Number of experiments in exploring new types of customers defining new

(Table 10.1 continued...)

(...Table 10.1)

No.	Parameter	Lead indicator	Lag indicator
		feasibility studies, invention disclosures, white papers in a year; average time for the first customer feedback; frequency of innovation review; average time to get support from a champion	offerings/ products, exploring new partnerships and new pricing models, average time from formal approval to cash/ saving/impact
3	Batting average	Number of innovation sandboxes, number of innovation platforms	Percentage of revenue from innovations in the last five years.
4	Participation	Number of people giving ideas/ comments/votes, mentors/catalysts/ champions	Number of active Communities of Practice (CoPs), role models, customers engaged

Let's look at each of the parameters in detail:

1. Pipeline: In chapter three we looked at how a challenge book prompted ideas. We saw challenge books in various forms. In Tihar Jail it was created through a physical petition box. In HCL it was an intranet portal where any employee could log problems while at the Bank of Baroda, a challenge book was created through customer complaints. We also saw examples of open challenge book contests by GE in the form of Ecomagination. It is interesting to note that a challenge book is relevant no matter what your scale is. A five-person team may have a challenge book and a $50 billion organization may also have one. If the challenge book is a lead indicator of the innovation pipeline, then the ideas which come as a response to the challenges posed constitute a lag indicator. There are two ways in which idea pipelines are tracked. One is through a parameter like ideas per person per year, which we saw in Toyota as well as in Tata Motors. The other way is to measure the actual number. For example, GE's imagination breakthrough pipeline measures the actual number of ideas. Similar to a challenge book, an idea pipeline can exist at multiple levels. A product manager may track an idea pipeline relevant for his product and a CEO may track a different idea pipeline at the organizational level.

2. Idea velocity: Ideas which remain on paper or on a white board or on a portal are of little use. Only when they move through a set of experiments towards creating an impact do they become useful. We divided the idea lifecycle into two loops: the idea-to-demo loop and the demo-to-impact loop. In the first loop, the best measurement of idea velocity is speed of prototyping. We saw that Paul Buchheit's first AdSense prototype was built in a few hours, the Nano team presented its first low-cost transportation survey within a day and Phalke's pea plant demo was built in a couple of weeks. When we see that experiments are being performed within hours, days or weeks, chances are that dynamic ideas are moving forward with satisfactory speed. If we see months or quarters for ideas to move forward, we know there is a problem.

On the programme management side, the regularity of the innovation review and the rigour with which idea selection and resource allocation happens is a good indicator of idea velocity. We saw in various organizations like GE, BMC and Cognizant that the first level of innovation review happens on a monthly cycle. In the Shell Game Changer programme, ideas reviewed by the screening panel and extended panel are responded to within forty-eight hours.[5]

The speed of experimentation plays an equally important role during the second loop when ideas are moving from demo to market. To figure out how many beds are appropriate for a primary care hospital in a tier-three town like Gadag or Hubli, Vaatsalya may have taken a year. On the other hand, it may have taken Husk Power Systems a few months to finalize the bundled offering of two CFL lamps and an unlimited mobile charge being offered for Rs 80 per month. The average time to implement and reach the market after formal approval is a fairly accurate lag indicator. For Google's AdSense, the launch happened in six months after a team was put in place to work on the idea.[6]

3. Batting average: Every time you try to score a run, there is a risk of getting out. The risk, in general, may be lower when you try to take a single than when you try to hit a sixer. However, at the end what counts is the team's batting average. Are you able to score well on an average? Similarly, incremental ideas as well as big-ticket ideas carry different kinds of risks. Both types are important in every organization and what counts is the net impact they create as a portfolio. Unlike a game of cricket, the potential impact of a big-ticket idea could be several hundred or thousand times that of a small idea. On the flip side, the damage due to the movement of the Tata Nano factory from

Singur to Sanand could be several hundred million dollars. An innovation programme should track both the upside and downside exposure.

We saw how an innovation sandbox increases the upside exposure, a possibility of hitting sixers. Hence, it is a good lead indicator. Companies like 3M also track the percentage of revenue from products launched within the last five years. 3M calls it the New Product Vitality Index and as of 2012, this index is at a healthy 33 per cent.[7] Cognizant tracks its total business impact (either revenue increase or cost savings) due to innovation every year.[8]

4. Participation: The number of people participating in an innovation activity month on month, year on year—submitting, reviewing, voting, mentoring, championing ideas gives an indication of how sustainable the innovation process is. Toyota's forty-year tracking table shows us how the participation went from a mere 8 per cent in the first year to a phenomenal 95 per cent in the thirty-fifth year. A social networking platform also enables us to track the number of people submitting, commenting/voting on others' ideas.

Self-organizing communities of practice—sometimes associated with specific technologies like Java or Android, sometimes related to a function like testing, sometimes related to a domain like cloud computing—make a big difference in sustaining innovation initiatives. Tracking active communities gives an indication of how sustainable the participation is. Keep track of the number of role models (Rajappas, Ajay Bhatts, Jaruhars and Paul Buchheits) in your organization. Another indicator is the number of contributions from customers into the idea bank and challenge book.

GETTING A QUICK WIN AND CELEBRATING THE BRIGHT SPARKS

In 2011, social activisit Anna Hazare became the torch-bearer for the anti-corruption movement in India.[9] Hazare began his indefinite fast on 5 April 2011 at Jantar Mantar in Delhi to press demands for forming a joint committee of people from government and civil society members to draft a stronger Lokpal (Ombudsman) bill against corruption. The Jan Lokpal Bill was drafted by N. Santosh Hegde, a former justice of Supreme Court, Prashant Bhushan, a senior lawyer in the Supreme Court and Arvind Kejriwal, a social activist along with the members of the 'India against Corruption' movement. The campaign attracted media attention and almost 150 people joined Hazare in his fast. Anna began a second wave of hunger strikes on 16 August demanding a stronger Lokpal bill. The twelve-day fast which ended on 28 August attracted unprecedented support from people across the nation.

Corruption is a formidable enemy and it is entrenched in the veins of the country. Hence, one of the objections raised against the Hazare campaign was, 'What difference will one Lokpal bill make?' And that is precisely the point many people miss when the change involved is a difficult one. Every long journey begins with a single step. Some steps are small, some are long and some have really difficult hurdles to surmount, such as Edmund Hillary's last step to ascend Mount Everest. However, every small step goes a long way in engaging the rider and the elephant in the journey together.

The rider needs a concrete goal to focus its energies. Otherwise it spins its wheels and keeps analyzing various options. The Jan Lokpal Bill created that concrete next step for the anti-corruption movement. It didn't matter that most people rallying in support of Anna Hazare didn't know the exact points and issues raised in the bill. What mattered was that the bill is a step in the right direction.

Any effort to change needs concrete steps to direct the rider, and a cause like anti-corruption that will motivate the elephant. An innovation programme is no exception. What could be such small steps in the innovation programme journey?

Let's look at three eight-to-twelve-week campaigns we came across in the book:

1. In chapter four (build participation) we saw how BMC Software ran an eight-week idea contest based on 'cloud computing' as the theme. It received 170 ideas out of which ten were selected for further execution. Mentors were identified to help the idea authors in taking the ideas further and as an incentive, awards were given to the selected ideas. In a span of two months, the campaign achieved several goals. One, it communicated the importance of 'cloud computing' as an area of focus for the organization. Second, it engaged a few hundred people in giving, commenting and reviewing ideas. Third, it encouraged a few senior people to mentor the juniors in expanding their ideas. Fourth, by sponsoring a few selected ideas for further development, the management communicated its commitment to the initiative. All this was done in a span of two months. If you are wondering where to begin the journey, a two- to three-month campaign as in the case of BMC Software could be a good start.

2. In chapter six (from prototyping to incubation), we looked at a twelve-week process at Tata Steel under the customer

value management (CVM) initiative. It involves partnering with one of the key customers and jointly identifying key problems in the customer's business process. The issues could be related to transportation, packaging, order progress reporting, complaints handling, furnishing samples and test certificates, billing etc. Then a joint brainstorming session is held at the customer premises where senior management from both sides participates. The selection committee narrows the ideas down to ten or twelve from a few hundred. An implementation plan is worked out and eventually handed over to a manager from either Tata Steel or its customers.

We saw how idea velocity can improve in a three-month period where ideas move from concept to implementation with the customer buy-in already in place.

3. In chapter eight (innovation sandbox), we saw how GE executed a four-month (July–November 2010) open challenge on 'Powering the grid' under the Ecomagination initiative. Compared to the previous two examples, this involved a lot more people (7,000) and many more ideas (3,844). However, within four months, GE was able to announce winners and fund selected ideas for further development. Twelve projects were selected in which GE would be a partner and some of these could even evolve into innovation sandboxes for GE.

Three to four months is a short time when you are trying to build innovation capacity for the entire organization. And yet these small wins create confidence among employees as well as people managing the innovation programme. Moreover, they create a sense of progress, of going forward.

What is also important to see in these initiatives is that they involved rewards and recognition in various forms. Getting your name listed in a full-page advertisement in the *Economic Times* in India is a significant recognition for the winning students who participated in the Ecomagination challenge. Spotting and celebrating the bright sparks creates an important reinforcement of what is valued as part of the initiative.

We also looked at the 'Dare to Try' awards in chapter five on experimentation. It is a special type of award Tata Group offers to teams from the Tata companies where failure generates significant learning. A bright spot is not necessarily only a winning idea. It could also be a non-selected idea that could provide inspiration to many innovators. Who knows, perhaps the learning from the plastic door experiment by the Taco-IPD team might lead to something totally new in an unrelated product. Perhaps each idea contest should have its own version of a 'Dare to Try' award.

STRUCTURES ENABLING INNOVATION

Throughout the book we saw organizations creating and supporting various structures to manage innovation programmes. In chapter two we saw how Toyota created formal committees at different levels to participate in the selection of ideas. Similarly, we saw how Toyota supported the informal group called the 'Good Idea Club', which innovators used as a platform to network and share knowledge. In chapter four we saw how Intel has created a career ladder parallel to the managerial ladder that encourages people like Ajay Bhatt to focus on a technical specialty and contribute towards innovations. We looked at laboratory structures such as Aravind Eye Hospital's Aurolab or

3M's optics technology centre where focused experiments are performed. We also looked at how Titan's Innovation School of Management and Cognizant's evangelists facilitate and train employees to become better at innovation. We saw how organizations like Cognizant and BMC software have created a separate fund for incubating new business ideas. The following table summarizes these structures:

TABLE 10.2: STRUCTURES ENABLING INNOVATION

Structure	Objective	Emphasis	Example
Innovation programme committee	Build a culture of innovation	Employee participation	Toyota, Cognizant, Tihar Jail
	Build and manage a large-impact idea pipeline	Challenge-based idea generation, participation from experts outside the organization	GE, P&G, BMC Software
Co-innovation department	Co-innovate in partnership with customers	Involve customer as early as one can in the innovation cycle	Tata Steel CVM, P&G Connect and Develop
Laboratory for incubation	Build technologies and other assets and establish	Incubate ideas relevant to an existing business	NPD (Mahindra)

(Table 10.2 continued...)

(...*Table 10.2*)

Structure	Objective	Emphasis	Example
	business viability	Incubate ideas outside the scope of existing businesses	Cognizant Capital, BMC, Software GE (Imagination) (breakthrough)
	Build an innovation platform	Creating technologies and/or capabilities of strategic importance	Biocon fermentation capability, 3M microreplication, Strand Avadis
Innovation sandbox	Innovation within a given set of constraints	Creating a large-impact innovation of strategic importance	Tata Nano, Biocon oral insulin
Structures for learning and development	Build competencies relevant for innovation	Build creative confidence	Innovation school of management (Titan),

(*Table 10.2 continued...*)

(...*Table 10.2*)

Structure	Objective	Emphasis	Example
		Create space for immersive research, experimentation and collaboration	Evangelists (Cognizant) Ideo (TechBox)
Specialist ladder	Encourage experts to go deeper into the subject matter	Value specialization in technical areas relevant to business	Ajay Bhatt (Fellow at Intel), Roger Appeldorn (3M), Narendra Kumar Jain (Tata Motors)

Who heads the innovation initiatives? Looks like there is no single function that is responsible for managing innovation. In some organizations like Wipro and BMC Software, it is the chief technology officer (CTO) who is the custodian of innovation efforts. In GE, it is the CMO who heads initiatives like Ecomagination. At Cognizant the head of the innovation programme is also the chief information officer (CIO). At Titan, the head of the innovation council is also the chief manufacturing officer. We believe that heads of functions such as Business Excellence, Strategy and Human Resources are also good candidates for leading the innovation initiatives.

THE ELEPHANT, THE RIDER AND THE INNOVATION PROGRAMME

In chapter one, we saw the elephant–rider model that represents the intuitive and analytical side of our brain. We also saw how it helps designing change management approaches that (1) direct the rider (2) motivate the elephant and (3) shape the path for the elephant. In Table 10.3 we classify various approaches we saw in the book into these three categories.

TABLE 10.3: SUMMARY OF APPROACHES IN MANAGING INNOVATION

Direct the Rider	Motivate the Elephant	Shape the Path
1. HOW TO BUILD AND SUSTAIN THE IDEA PIPELINE		
Build a challenge book (U&I Portal, HCL, Petition box, Tihar Jail)	Create internal role models (Ajay Bhatt, Intel)	Roll out an idea management process (Maruti, GE, P&G)
Launch a campaign (e.g. 'Heavier, faster and longer', Indian Railways)	Rewards and recognition (Tata Group, Maruti Motors)	Establish a regularity to innovation programme review (GE, P&G, BMC Software)
	Create innovation catalysts (Cognizant, Intuit); create communities of practice (MindTree, Tihar Jail)	

(Table 10.3 continued...)

(...*Table 10.3*)

Direct the Rider	Motivate the Elephant	Shape the Path
2. HOW TO IMPROVE IDEA VELOCITY		
Define low-cost high-speed experiments (quick wins)	Showcase prototypes (Ideo)	Ensure effectiveness to the innovation reviews (P&G, Google)
Publish a metric on idea velocity	Reward learning from failed experiments ('Dare to Try', Tata Group)	Create a lab for experimentation (Edison, Ideo)
Find champions for selected ideas (Tata Steel, 3M)	Get customer feedback (Lego, Tata Steel)	Assign a dedicated team to the project (Nano)
3. HOW TO IMPROVE BATTING AVERAGE		
Give tough challenges (Aravind Eye Hospital, Nano)	Senior management attention (Tata Motors, P&G)	Create an innovation sandbox (Nano)
Affordable loss heuristic (Biocon)	Create a compelling vision ('Eradicate needless blindness', Aravind)	Create a venture fund (Cognizant)
Surf big waves (Oral insulin, Biocon) Do the last experiment first		Create an innovation platform (3M) Premortem

We began this book by asking the question, 'Can anyone innovate?' A tentative answer we offered was, 'Maybe, as long as the conditions are right.' Throughout the book we have presented suggestions about how we can go about setting those right conditions. We talked about setting up an idea management process, championing good ideas, creating labs for experimentation, developing an innovation sandbox, managing an innovation portfolio etc. Who will create and manage these? Every organization needs to build leaders who can do this. You are going to need the Rajappas and you are going to need the Patils (HMT), Paul Buchheits and Marissa Mayers (Google), people like Girish Wagh who led the Tata Nano sandbox, the Jaruhars and Sudhir Kumars (railways), the Kalams and V.K. Krishna Menons (ADE), the David Greens and Balakrishnans (Aravind), and the E. Sreedharans, not to forget George Fernandes. We are in no way underestimating the importance of the Jamsetji Tatas and Mahatma Gandhis, but facing reality; we know that they are not easy to find.

The good news is that the Rajappas and Patils exist in every organization. We only need to spot and encourage them. In fact, we believe there are capable people who are always striving, always seeking solutions to problems—big or small—and who can think out of the box. One of those people could be you. We believe in you, and you could be a potential candidate to play one of the innovation leadership roles.

Are you ready for the first step?

Acknowledgements

Innovation often appears to be some kind of mysterious activity, a process that somehow 'happens'. It tends to be closely identified with technology and R&D and this scares many people. Many organizations want to be innovative but don't know how to go about it. Or, they have embarked on an innovation journey but lost their way, and are keen to get back on the right road. Some are on the right track and want to know the next step in their journey.

We wrote this book to de-mystify the management of innovation. Though there are hundreds if not thousands of books written on innovation, we could not find one that presented a structured approach to building innovation excellence, and at the same time incorporated contemporary ideas from social psychology, behavioural economics and change management. We were driven largely by the needs of Indian companies, but the ideas in this book are not constrained by context or geography.

For Vinay, this was an opportunity to codify concepts and ideas that have emerged from his consulting and training practice with leading Indian and multinational companies. For Rishi, this was a way of countering critics of his earlier book *From Jugaad to Systematic Innovation* since many of his corporate friends found the book to be of too high a level and policy-oriented, and wanted something more practical and down-to-earth.

We believe that we have brought our respective strengths to the table: Vinay's emphasis on simplicity, structure, experimentation, measurement, management of risk and conveying ideas through stories; and Rishi's vast experience in the domain, understanding of strategy–innovation links, and the ability to synthesize different concepts. We hope this came through in the book.

In a crowded discipline like innovation, any addition to the literature has to ride on the shoulders of giants—people who have worked in, and written on, this field over the years. We are indebted to all the thought leaders mentioned in the book and notes.

We were disproportionately influenced by the work of Chip and Dan Heath. The framework for effective communication of ideas that they presented in their book, *Made to Stick*, was the source of inspiration for writing this book around stories. We found their 'elephant and rider' model for change management in *Switch* to echo our own experiences in bringing about change, and we therefore used this metaphor across the book.

The conceptual framework for this book emerged from thought and experience. But once we had taken the decision to use stories to illustrate our ideas, we had the challenge of finding stories that communicated these ideas effectively. Here, apart from stories we had ourselves heard or been a part of, we drew on the work by many others and re-told their stories to suit our themes. Most knowledge builds on the work of others, and this book is no exception.

Innovation leaders in various companies graciously agreed to meet with us and explain how the management of innovation was working or not working in their organizations. We would like to thank each of them for sharing their thoughts with us: Preethi Pradhan and Thulasiraj Ravilla of Aravind Eye Care System, Suhas Kelkar and Nikhil Sahasrabudhe of BMC Software, Sukumar R. and members of the innovation council of Cognizant, Subu Goparaju of Infosys, Vijay Anand and members of the innovation programme at Intuit, India, Nirmal Koshti of Galaxy Surfactants and Vijay Ivaturi of Wipro. We would also like to thank Jayesh Badani of Ideaken for sharing his experience with running open innovation challenges, especially in the Indian context.

Apart from the companies with whom we have worked, we are thankful to Vijay Ramachandran, editor-in-chief of CIO magazine in India for giving us the opportunity to jointly offer a workshop on innovation to Indian CIOs. This was an important step in our collaboration process. Another useful platform to clarify our ideas was the Executive Education Programme on Going Beyond Jugaad that we offered with Professor S. Rajeev at IIM Bengaluru in October 2011.

We benefited from the feedback and insightful comments given by friends who generously spared their time to read our manuscript at different stages. Ramprasad Moudgalya and Dr Ardhendu Pathak deserve special thanks in this regard.

Geetika and Anju, two diligent students from IIT Kharagpur, interned with us in the summer of 2010 and raised several questions that triggered fresh thinking.

Rishi would like to thank the following people who have helped him understand the challenges involved in corporate innovation: Vijay Anand, Sanjay Anandaram, K. Ananth Krishnan, Deepa Bachu, Subroto Bagchi, Bhaskar Bhat, Charles Dhanaraj, Kris Gopalakrishnan, Subu Goparaju, Ivaturi Vijay,

Meera Harish, Srivardhini K. Jha, Gopichand Katragadda, Nirmalya Kumar, Mano Manoharan, Kamalaksha Naik, Ajay Nanavati, Narayan Murthy, L.R. Natarajan, Sanjay Nayak, Phanish Puranam, Kumar Ranganathan, Mitrabarun Sarkar, D.V.R. Seshadri, Vishwanathan Seshan, Kiran Mazumdar-Shaw, Pavan Soni and Niranjan Thirumale.

Rishi also offers a special word of thanks to Srikant Datar, Rejie George, Vidyanand Jha, Pankaj Rai, J. Ramachandran, Pramath Raj Sinha and Vasanthi Srinivasan for their continuing support. Two institutions—the Indian School of Business and IIM Bengaluru—provided a facilitating environment.

Kajoli was not directly involved in writing this book, but has always been behind Rishi's endeavours. Her dogged persistence in her own innovation efforts is always a source of inspiration.

Vinay would like to thank his parents for providing constant encouragement. Without patience and support from Gauri and Kabir, this project wouldn't have moved far.

Vinay would like to thank Swami Krishnan for providing an opportunity to teach a course on innovation management at IFIM Business School in the fall of 2009. He would also like to thank all those who provided encouragement and constructive inputs on his innovation consulting journey. Among these special thanks go to Rahul Abhyankar, Pearl Abraham, Manish Agarwal, Ravikiran Aranke, Swaroop Bachireddy, Kalyan Banarjee, Yogesh Bhagwat, Manoj Bhalerao, V.N. Bhattacharya, Akkiraju Bhattiprolu, Malla Chakravarthy, Raja Chidambaram, Madhav Dabholkar, Vivek Dabholkar, Padmanabh Dabke, Raj Datta, Deepa C., Pradeep Desai, Gururaj Deshpande, K. Ganesh, Ketan Goswami, Anuradha Goyal, Umesh Gupta, Hari Iyer, Halasyam S., Jaykumar P., Ravindra Keskar, Srinivas Konidena, Sanjeev Krishnan, Ganapathy Lakshman, Sanjay Malpani,

Mahesh Mehendale, Deepa Mahesh, Satyajit Majumdar, Manish Malhotra, Madhav Manthri, Vipul Mathur, Susanta Misra, Rajiv Mody, Sachin More, Edwin Moses, Ramprasad Moudgalya, Sourav Mukherji, Nilesh Naik, Murthy Narayanan, Rajasekhar Padala, Paresh Padgaonkar, Ishwar Parulkar, S. Poovannan (Poo), C.K. Prahalad, Shambu Prasad, N. Ramesh, S. Ramesh, Ramya T.V., Rajeev Redkar, Sanjeev Redkar, Lakshman Seshadri, Balaji Setlur, Pavan Soni, K.T. Suresh, Arun Tanksali, Richard Tedlow, Stefan Thomke, Abhijit Tongaonkar, Naresh Tyagi, A. Thiagarajan, Ushasri T., G. Venkatesh and S. Yegneswar.

Two industry forums have been of great help during this research. One, the CII Karnataka Innovation Forum spearheaded by Kris Gopalkrishnan. Since 2008, it hosted several speakers at IIM Bengaluru sharing their insights on managing innovation. Two, the Indian Suggestion Scheme Association (INSSAN), a twenty-year-old organization benchmarking data on suggestion schemes in the Indian industry. Special thanks to Sudhir Date and Bhushan Ganjoo for providing the INSSAN data.

We would like to thank the team at HarperCollins India for making the book reader-friendly. Special thanks to Bidisha Srivastava for her diligent editing of the stories and the flow, Amit Agarwal for excellent coordination among all the stakeholders and Krishan Chopra for believing in us.

Notes and References

PART 1: BUILD AN IDEA PIPELINE

Introduction

1. A.P.J Abdul Kalam, *Wings of Fire*, Universities Press, 2000, p. 28. Kalam said this after building a working prototype of a hovercraft named 'Nandi'. Before the work began the team felt it was beyond their capability.
2. http://articles.economictimes.indiatimes.com/2010-07-16/news/28406676_1_d-udaya-kumar-rupee-symbol-industrial-design-centre, accessed on 27 May 2012.
3. Gopichand Katragadda, *Smash Innovation: Smashing the Hand-Mind-Market Barrier*, Wiley India, 2009, pp. 56–58.
4. Ibid., pp. 55–56.
5. http://www.super30.org/history1.html, accessed on 28 April 2012.
6. 'Innovator Saves Crores of Rupees for BEL', the *Hindu*, 23 October 2011; http://www.thehindu.com/todays-paper/tp-national/tp-karnataka/article2564006.ece
7. L.R. Natarajan, 'Innovation Journey: Titan Industries Ltd', presented at the Innovation Educators' Conference, Indian Business School (ISB), Hyderabad, 29–30 April 2011.
8. S.M. Patil, *25 Years with HMT*, Bharatiya Vidya Bhavan, 1998, p. 80.

9. Ibid., pp. 81–82.

10. 'The Man who Started the Suggestion Box Scheme Rolling'; http://www.tatamotors.com/50years/diary/pop_15.php, accessed on 10 October 2010.

11. Ibid.

12. Personal communication with Mukesh Prasad who spent thirty years with Tata Steel, 1 August 2011.

13. http://www.businessweek.com/interactive_reports/ innovative_50_2009.html, accessed on 4 November 2011. This classification is not very different from the one proposed by Joseph Schumpeter in 1911. For more, see Vinay Dabholkar, 'A Century of Innovation Economics: Schumpeter's 5 Types of Innovations', a blog; http://cataligninnovation.blogspot.in/2010/ 04/century-of-innovation-economics.html, accessed on 4 June 2012.

14. 'Who Says Money Doesn't Grow on Trees?' *Economic Times*, 21 April 2010.

15. Porus Munshi, *Making Breakthrough Innovation Happen*, Collins Business, 2009, pp. 34–52.

16. Gideon Parchomovsky and R. Polk Wagner, 'Patent Portfolios', Working paper 04–16, University of Pennsylvania Law School, 1 March 2005.

17. R.M. Lala, *For the Love of India: The Life and Times of Jamsetji Tata*, Penguin, 2006, pp. 33–34.

18. Timothy Leunig, 'New Answers to Old Questions: Explaining the Slow Adoption of Ring Spinning in Lancashire, 1880–1913', working paper no. 60/00, London School of Economics, 2000; http://eprints.lse.ac.uk/22378/1/wp60.pdf, accessed on 6 October 2011.

19. Alan Robinson and Sam Stern, *Corporate Creativity: How Innovation and Improvement Actually Happens*, Berret-Koehler Publishers, 1998, p. 65.

20. Ibid., pp. 65–68.

21. Stephen Dubner, 'John Unitas, Steel-Town Quarterback', *New York Times Magazine*, 2002; http://stephenjdubner.com/journalism/unitas.html, accessed on 12 August 2011.

22. Alan Axelrod, *Edison on Innovation: 102 Lessons in Creativity for Business and Beyond*, Jossey-Bass, 2008, p. 145.

23. Ibid., p. 50.

24. Henry Ford, *Edison as I Know Him*, Atomica Creative Group, 2006, p. 30; www.atomicacreative.com/images/ACG_EdisonAsI KnowHim.pdf, accessed on 11 August 2011.

25. Ibid., p. 25.

26. We have used the term 'idea velocity' after reading about 'velocity metrics' in Alan Robinson and Dean Schroeder's, *Ideas Are Free: How the Idea Revolution is Liberating People and Transforming Organizations*, Berrett-Koehler Publishers, 2006, p. 143. However, Robinson and Schroeder associate the term primarily with responsiveness (rate of evaluation, feedback to idea's author). We also include the rate of experimentation and learning as in Edison's case.

27. Vinay Dabholkar, 'Thomas Edison's Method of Innovation'; http://cataligninnovation.blogspot.in/2009/11/thomas-edisons-method-of-innovation.html, accessed on 22 May 2012.

28. Larry Huston and Nabil Sakkab, 'Connect and Develop: Inside Procter & Gamble's New Model for Innovation', *Harvard Business Review*, March 2006.

29. A.G. Lafley and Ram Charan, *The Game-changer: How Every Leader can Drive Everyday Innovation*, Portfolio, 2008, p. 136. Also see Huston and Sakkab, 'Connect and Develop', pp. 58–66.

30. Lafley and Charan, *The Game-changer*, p. 5.

31. Kishore Biyani, *It Happened in India*, Rupa Publications, 2007, p. 41.

32. Ibid., p. 42.

33. Christabelle Noronha, 'Making of the Nano', interview of Ratan Tata; http://www.tata.com/media/interviews/inside.aspx?artid=Sd75BUBmzSM=, accessed on 6 November 2011.

34. Nassim Taleb, *The Black Swan*, Penguin, 2007, p. 137.

35. Reeba Zachariah and Namrata Singh, 'Denim Man Turns Focus to Retail Business', *Times of India*, 2 November 2010.

36. Ibid.

37. Daniel Kahneman, *Thinking, Fast and Slow*, Farrar, Straus and Giroux, 2011, pp. 20–24.

38. Chip and Dan Heath, *Switch: How to Change Things When Change is Hard*, Broadway Books, 2010.

39. R.C. Bhargava, *The Maruti Story*, Collins Business, 2010, pp. 317–320.

40. http://en.wikipedia.org/wiki/Quality_circle, accessed on 3 November 2011.

41. Heath, *Switch*, p. 183.

42. 'Interview with I.V. Rao, Managing Executive Officer, Maruti Suzuki', 31 August 2010; http://suzukifan.com/2010/08/31/interview-with-i-v-rao-managing-executive-officer-maruti-suzuki/, accessed on 29 April 2012.

43. Results of the Excellence in Suggestion Scheme contest, *INSSAN Bulletin*, October–December 2010, vol. 22, no. 4.

44. Nandini Sen Gupta, 'Maruti Suzuki Giving Shape to Small Car', *Economic Times*, 12 January 2011.

chapter one
Step 1: Lay the Foundation

1. A.G. Lafley and Ram Charan, *The Game-changer: How Every Leader Can Drive Everyday Innovation*, Portfolio, 2008, p. 7.

2. Stefan Thomke and Briana Doerr Luthra, 'Innovation at Mahindra and Mahindra (A)', *Harvard Business School*, case study 9-609-065, Revision: 5 May 2009, p. 2.

3. Ibid., pp. 2–3.

4. Rishikesha T. Krishnan, *From Jugaad to Systematic Innovation: The Challenge for India*, The Utpreraka Foundation, 2010, pp. 62–71.

5. 'Century of innovation: The 3M storybook'; http://solutions.3m.com/wps/portal/3M/en_WW/History/3M/Company/century-innovation/, accessed on 13 August 2011, pp. 22–23.

6. Ibid., p. 23.

7. 'Jeff Immelt on taking swings', *Bloomberg Businessweek*, 28 March 2005; http://www.businessweek.com/magazine/content/05_13/b3926093_mz056.htm, accessed on 9 May 2012.

8. 'GE finds its inner Edison', interview of Jeff Immelt by Robert Buderi in *Technology Review*, MIT, October 2003; http://www.technologyreview.com/business/13307/, accessed on 29 April 2012.

9. Yuzo Yasuda, *40 Years, 20 Million Ideas*, Productivity Press, 1991.

10. Ibid., pp. 102–05.

11. Personal communication with Dr Nirmal Koshti, Head, Innovation Process, Galaxy Surfactants, 24 April 2011.

12. Personal communication with Vijay Anand, MD of Intuit India, 24 February 2011.

13. Laura Messerschmitt, 'What is "Follow-me-home"?'; http://blog.intuit.com/trends/what-is-a-follow-me-home/, accessed on 9 May 2012.

14. Rishikesha T Krishnan, 'Intuit: Innovating for India', http://jugaadtoinnovation.blogspot.in/2012/02/intuit-innovating-for-india.html, accessed on 4 April 2012.

15. Yasuda, *40 Years, 20 Million Ideas*, p. 70.

16. Indian National Suggestion Scheme Association (INSSAN), www.inssan.org.

17. Sunil Kumar and Amrita Singh, 'Initiate, Innovate, Implement', *Proceedings of the 20th National INSSAN Convention*, 21–23 January 2010, pp. 187–92.

18. Ibid., pp. 154–65.

19. 'Lessons from Toyota's Long Drive', interview with Katsuaki Watanabe, CEO of Toyota, *Harvard Business Review*, July–August 2007, pp. 74–83.

20. Alan Robinson and Dean Schroeder, *Ideas Are Free: How the Idea Revolution is Liberating People and Transforming Organizations*, Berrett-Koehler Publishers, 2006, pp. 46–52.

21. Muhammad Yunus, *Banker to the Poor*, Penguin, 2007, pp. 3–11.

22. Robinson and Schroeder, *Ideas Are Free*, pp. 127–30.

23. 'Nokia's Chief Executive to Staff: "We are standing on a burning platform"'; http://www.guardian.co.uk/technology/blog/2011/feb/09/nokia-burning-platform-memo-elop, accessed on 28 May 2012. Nokia did not publicly accept or deny the memo.

24. John P. Kotter, *Leading Change*, Harvard Business Review Press, 1996, pp. 35–49.

25. http://en.wikipedia.org/wiki/Operation_Lighthouse, accessed on 30 October 2011.

26. Balbir Pasha AIDS campaign; http://www.youtube.com/watch?v=N41pGKlQZtU, accessed on 30 October 2011.

27. Barbara Fredrickson, 'What Good are Positive Emotions?', *Review of General Psychology*, 1998, vol. 2, no. 3, pp .300–19.

28. 'The Power of Ideas Delivers on India Inc's Dream', *Economic Times*, 23 June 2010.

29. Ibid.

30. V. Nilakant and S. Ramnarayan, *Changing Tracks: Reinventing the Spirit of Indian Railways*, Collins Business, 2009.

31. Ibid.

32. Ibid., p. 127.

33. L.R. Natarajan, 'Innovation Journey: Titan Industries Ltd', presented at *Innovation Educators' Conference*, ISB, Hyderabad, 29–30 April 2011.

34. Ibid.

35. Ibid.

36. Ibid.

37. Ibid.

38. Vinay Dabholkar, 'Building Creative Confidence: Insights from Sukumar Rajgopal of Cognizant'; http://cataligninnovation.

blogspot.in/2011/12/building-creative-confidence-insights.html, accessed on 9 May 2012. The term 'creative confidence' was coined by David Kelley, a Standford University professor and the founder of IDEO, a leading global design firm. For more see Tom Kelley and David Kelley, 'Reclaim Your Creative Confidence', Harvard Business Review, December 2012; http://wor.org/2012/12reclaim-your-creative-confidence, accessed on 15 January 2013.

39. Tom Kelley, *The Art of Innovation*, Profile Books, 2004.

40. Tim Brown, *Change by Design*, Harper Business, 2009.

41. http://en.wikipedia.org/wiki/TRIZ, accessed on 27 May 2012.

42. http://trizindia.org/, accessed on 27 May 2012.

43. Peter Senge, *The Fifth Discipline*, Random House, 2006.

44. Eliyahu Goldratt, *Theory of Constraints*, North River, 1999.

45. http://en.wikipedia.org/wiki/Six_Thinking_Hats, accessed on 27 May 2012.

46. Peter Coughlan, et. al., 'Prototypes as Design Tools for Behavioural and Organizational Change', *Journal of Applied Behavioural Science*, vol. 43, no. 1, March 2007, pp. 1–13.

47. Hasso Plattner Institute of Design at Stanford; http://dschool.stanford.edu/; HPI School of Design Thinking at Potsdam; http://www.hpi.uni-potsdam.de/d_school/home.html

48. Donella Meadows, 'Leverage points: Places to Intervene a System', *Sustainability Institute*, December 1999.

49. Peter Senge, *The Fifth Discipline*, Random House, 2006

50. http://en.wikipedia.org/wiki/Theory_of_constraints, accessed on 27 May 2012.

51. http://en.wikipedia.org/wiki/Lateral_thinking, accessed on 27 May 2012.

52. http://en.wikipedia.org/wiki/Six_Thinking_Hats, accessed on 27 May 2012.

chapter two
Step 2: Create a Challenge Book

1. Kiran Bedi, *It's Always Possible*, Sterling Publishers, 2010, p. 172.
2. *Gandhi*, a film directed and produced by Richard Attenborough, 1982; http://en.wikipedia.org/wiki/Gandhi_movie, accessed on 27 May 2012.
3. M.K. Gandhi, *An Autobiography or The Story of my Experiments with Truth*, Navjivan Trust, 2001, p. 311.
4. Ibid., p. 319.
5. Ibid.
6. Louis Fischer, *The Life of Mahatma Gandhi*, HarperCollins, 2009, pp. 126–27.
7. G. Sreekala and R. Sriram, 'No Indian Co is a Tier 1 Pharma Play', Q&A with vice-chairman and managing director of Dr Reddy's Laboratories, G.V. Prasad, *Economic Times*, 21 September, 2010.
8. Pradeep Thakur, *Tata Nano: The People's Car*, Shree Book Centre, 2009, p. 88.
9. Vineet Nayar, *Employees First, Customers Second*, Harvard Business Review Press, 2011.
10. Kiran Bedi, *It's Always Possible*, pp. 155–77.
11. J.K. Rowling, *Harry Potter and the Philosopher's Stone*, Bloomsbury, 2001, chapter 12.
12. en.wikipedia.org/wiki/Thomas_Savery, accessed on 27 May 2012.
13. 'The World's Billionaires', Forbes, 10 March 2010; http://www.forbes.com/lists/2010/10/billionaires-2010_Kavitark-Ram-Shriram_PED7.html, accessed on 24 April 2012.
14. Archana Rai, 'The Digital Guru Betting on India for His Next Billion', *Economic Times*, 17 September 2010, p. 6.
15. Featured interview of Sumir Chadha, MD of Sequoia Capital India, 18 May 2008; http://iinnovate.blogspot.com/2008/05/chadha.html, accessed on 17 September 2010.
16. Vinay Dabholkar, 'INSSAN 20th Annual Convention: where

shop-floor innovators are the heroes'; http://cataligninnovation. blogspot.in/2010/01/inssan-20th-annual-convention-where. html, accessed on 22 May 2012.

17. Ibid.

18. 'Thinkpad working on thinner, lighter form factor, says Naitoh', *Economic Times*, 3 November 2010.

19. Anil Khandelwal, *Dare to Lead: The transformation of Bank of Baroda*, Sage Publications, 2011, p. 238.

20. Ibid., p. 238.

21. A.G. Lafley and Ram Charan, *The Game-changer: How Every Leader Can Drive Everyday Innovation*, Portfolio, 2008, pp. 47–52.

22. Shramana Ganguly Mehta, 'Innovation at Your Doorstep', *Economic Times*, 20 May 2011.

23. Ibid.

24. Kala Vijayraghava, 'HUL sharpening its consumer focus: Nitin Paranjpe', *Economic Times*, 14 January 2011; http://articles. economictimes.indiatimes.com/2011-01-14/news/28425800_ 1_hul-managers-nitin-paranjpe-consumer, accessed on 9 May 2012.

25. Ibid.

26. Talk by Professor Huggy Rao at a Stanford GSB event, Hotel Taj West End, Bangalore, December 2007.

27. Ibid.

28. Anshul Dhamija and Sujit John, 'Indian pharma companies must be more creative', *Times of India*, interview with Kiran Mazumdar-Shaw, 22 May 2010.

29. Dan P. Lovallo and Lenny T. Mendonca, 'Strategy's Strategist: An interview with Richard Rumelt', *McKinsey Quarterly*, August 2007.

30. Ibid, p. 4.

31. Ibid.

32. 'Gartner Hype Cycle'; http://www.gartner.com/technology/ research/methodologies/hype-cycle.jsp, accessed on 13 August 2011.

33. http://www.gartner.com/it/page.jsp?id=1447613, accessed on 23 May 2012.

34. Peter Drucker, *Innovation and Entrepreneurship*, HarperBusiness, 1993, pp. 88–98.

35. Joji Thomas Philip, 'Augmenting customer experience is the key', interview with Sanjay Kapoor, Bharati Airtel, *Economic Times*, 27 January 2011; http://articles.economictimes.indiatimes.com/2011-01-27/news/28427851_1_offering-3g-services-airwaves-circles, accessed on 30 April 2012.

36. 'Disney, China Partner Will Spend $4.4 Billion Building Resort in Shanghai', *Bloomberg News*, 8 April 2011.

37. Rishikesha T. Krishnan, 'Infosys: Innovation to Build Tomorrow's Enterprise', 14 April 2012; http://jugaadtoinnovation.blogspot.in/2012/04/infosys-innovation-to-build-tomorrows.html, accessed on 9 May 2012.

38. Sarah Jacob, 'Ready-to-cook idlis, vegetarian sausages lead India's frozen food revolution', *Economic Times*, 12 September 2011.

39. Talk by V.R. Ferose in an Innovation Forum meeting at IIM Bangalore, August 2011.

40. F.M. Scherer, 'Invention and innovation in the Watt-Boulton steam engine venture', *Technology and Culture*, vol. 6, no. 2, Spring 1965, pp. 165–87.

41. Richard Tedlow, *Giants of Enterprise: Seven Business Innovators and the Empires They Built*, HarperBusiness, 2001, p. 393.

chapter three
Step 3: Build Participation

1. Stephen Wozniak, 'Homebrew and How the Apple Came to Be'; http://www.atariarchives.org/deli/homebrew_and_how_the_apple.php, accessed on 10 May 2012.

2. Kameshwar Wali, *Chandra: A Biography of S. Chandrasekhar*, University of Chicago Press, 1992, p. 62.

3. Ibid., p. 63.

4. P.C. Deshmukh, 'Life and Works of C.V. Raman', talk at IIT Madras, 18 January 2009; available at www.physics.iitm.ac.in/~labs/amp/CVRaman-Life-and-Works.pdf, accessed on 31 October 2011.

5. Interviews of S. Chandrasekhar by S. Weart on 17 May 1977, Neils Bohr Library and Archives, American Institute of Physics, College Park, MD, USA, http://www.aip.org/history/ohilist/45511.html., accessed on 28 November 2012.

6. Wali, *Chandra*, p. 47.

7. Kishore Biyani, *It Happened in India*, Rupa Publications, 2007, pp. 36–37.

8. Edgar Schein, *Organization Culture and Leadership*, John Wiley & Sons, 2004, pp. 327–28.

9. Yasuda, *40 Years, 20 Million Ideas*, pp. 97–101.

10. Ibid., p. 97.

11. Ibid., pp. 86–87.

12. Intel commercial: 'Our rock stars are not like your rock stars'; http://www.youtube.com/watch?v=q-8GVi2Fdi4, accessed on 27 April 2012.

13. http://en.wikipedia.org/wiki/Ajay_Bhatt, accessed on 27 May 2012.

14. http://en.wikipedia.org/wiki/Indian_Association_for_the_Cultivation_of_Science; accessed on 27 May 2012.

15. Subrata Dasgupta, *The Bengal Renaissance*, Permanent Black, 2007, pp. 146–60.

16. Etienne Wenger and William Snyder, 'Communities of Practice: The Organizational Frontier', *Harvard Business Review*, January–February 2000, pp. 139–45.

17. David Garvin and Rachna Tahilyani, 'MindTree: A Community of Communities', *Harvard Business School*, case 9-311-049, 27 August 2010.

18. Ibid.

19. Bedi, *It's Always Possible*, pp. 217–33.
20. Ibid., pp. 241–44.
21. Henry Ford, *My Life and Work*, p. 21, Project Gutenberg; http://www.gutenberg.org/ebooks/7213, accessed on 29 April 2012.
22. Ibid., p. 21.
23. Ibid., p. 1.
24. Ibid., p. 2.
25. Ibid., p. 2.
26. Peter Skarzynski and Rowan Gibson, *Innovation to the Core: A Blueprint for Transforming the Way your Company Innovates*, Harvard Business Press, 2008, pp. 22–25.
27. Alan Robinson and Dean Schroeder, *Ideas Are Free: How the Idea Revolution is Liberating People and Transforming Organizations*, Berrett-Koehler Publishers, 2006, pp. 66–84.
28. Chetan Bhagat, 'A Book, a Film and the Truth', 31 December 2009; http://www.chetanbhagat.com/blog/general/a-book-a-film-and-the-truth, accessed on 11 December 2010.
29. Robinson and Schroeder, *Ideas Are Free*, pp. 66–70.
30. Ibid., pp. 70–78.
31. Ibid., p. 78.
32. 'Employee inventor scheme practices survey', *Intellectual Property Owners Association*, Report of the Asian Practice Committee, February 2004; http://www.ipo.org/AM/Template.cfm?Section=Past_Meetings_and_Events&Template=/CM/ContentDisplay.cfm&ContentFileID=55127, accessed on 9 May 2012.
33. 'Tata InnoVista awards 2011', 26 April 2011, from the Tata Quality Management Services website; http://www.tataquality.com/ui/otherarticle.aspx?contentid=042711183458504454&tabs= y, accessed on 17 August 2011.
34. Ibid.
35. http://en.wikipedia.org/wiki/Tony_Fadell, accessed on 27 May 2012.
36. Vinay Dabholkar, 'Entering the game-changer funnel: Story of

SAP Labs India', 20 August 2010; http://cataligninnovation. blogspot.com/2010/08/entering-game-changer-funnel-story-of.html, accessed on 17 August 2011.

37. Theresa Amabile, 'How to Kill Creativity', *Harvard Business Review*, September–October 1998, pp. 77–87.

PART 2: IMPROVE IDEA VELOCITY

1. http://en.wikipedia.org/wiki/Von_Neumann_architecture, accessed on 27 May 2012.
2. M.G.K. Menon, 'Homi Bhabha and the Self-reliance in Electronics and Information Technology', in R.K. Shyamasundar and M.A. Pai, *Homi Bhabha and the Computer Revolution*, Oxford University Press, 2011, pp.107–18.
3. Ibid., p. 110.
4. R.K. Shyamasundar and M.A. Pai, 'Bhabha, "Big Science", and the IT revolution in India', in Shyamasundar and Pai, *Homi Bhabha and the Computer Revolution*, pp. xix–xxxiii.
5. P.V.S. Rao, 'TIFRAC: India's First Computer', in Shyamasundar and Pai, *Homi Bhabha and the Computer* Revolution, pp. 3–16.
6. http://en.wikipedia.org/wiki/HAL_Tejas, accessed on 27 May 2012.
7. G.B. Meemamsi, *The C-DoT Story*, Kedar Publications, 1993.

chapter four
Step 4: Experiment with Low Cost at High Speed

1. Allen Webb, 'Taking improbable events seriously: An interview with the author of *The Black Swan*', *McKinsey Quarterly*, Corporate Finance, December 2008, p. 3.
2. Jaya Dadkar, *Dadasaheb Phalke: Kaalani Kartutva (Dadasaheb Phalke: Time and Works)*, Mauj Publishers, 2012, pp. 76–79.
3. Mihir Bose, *Bollywood: A History*, Roli Books, 2006, p. 55.

4. Dadkar, Dadasahab Phalke, p. 49.

5. 'The Start-up Artist, interview by Vinod Mahanta with Guy Kawasaki, *Economic Times*, 19 September 2008.

6. Peter Coughlan, et. al, 'Prototypes as (design) tools for behavioural and organizational change', *Journal of Applied Behavioural Science*, vol. 43, no. 1, March 2007, pp. 1–13.

7. *Jim Blasingame interview* with *Stefan Thomke*; www.smallbusiness advocate.com/small-business-interviews/stefan-thomke-973, accessed on 1 March 2009.

8. Bose, *Bollywood*, p. 49.

9. Stefan Thomke, *Managing Product and Service Development: Text and Cases*, McGraw Hill, 2007, pp. 4–5.

10. Bose, *Bollywood*, pp. 49–50.

11. Ibid., p. 51.

12. Stefan Thomke, *Experimentation Matters*, Harvard Business School Press, 2003, p. 2.

13. Talk by Sandeep Dhar on innovation at Tesco, CII Innovation Forum, IIM Bangalore, August 2011.

14. Khandelwal, *Dare to Lead*, p. 238.

15. Stefan Thomke, 'Bank of America (A)', *Harvard Business School case study 9-603-022*, 28 October 2002.

16. Thomke, *Experimentation Matters*, pp.167–70.

17. The design of complex experiments is out of the scope of this book. However, the reader may refer to wikipedia for more information on this topic where methods such as the Taguchi method and randomized experimentation are described; http://en.wikipedia.org/wiki/Design_of_experiments, accessed on 31 October 2011.

18. Tom Kelley, *The Art of Innovation*, Profile Books, 2004, pp. 142–246.

19. Ibid., p. 142.

20. http://en.wikipedia.org/wiki/Thomas_Edison, accessed on 27 May 2012.

21. Theresa Mary Collins, et al., *Thomas Edison and Modern America: A Brief History with Documents*, Bedford Books, 2002, pp. 50–151 (The site of invention: Edison's draft letter to James Hood Wright, 1887).

22. Biyani, *It Happened in India*, p. 204.

23. Ibid. p. 204.

24. 'How Google makes improvements to its search algorithm', YouTube video uploaded by Google on 24 August 2011; http://www.youtube.com/watch?v=J5RZOU6vK4Q, accessed on 10 September 2011.

25. Roger Martin, 'Innovation Catalysts', *Harvard Business Review*, June 2011.

26. 'Culture of experimentation', talk by Scott Cook at 2011 CEO Conference; http://www.khoslaventures.com/culture-of-experimentation-2/, accessed on 6 April 2012.

27. V. Nilakant and S. Ramnarayan, *Changing Tracks: Reinventing the Spirit of Indian Railways*, Collins Business, 2009, pp. 151–61.

28. Kalam, *Wings of Fire*, pp. 27–31.

29. 'A Culture of Creativity', April 2011; http://www.tata.com/article.aspx?artid=9utBf9+SGyI=, accessed on 1 May 2012.

30. Jackie Freiberg, et al., *Nanovation: How a little car can teach the world to think big and act bold*, Dain Dunston, Portfolio, 2010, pp. 469–70.

31. 'Innovation at Tata Group, talk by Dr Murali Sastry, *Innovation Educators' Conference*, ISB, April, 2011, pp. 29–30.

32. 'Century of Innovation: The 3M Storybook'; http://solutions.3m.com/wps/portal/3M/en_WW/History/3M/Company/century-innovation/, accessed on 13 August 2011.

33. Chip and Dan Heath, *Switch: How to Change Things When Change is Hard*, Broadway Books, 2010, p. 173.

34. Kalam, *Wings of Fire*, p. 28.

chapter five
Step 5: Go Fast from Prototyping to Incubation

1. 'Champion', *The Economist*, 15 December 2008 (article adapted from Tim Hindle) *The Economist Guide to Management Ideas and Gurus*; http://www.economist.com/node/12677035, accessed on 24 May 2012.

2. 'Century of Innovation: The 3M Storybook'; http://solutions.3m.com/wps/portal/3M/en_WW/History/3M/Company/century-innovation/, accessed on 13 August 2011, pp. 38–40.

3. E. Sreedharan, 'The Story of Konkan Railway of India: How the Ideas have Worked'; http://praja.in/files/The-Story-of-Toughest-Konkan-Railways-Project-India-by-Its-Project-Director-E-Shreedharan.pdf, accessed on 17 August 2011.

4. Ibid., p. 2.

5. Vikas Singh, 'Indian Railways in Postal Stamps'; http://www.irfca.org/articles/vikas/stamps.html, accessed on 7 October 2011.

6. Sreedharan, 'The Story of Konkan Railway of India', p. 3.

7. *Century of Innovation: The 3M Storybook*; http://solutions.3m.com/wps/portal/3M/en_WW/History/3M/Company/century-innovation/, accessed 13 August 2011, pp. 70–71.

8. http://en.wikipedia.org/wiki/Satyendra_Nath_Bose, accessed on 27 May 2012.

9. Ibid.

10. Dr Subodh Mahanti, 'Satyendra Nath Bose: The Creator of Quantum Statistics', *Vigyan Prasar Science Portal*; http://www.vigyanprasar.gov.in/scientists/snbose/bosenew.htm, accessed on 2 May 2012.

11. http://en.wikipedia.org/wiki/Gabriel_Tarde, accessed on 27 May 2012.

12. Thomas McCraw, *Prophet of Innovation: Joseph Schumpeter and Creative Destruction*, Harvard University Press, 2009, p. 72.

13. Everett Rogers, *Diffusion of Innovations*, Focal Press, 2003.

14. http://en.wikipedia.org/wiki/Diffusion_of_innovations, accessed on 27 May 2012.

15. Geoffrey Moore, *Crossing the Chasm*, Harper Paperbacks, 2002.

16. 'Customer Value Management at Tata Steel', case study by D.V.R. Seshadri and Arabinda Tripathy, IIM Ahmedabad and Peeyush Gupta and Subodh Pandey of Tata Steel, 2004.

17. Emanuel Rosen, *The Anatomy of Buzz Revisited*, Doubleday, 2009, pp. 212–14.

18. Malcolm Gladwell, *The Tipping Point*, Abacus, 2008.

19. Chip and Dan Heath, *Made to Stick: Why Some Ideas Survive and Others Die*, Arrow Books, 2008.

20. M.K. Gandhi, *The Story of my Experiments with Truth*, Navjivan Publishing House, 2001, pp. 266–67

21. Louis Fischer, *The Life of Mahatma Gandhi*, HarperCollins, 2009, p. 332.

22. Ibid., pp. 335–36.

23. Ibid., p. 336.

24. Ibid., p. 337.

25. Heath, *Made to Stick*, pp. 14–19.

26. Yasuda, *40 Years, 20 Million Ideas*, p. 95.

27. http://www.youtube.com/watch?v=kN0SVBCJqLs, accessed on 2 May 2012.

28. Heath, *Made to Stick*.

29. Ibid., p. 157.

30. Paul Buchheit, 'Communicating with code'; http://paulbuchheit.blogspot.com/2009/01/communicating-with-code.html, accessed on 30 August 2011.

31. Interview with Marissa Mayer; http://iinnovate.blogspot.com/2007/08/marissa-mayer-vp-of-search-products-and.html, accessed on 31 August 2011.

32. Buchheit, 'Communicating with code'.

33. A.G. Lafley and Ram Charan, *The Game-changer: How Every Leader Can Drive Everyday Innovation*, Portfolio, 2008, pp.178–79.

34. Ibid., p. 178.

35. 'Innovation at Procter & Gamble', interview of A.G. Lafley; http://www.youtube.com/watch?v=xvIUSxXrffc, accessed on 24 May 2012. A.G. Lafley presents the key questions asked during the interview of six minutes and fifteen seconds.

36. Talk by D. Shivakumar, CEO, Nokia India, at IIM Bangalore on 2 August 2011.

37. Lafley and Charan, *The Game-changer*, p. 289.

38. Raghunath Mashelkar, *Reinventing India,*10 May 2011, pp. 106–07.

39. R. Mashelkar, 'Fun and Joy of Science: Learning from Anomalies and Discontinuities', Professor Brahma Prakash Memorial Lecture, 21 August 2002, delivered at Indian Institute of Metals, Bangalore chapter; www.csir.res.in/External/Heads/aboutcsir/leaders/dg/dgsp1.pdf, accessed on 14 September 2011.

40. Personal communication with Suhas Kelkar and Nikhil Sahasrabudhe of BMC Software, 7 September 2011.

41. Pranav Nambiar 'Technology companies adopt venture capital model', *Times of India*, 31 May 2011; http://articles.timesofindia.indiatimes.com/2011-05-31/india-business/29603358_1_venture-capital-vc-firms-ideas, accessed on 27 May 2012.

chapter six
Step 6: Iterate on the Business Model

1. Peter Drucker, *The Daily Drucker*, HarperBusiness, 2004, p. 204.

2. http://www.shaadi.com/, accessed on 9 May 2012.

3. 'Customer Focus at People Group', interview with Anupam Mittal; http://www.cio.in/view-top/customer-focus-people-group, accessed on 25 August 2011.

4. Joan Magretta, 'Why Business Models Matter', *Harvard Business Review*, May 2002, pp. 86–92.

5. Tim Harford, *Adapt: Why Success Always Starts with a Failure*, Little Brown, 2011, p. 10.

6. G.R. Gopinath, *Simply Fly: A Deccan Odyssey*, Collins Business, 2010, pp. 183–85.

7. Ibid., pp. 183–87.

8. Henry Ford, *Edison as I Know Him*, Atomica Creative Group, 2006; www.atomicacreative.com/images/ACG_EdisonAsIKnowHim.pdf, accessed on 11 August 2011, pp. 17–18.

9. Frank Dyer and Thomas Martin, *Edison: His Life and Inventions*, available from Project Gutenberg; http://www.gutenberg.org/ebooks/820, chapter X, 'Phonograph'.

10. Vishnu Narasimhan, 'Power of ideas: Ticket to comfortable ride', *Economic Times*, 3 September 2010; http://articles.economictimes.indiatimes.com/2010-09-03/news/27578069_1_bus-operators-bus-ticket-travel-agents, accessed on 25 August 2011.

11. Ibid.

12. 'Journey from Micro to Max' *Economic Times*, 29 April 2010, p. 5.

13. 'iON brings the power of world-class technology to India's SMBs', 21 February 2011; http://www.tcs.com/news_events/press_releases/pages/ion_power_world_class_technology_india_smbs.aspx, accessed on 25 May 2012.

14. Richard Tedlow, *Giants of Enterprise*, Harper Business, 2003, pp. 95–97.

15. http://en.wikipedia.org/wiki/Sherman_Act, accessed on 25 May 2012.

16. Tedlow, *Giants of Enterprise*, p. 100.

17. Ibid.

18. Ibid., p. 104.

19. J.B. Harreld et al., 'Dynamic Capabilities at IBM', *California Management Review*, vol. 49, no. 4, Summer 2007, pp. 21–43.

20. Joji Thomas Philips, 'IBM deal to support up to 500 million global Bharti users,' *Economic Times*, 28 September 2010.

21. Michael Cusumano, *The Business of Software*, Free Press, 2004.

22. Shrabonti Bagchi, 'Saving Little Lives', *Times of India*, 19 September 2011, p. 4.

23. Sourav Mukherji, 'Vaatsalya Hospitals: Inclusiveness through Proximity', case study, UNDP, 2011; www.growing inclusivemarkets.org/media/cases/India_Vaatsalya_ 2011.pdf, accessed on 19 September 2011.

24. 'Innovation in the Indian Context: The Sasken Experience', talk at the Indian Institute of Management, Bangalore by Rajiv C. Mody, 2004; http://www.iimb.ernet.in/~review/ DOCUMENTS/Rajiv%20C%20Mody.pdf, accessed on 28 May 2012.

25. Ibid., p. 3.

26. http://en.wikipedia.org/wiki/Flash_of_Genius_(film), accessed on 27 May 2012.

27. V.K. Narayanan, *Managing Technology and Innovation for Competitive Advantage*, Pearson Education, 2001, pp. 445–48.

28. Allen Afuah, *Business Models: A Strategic Management Approach*, McGraw Hill 2004.

29. http://en.wikipedia.org/wiki/Husk_Power_Systems, accessed on 5 June 2012.

30. Vinay Dabholkar, 'Gyanesh Pandey Tells Husk Power Systems Story', 24 November 2011; http://www.catalign.com/data/ Gyanesh-hps-story.pdf, accessed on 5 June 2012.

31. Ibid.

32. Ibid.

33. Ibid.

34. Ibid. and http://en.wikipedia.org/wiki/Husk_Power_Systems, accessed on 5 June 2012.

35. Dabholkar, 'Gyanesh Pandey Tells Husk Power Systems Story'.

36. Gireesh Shrimali, et al., 'Husk Power Systems', a case study from the Indian School of Business (ISB) and Richard Ivey School of Business, version 2011-02-13.

37. Dabholkar, 'Gyanesh Pandey Tells Husk Power Systems Story'.

38. http://www.doblin.com/thinking/, accessed on 29 April 2012.

PART 3: INCREASE THE BATTING AVERAGE

1. Gita Piramal, *Business Legends*, Penguin, 1999, pp. 243–49.
2. Clay Chandler 'Wireless Wonder: India's Sunil Mittal', *Fortune*, 17 January 2007; http://money.cnn.com/magazines/fortune/fortune_archive/2007/01/22/8397979/index.htm, accessed on 21 September 2011.
3. Ibid.
4. Gita Piramal, *Business Legends*, Penguin, 1999, pp. 247–248.
5. Clay Chandler 'Wireless Wonder: India's Sunil Mittal', *Fortune*, 17 January 2007; http://money.cnn.com/magazines/fortune/fortune_archive/2007/01/22/8397979/index.htm, accessed on 21 September 2011.

chapter seven
Step 7: Build an Innovation Sandbox

1. C.K. Prahalad, 'Innovation Sandbox', *Strategy + Business*, issue 44, Autumn 2006.
2. Pradeep Thakur, *Tata Nano: The People's Car*, Shree Book Centre, 2009.
3. Jackie Freiberg, Kevin Freiberg and Dain Dunston, *Nanovation: How a Little Car Can Teach the World to Think Big and Act Bold*, Portfolio, 2010; Philip Chako, *Small Wonder: The Making of the Nano*, Westland, 2010; Pradeep Thakur, *Tata Nano: The People's Car*, Shree Book Centre, 2009.
4. Jackie Freiberg, et al, *Nanovation*, p. 66.
5. Prahalad, 'Innovation Sandbox'.
6. Frans Johansson, *The Medici Effect*, Harvard Business School Press, 2006, pp. 79–83.
7. S. Manikutty and Neharika Vohra, 'Aravind Eye Care System: Giving them the most precious gift (R1)', a case study (revision 1) at the Indian Institute of Management, Ahmedabad, 2004; https://wiki.brown.edu/confluence/download/attachments/9994241/Aravind+case.pdf?version=1, accessed on 29 April 2012.

8. Kasturi V. Rangan and R.D. Thulasiraj, 'Making Sight Affordable', *Innovations*, MIT Press Journals, Fall 2007, pp. 35–49; http://www.mitpressjournals.org/doi/abs/10.1162/itgg.2007.2.4.35, accessed on 15 June 2012.

9. 'Compassionate High Quality Health Care at Low Cost: The Aravind Model', in conversation with Dr G. Venkataswamy and R.D, Thulasiraj, interview by Janat Shah and L.S. Murthy, *IIMB Management Review*, September 2004, vol. 16, no. 3, pp. 31–43.

10. M. Ibrahim et al., 'Making the Sight Affordable (part I)', *Innovations*, Summer 2006, pp. 25–41.

11. Tim Brown, *Change by Design*, HarperCollins, 2009, p. 208.

12. Jaspal Sandhu, et al., 'Appropriate design of medical technologies for emerging regions: The case of Aurolab', *Proceedings of International Mechanical Engineering Conference and Exposition*, 5–11 November 2005, Orlando, Florida.

13. Porus Munshi, *Making Breakthrough Innovation Happen*, Collins Business, 2009, p. 43.

14. Sandhu, et al., 'Appropriate design of medical technologies for emerging regions: The case of Aurolab'.

15. Ibid., p. 3.

16. Rishikesha T. Krishnan, and Srivardhini K. Jha, 'Innovation strategies in emerging markets: What can we learn from Indian market leaders", *ASCI Journal of Management*, vol. 41, no. 1, pp. 21–45.

17. Charles Dhanaraj and Nita Sachan, 'Oral Insulin: Managing Breakthrough Innovation at Biocon, a case study by the ISB and Richard Ivey School of Business, version 2011-01-01.

18. Saras Sarasvathy, 'What Makes Entrepreneurs Entrepreneurial?', 1 June 2001; http://faculty.darden.virginia.edu/SarasvathyS/documents/0_Own%20Notes/What%20makes%20entrs%20entl.doc, accessed on 25 August 2011.

19. Chip and Dan Heath, *Switch: How to Change Things When Change is Hard*, Broadway Books, 2010, Chapter 6, 'Shrink the change', p. 124.

20. Vijay Chandru's talk at the Innovation Educators' Conference, ISB, Hyderabad, 29–30 April 2011.

21. 'Strand and Narayana Hrudalaya Collaborate in Translational Cancer Research'. Press release from Strand, 18 August 2010; http://www.strandls.com/viewnews.php?param=5&param1=62, accessed on 22 September 2011.

22. David Kirkpatrick, *The Facebook Effect: The Inside Story of the Company that is Connecting the World*, Virgin Books, 2010, pp. 153–56.

23. Ibid., p. 217.

24. 'Zynga in talks to raise funds; valued at $10 billion', *Economic Times*, 16 February 2011.

25. 3M Technologies; http://solutions.3mindia.co.in/wps/portal/3M/en_IN/3M-Tech3/Technology/, accessed on 10 May 2012.

26. 'Innovation at 3M', talk by Bert O'Donoghue, MD, 3M India at Innovation Summit, 20–21 June 2008, Bangalore.

27. 'Century of Innovation: The 3M Storybook'; http://solutions.3m.com/wps/portal/3M/en_WW/History/3M/Company/century-innovation/, accessed on 13 August 2011; pp. 57–65.

28. Ibid.

29. 'None of our M&As are done for ego or size', interview with Anand Mahindra, *Economic Times*, 29 June 2012; http://m.economictimes.com/PDAET/articleshow/msid-6103169,curpg-1.cms, accessed on 10 May 2012.

30. Rishikesha T. Krishnan and Srivardhini K. Jha, 'Innovation Strategies in Emerging Markets: What can we learn from Indian market leaders', *ASCI Journal of Management*, vol. 41, no. 1, pp. 21–45.

31. 'Tata Motors Celebrates Silver Jubilee of Tata 407', *The Hindu*, 19 October 2011.

32. Rishikesha T. Krishnan, 'Infosys: Innovation to build tomorrow's enterprise', blog posted on 14 April 2012; http://

jugaadtoinnovation.blogspot.in/2012/04/infosys-innovation-to-build-tomorrows.html, accessed on 12 May 2012.

33. Ibid.

34. Gail Edmondson, 'GE Ecomagination challenge puts $63M into 10 home energy start-ups'; http://bulletin.sciencebusiness.net/news/75193/GE-ecomagination-Challenge-puts-$63M-into-10-home-energy-start-ups, accessed on 30 August 2011.

35. 'Ecomagination challenge: Powering the grid', case study from BrightIdea www.brightidea.com/pdf_casestudy/casestudy_ge.pdf, accessed on 31 August 2011.

36. Ibid., p. 2.

37. 'Realization of khadi mission', *MIGIRI Newsletter*, vol. 2, nos. 6–7, June–July 2010.

38. Karim Lakhani and Jill Panetta, 'The Principles of Distributed Innovation', *Innovations from MIT Press Journal*, Summer 2007.

39. Rob Norton, 'The Thought Leader Interview: Henry Chesbrough', 24 May 2011, *Strategy+Business*, Summary 2011, no. 63.

chapter eight
Step 8: Create a Margin of Safety

1. Christopher Reed, 'The Damn'd South Sea'; http://harvardmagazine.com/1999/05/damnd.html, accessed on 10 May 2012.

2. 'Debt-hit Mallya flies out of low-cost space', *Times of India*, 29 September 2011.

3. Captain G.R. Gopinath, *Simply Fly: A Deccan Odyssey*, Collins Business, 2010, pp. 341–45.

4. Interview with Warren Buffet, Bloomberg; http://www.youtube.com/watch?v=X23tTykwpiY, accessed on 30 September 2011.

5. Jeffrey Young and William Simon, *iCon: Steve Jobs: The Greatest Second Act in the History of Business*, Wiley-India, 2005, pp. 59–97.

6. Ibid., p. 60.

7. Walter Isaacson, *Steve Jobs*, Little Brown, 2011, pp. 98–99.

8. Daniel Kahneman, *Thinking, Fast and Slow*, Allen Lane, 2011, p. 255.

9. Ibid., p. 256.

10. Ibid., p. 257. Inventor's Assistance Programme website; http://innovationcentre.ca/services/entrepreneur-support/innovators-assistance-program/, accessed on 4 May 2012.

11. 'The critical factor assessment: Planning for venture success', by the Canadian Innovation Centre; http://dev.innovationcentre.ca/wp-content/uploads/2011/02/Critical-Factor-Assessment-White-Paper.pdf, accessed on 4 May 2012.

12. 'How the Suzlon story came undone', *Economic Times*, 30 December 2010.

13. Gopinath, *Simply Fly*, pp. 335–36.

14. Ibid., p. 336.

15. Lisa Endlich, *Goldman Sachs: The Culture of Success*, Sphere, 2008, pp. 107–09.

16. http://en.wikipedia.org/wiki/Popular_Delusions.

17. http://en.wikipedia.org/wiki/General_Zorawar_Singh.

18. Gary Klein, *The Power of Intuition*, Doubleday, 2004, pp. 215–18.

19. http://en.wikipedia.org/wiki/Zappos.com, accessed on 8 May 2012.

20. Jay Yarow, 'The Zappos Founder Told us all Kinds of Crazy Stories', interview of Nick Swinmurn in *Business Insider,* 28 November 2011; http://articles.businessinsider.com/2011-11-28/tech/30449388_1_zappos-nick-swinmurn-tony-hsieh, accessed on 8 May 2012.

21. Lafley and Charan, *The Game-changer*, p. 202.

22. John Mullins and Randy Komisar, *Getting to Plan B*, Harvard Business Press, 2009, p. 18. The Zappos story and associated experimentation is also presented in Eric Ries, *The Lean Startup*, Crown Business, 2011, pp. 57–58.

23. Eric Bonabeau, et al., 'A more rational approach to new product development', *Harvard Business Review*, March 2008, pp. 96–102.

24. Benjamin Graham and David Dodd, *Security Analysis*, McGraw-Hill, 1996.

25. Dan Senor and Saul Singer, *Start-up Nation: The Story of Israel's Economic Miracle*, Twelve, 2011, pp. 147–51.

26. S.M. Edwards, *A Memoir of Rao Bahadur Ranchhodlal Chhotalal*, William Pollard and Co. Ltd., 1920; http://www.archive.org/stream/memoirofraobahad00edwa/memoirofraobahad00edwa_djvu.txt, accessed on 29 April 2012.

27. Rishikesha T Krishnan and Swarna Kumar Vallabhaneni, 'Innovation, technology and competitive strategy: Bajaj Auto and the motorcycle market (A) & (B)', IIMB case study, November 2009.

28. 'TVS Motors targets 2 million sales, 10% EBITDA margin in 2010, interview of with Venu Srinivasan, TVS Chairman and MD; http://www.moneycontrol.com/news/business/tvs-motor-targets-2m-sales-10-ebitda-margin2010_435076.html, accessed on 3 November 2011.

29. Michael Peterson, 'Thomas Edison, Failure', *American Heritage of Invention and Technology*, 6, Winter 1991, pp. 8–14.

30. Ibid.

31. Ibid.

32. Ibid.

33. Leonard DeGraaf, 'Confronting the Mass Market: Thomas Edison and the Entertainment Phonograph', *Business and Economic History*, vol. 24, no. 1, Fall 1995; http://www.h-net.org/~business/bhcweb/publications/BEHprint/v024n1/p0088-p0096.pdf, accessed on 27 May 2012.

34. Andrew S. Grove, *Only the Paranoid Survive*, Currency Doubleday, 1999, p. 3.

Conclusion

1. http://www.bbc.co.uk/worldservice/learningenglish movingwords/ shortlist/laotzu.shtml, accessed on 27 May 2012.

2. 'Chidambaram Sings Tihar Praises', *Times of India*, 24 September 2009; http://tihartj.nic.in/images/in_the_news/toi/24-09-2009.jpg, accessed on 27 May 2012.

3. Information on the Tihar Jail factory; http://delhi.gov.in/wps/wcm/connect/lib_centraljail/Central+Jail/Home/Factory, accessed on 24 September 2011.

4. 'Second campus recruitment in Tihar Jail', 27 June 2011; http://alpha.newsx.com/story/second-campus-recruitment-tihar-jail, accessed on 27 May 2012.

5. http://www.shell.com/home/content/innovation/innovative_thinking/game_changer/what_can_we_do/step_by_step/, accessed on 27 May 2012.

6. Paul Buchheit, 'Communicating with Code', blog; http://paulbuchheit.blogspot.in/2009/01/communicating-with-code.html, accessed on 27 May 2012.

7. Rishikesha T. Krishnan, 'What makes 3M the most sustainably innovative tech company in the world'; http://jugaadtoinnovation.blogspot.in/2012/05/what-makes-3m-most-sustainably.html, accessed on 15 June 2012.

8. Personal communication with Cognizant Innovation group leadership, 20 July 2011.

9. http://en.wikipedia.org/wiki/2011_Indian_anti-corruption_movement, accessed on 27 May 2012.

Index

OTHER BOOKS FROM COLLINS BUSINESS

COLLINS BUSINESS

MAKING BREAKTHROUGH INNOVATION HAPPEN
How 11 Indians Pulled Off the Impossible

Porus Munshi

Through the breakthroughs achieved by eleven organizations, Porus Munshi, an innovation consultant, shows that to do what is considered 'impossible' in your particular industry, you have to be subversive and think differently. For only a subversive mindset can challenge and transform the status quo and make breakthrough innovation happen. In the process, if the existing business model needs to be turned on its head, then so be it!

'In a knowledge society, we have to make innovations continuously. Innovation can start anywhere—from a fisherman's hamlet or a farmer's household or a classroom to a lab or an industry or an R&D centre'

—Dr A.P.J. Abdul Kalam

'Provides insightful case studies from diverse contexts . . . highly relevant'

—N.R. Narayana Murthy, Chairman and Chief Mentor, Infosys

INFINITE VISION

How Aravind Became the World's Greatest Business Case for Compassion

Pavithra K. Mehta & Suchitra Shenoy

When a crippling disease shattered his lifelong ambition, a young surgeon named Dr Govindappa Venkataswamy chose an impossible new dream: to eliminate curable blindness. By 1976 he had personally performed over 100,000 sight-restoring surgeries. That same year he founded Aravind, an 11-bed eye clinic in south India, with no money, business plan or safety net. Dr V (as he came to be known) was fifty-eight years old at the time, and over the next three decades his humble clinic would defy the odds to become the largest provider of eye care in the world. *Infinite Vision* tells an unforgettable story . . . one that has lit the eyes of millions.

'Aravind is an organization built on hope, possibility, purpose, deep insights and transformational, measurable impact. *Infinite Vision* brings all this alive. E.F. Schumacher would probably have called it *Innovation As If People Mattered.* Aravind is *the* global bellwether for innovations where people matter'

—Porus Munshi, Author of *Making Breakthrough Innovation Happen: How 11 Indians Pulled Off the Impossible*

'Reveals the power of a model that combines business discipline with compassion. May the wisdom of Dr V and Aravind shared here inspire many such initiatives for the well-being of future generations'

—Muhammad Yunus, Nobel Peace Prize Laureate and Founder, Grameen Bank

WHAT THE CEO REALLY WANTS FROM YOU
The 4 As for Managerial Success

R. Gopalakrishnan

There are many books on leadership and how to lead. *What the CEO Really Wants from You* is distinctive in so far as it addresses the question that is uppermost in the mind of any manager: What should he or she do to make the boss a partner rather than perceive the boss as an extractor of work or an adversary? In this immensely practical book informed by the wisdom he has gleaned over the years, R. Gopalakrishnan offers the reader the benefit of all he has learnt, summarized in the four As—Accomplishment, Affability, Advocacy and Authenticity.

'I am very happy to provide a few words as a perspective foreword to a remarkable book by Gopal. It is important for the development of any profession that experienced practitioners share their views with future practitioners—and that is exactly what Gopal has set out to do. All managers do not write and neither are all writers, good managers. Gopal combines both skills and so this book is special'

—Ram Charan,
CEO and Board Advisor and Bestselling Author

'Many management books outline what it takes for you to be a great leader once you have arrived. In reality, few of us spend the majority of our careers at the top. In *What the CEO Really Wants from You*, Gopal provides a refreshing perspective on how winning careers are built on great relationships between a rising leader and his or her boss; it focuses on what the CEO truly cares about— qualities that contribute to the company's overall success—and how they ultimately lead to career success'

—Shantanu Narayen,
President and CEO, Adobe Systems